BETTER HOMES AND GARDENS®

Great COOKING for TWO

BETTER HOMES AND GARDENS® BOOKS
Des Moines

GREAT COOKING FOR TWO

Editors: Jennifer Darling, Shelli McConnell, Heidi McNutt
Graphic Designer: Harijs Priekulis
Project Manager: Liz Anderson

Associate Department Editor: Liz Woolever
Associate Art Directors: Neoma Thomas, Linda Ford Vermie
Publishing Systems Text Processor: Paula Forest
Test Kitchen Product Supervisor: Colleen Weeden
Food Stylists: Suzanne Finley, Carol Grones, Janet Herwig
Photographers: Dennis Becker, Mike Dieter (cover and page 41),
    M. Jensen Photography, Scott Little (page 55)

BETTER HOMES AND GARDENS® BOOKS
An Imprint of Meredith® Books
Vice President and Editorial Director: Elizabeth P. Rice
Food and Family Life Editor: Sharyl Heiken
Art Director: Ernest Shelton
Managing Editor: David A. Kirchner
Art Production Director: John Berg
Test Kitchen Director: Sharon Stilwell

President, Book Group: Joseph J. Ward
Vice President, Retail Marketing: Jamie L. Martin
Vice President, Book Clubs: Richard L. Rundall

WE CARE!

All of us at Better Homes and Gardens® Books are dedicated
to providing you with the information and ideas you need to
create tasty foods. We welcome your comments or
suggestions. Write us at: Better Homes and Gardens® Books,
Cookbook Editorial Department, LS-348, 1716 Locust Street,
Des Moines, IA 50309-3023

Our seal assures you that every recipe in
Great Cooking for Two has been tested in the
Better Homes and Gardens® Test Kitchen.
This means that each recipe is practical and
reliable, and meets our high standards of
taste appeal. We guarantee your satisfaction
with this book for as long as you own it.

Contents

6 MEATS
A tempting sampling of beef, veal, pork, and lamb main dishes.

48 POULTRY
Pick from a scrumptious collection of light, fresh-tasting chicken and turkey recipes.

82 FISH AND SHELLFISH
Impressive entrées highlighting cod, salmon, shrimp, and more.

100 MEATLESS MAIN DISHES
A medley of cheese, bean, lentil, and grain recipes to add variety to your menus.

114 SALADS
A fresh and tasty selection of main-dish and side-dish salads.

142 SANDWICHES AND SOUPS
Together or on their own, savory soups and sandwiches offer easy-to-fix meal options.

172 SIDE DISHES
Simple, satisfying accompaniments to nestle alongside a main dish.

190 BAKED DESSERTS AND BREADS
Savor mouth-watering desserts and fresh breads with a meal or as a luscious treat.

218 BREAKFASTS
Warm up to delightful breakfast breads and egg dishes morning, noon, or night.

233 INDEX

On the cover: Glazed Chicken and Grapes (see recipe, page 55)

INTRODUCTION

Cooking has been a passion of mine for years. From baking cookies in Mom's kitchen to cooking meals for 60 or more at a guest ranch, I've loved it all. But when I got married and began cooking for two people, I encountered some new challenges. I found few recipes for only two servings, and we soon grew tired of eating leftovers from larger recipes.

That's why I've completely enjoyed creating *Great Cooking for Two* with co-editor Shelli McConnell (another cooking enthusiast who cooks for two). It's brimming with fresh-tasting recipes tailored *just* for two. You'll find tantalizing selections for every day, such as Marinated Beef with Spicy Pecan Sauce and Corn Salsa over Chicken. And, for special celebrations, Salmon and Green Peppercorn Strudel, Maple-Glazed Stuffed Cornish Hens, and other outstanding recipes will lend a splashy presentation to your occasion.

Each recipe is streamlined so you can minimize time spent in the kitchen but still make meals from scratch. Plus, *Great Cooking for Two* has several special features including the Eat Two/Freeze Two recipes and the Menu Ideas.

Whether you're just beginning to cook for two or you're returning to that life-style after raising a family, I think you'll find *Great Cooking for Two* meets your needs anytime the meal's for two.

Jennifer Darling

SPECIAL FEATURES

The Eat Two/Freeze Two recipes give you a meal to eat now and another one to freeze for later. Or, you can prepare the entire recipe when entertaining four.

EAT TWO/FREEZE TWO

MENU IDEA

Next to most recipes you'll find a Menu Idea box suggesting flavorful foods to round out your meal.

Use the Time Estimate given with every recipe as a guide to how long a recipe will take from the first step through the last.

TIME ESTIMATE

SALAD SPECTACULAR

Jazz up your salads with a variety of salad dressings and toppers and use the dressings as meat marinades or brush-ons, too.

Homemade bread in sizes just right for two are made from a no-knead yeast bread dough that you mix, chill or freeze, and use when you need it.

BEVY OF BREADS

PER SERVING

A nutrition analysis of every recipe lists calories and fat content plus the amounts of five other common nutrition elements.

MEAT

APRICOT-AND-ALMOND-STUFFED STEAK

APRICOT-AND-ALMOND-STUFFED STEAK

Mix and match the apricot sauce with pork, poultry, and fish.

1 8-ounce beef top loin
   steak, cut 1 to 1½
   inches thick
⅛ teaspoon pepper
4 dried apricot halves *or* 2
   dried peach halves,
   finely snipped
1 tablespoon toasted sliced
   almonds

■ Make a pocket in the steak by cutting a deep horizontal slit. Sprinkle the pepper on the cut surfaces of the pocket. Spoon the apricots or peaches and almonds into the pocket. If necessary, secure opening of pocket with a wooden toothpick.

To broil, place steak on the unheated rack of a broiler pan. Broil 3 to 4 inches from the heat to desired doneness, turning once. (Allow 8 to 12 minutes for rare, 13 to 17 minutes for medium, or 18 to 22 minutes for well-done.)

Or, to grill, place steak on the rack of an uncovered grill. (See tip, page 27.) Grill directly over *medium-hot* coals to desired doneness, turning once. (Allow 8 to 12 minutes for rare, 12 to 15 minutes for medium, or 16 to 20 minutes for well-done.)

⅓ cup apricot *or* peach
   nectar *or* orange juice
4 dried apricot halves *or* 2
   dried peach halves,
   finely snipped
1 tablespoon thinly sliced
   green onion
½ teaspoon cornstarch
½ teaspoon instant chicken
   bouillon granules
⅛ teaspoon pepper
1 tablespoon toasted sliced
   almonds (optional)

■ Meanwhile, for sauce, in a small saucepan combine the apricot nectar, peach nectar, or orange juice; apricots or peaches; green onion; cornstarch; bouillon granules; and pepper. Cook and stir over medium heat till thickened and bubbly. Cook and stir for 1 minute more.

To serve, cut steak in half. Transfer each half of the steak to an individual plate. Pour sauce over the steak. If desired, sprinkle with almonds. Makes 2 servings.

TIME ESTIMATE
Start to finish _ 20 min.

MENU IDEA
Drizzle whole green beans or asparagus spears with melted Mustard-Sage Butter or Sesame Butter (see recipes, page 177) and serve red grapes to complete your meal.

PER SERVING
Calories _____ 251
Protein _____ 26 g
Carbohydrate _____ 16 g
Fat (total) _____ 9 g
  Saturated _____ 3 g
Cholesterol ____ 65 mg
Sodium _____ 286 mg
Potassium _____ 610 mg

PEPPERED BEEF STEAK WITH VINAIGRETTE

1 8-ounce beef top loin *or* tenderloin steak, cut 1 to 1½ inches thick
½ teaspoon cracked black pepper

■ Sprinkle both sides of steak with pepper, pressing into surface.

■ *To broil,* place steak on the unheated rack of a broiler pan. Broil 3 to 4 inches from the heat to desired doneness, turning once. (Allow 8 to 12 minutes for rare, 13 to 17 minutes for medium, or 18 to 22 minutes for well-done.)

Or, to grill, place steak on the rack of an uncovered grill. (See tip, page 27.) Grill directly over *medium-hot* coals to desired doneness, turning once. (Allow 8 to 12 minutes for rare, 12 to 15 minutes for medium, or 16 to 20 minutes for well-done.)

2 tablespoons white wine vinegar *or* vinegar
2 teaspoons olive oil *or* cooking oil
½ teaspoon Dijon-style mustard
⅛ teaspoon dried rosemary, tarragon, *or* basil, crushed

■ Meanwhile, for vinaigrette, in a small saucepan stir together the white wine vinegar or vinegar, olive oil or cooking oil, mustard, and rosemary, tarragon, or basil. Heat mixture through over medium-low heat.

1 cup fresh spinach leaves or Bibb lettuce leaves (optional)

■ To serve, if desired, arrange spinach or Bibb lettuce leaves on individual plates. Slice steak across the grain into thin slices. Arrange the steak atop spinach or Bibb lettuce. Drizzle vinaigrette over steak and spinach or lettuce. Makes 2 servings.

TIME ESTIMATE
Start to finish _ 20 min.

MENU IDEA
Pass a small basket of sourdough, whole wheat, or hard rolls with the steak.

PER SERVING
Calories _____ 224
Protein _____ 25 g
Carbohydrate _____ 2 g
Fat (total) _____ 13 g
　Saturated _____ 4 g
Cholesterol _____ 65 mg
Sodium _____ 123 mg
Potassium _____ 510 mg

MARINATED BEEF WITH SPICY PECAN SAUCE

8 ounces boneless beef
   sirloin steak, cut ¾ to 1
   inch thick

■ Cut steak into 2 equal portions. Place steak in a plastic bag set in a deep mixing bowl.

TIME ESTIMATE
Preparation ____ 10 min.
Marinating ____ 30 min.
Cooking _____ 20 min.

2 tablespoons olive oil *or*
   cooking oil
2 tablespoons balsamic *or*
   red wine vinegar
1 small jalapeño pepper,
   finely chopped (see tip,
   page 12), *or* 2
   tablespoons canned
   diced green chili
   peppers, drained
1 clove garlic, minced
⅛ teaspoon ground red
   pepper

■ For marinade, in a bowl combine olive oil or cooking oil, balsamic or red wine vinegar, jalapeño pepper or green chili peppers, garlic, and ground red pepper. Pour over steak in bag. Close bag and turn steak to coat well. Marinate at room temperature for 30 minutes or in the refrigerator for 2 to 24 hours, turning bag occasionally. Remove steak from marinade; discard marinade.

MENU IDEA
Cooked long grain or brown rice or noodles is great teamed with this saucy steak.

PER SERVING
Calories _____ 446
Protein _____ 27 g
Carbohydrate _____ 4 g
Fat (total) _____ 36 g
  Saturated _____ 7 g
Cholesterol ____ 76 mg
Sodium_____ 491 mg
Potassium ____ 404 mg

1 tablespoon margarine,
   butter, olive oil, *or*
   cooking oil

■ In a medium skillet cook steak portions in hot margarine, butter, olive oil, or cooking oil over medium heat to desired doneness, turning once. (Allow 8 to 11 minutes for rare, 12 to 14 minutes for medium, or 15 to 17 minutes for well-done.) Transfer steak portions to individual plates; keep warm.

1 tablespoon margarine *or*
   butter
2 tablespoons chopped
   pecans
1 clove garlic, minced
⅛ teaspoon ground red
   pepper
⅓ cup water
½ teaspoon instant beef
   bouillon granules

■ For sauce, melt margarine or butter in the same skillet. Add pecans, garlic, and ground red pepper. Cook and stir for 2 to 3 minutes or till pecans are toasted. Carefully add water and bouillon granules to hot skillet, stirring and scraping crusty browned bits off the bottom. Simmer gently about 2 minutes or till liquid is reduced by half. To serve, spoon warm sauce over steak. Makes 2 servings.

ONION-STUFFED SIRLOIN WITH MUSHROOM SAUTÉ

Mix a variety of mushrooms, such as shiitake, oyster, brown, or buttons, in the sauce for a rich, earthy taste.

½ of a small onion, thinly
    sliced and separated
    into rings
1 clove garlic, minced
1 tablespoon margarine *or*
    butter
⅛ teaspoon lemon-pepper
    seasoning *or* pepper
1 8-ounce boneless beef
    top sirloin steak, cut 1½
    inches thick

■ For stuffing, in a small saucepan cook the onion and garlic in margarine or butter till onion is tender but not brown. Remove from heat. Stir in the lemon-pepper seasoning or pepper. Set aside.

Make a pocket in the steak by cutting a deep horizontal slit. Spoon the stuffing into the pocket. If necessary, secure opening of the pocket with a wooden toothpick.

To grill, place steak on the rack of an uncovered grill. (See tip, page 27.) Grill directly over *medium-hot* coals to desired doneness, turning once. (Allow 14 to 18 minutes for rare, 18 to 22 minutes for medium, or 24 to 28 minutes for well-done.)

Or, to broil, place steak on the unheated rack of a broiler pan. Broil 4 to 5 inches from the heat to desired doneness, turning once. (Allow 14 to 18 minutes for rare, 19 to 22 minutes for medium, or 23 to 28 minutes for well-done.)

TIME ESTIMATE

Start to finish _*35 min.
*Allow extra time
to heat coals.*

MENU IDEA

Grill new potatoes (see chart, page 181) to round out the meal.

PER SERVING

Calories _____ 319
Protein _____ 27 g
Carbohydrate ____ 12 g
Fat (total) _____ 18 g
  Saturated _____ 5 g
Cholesterol ____ 76 mg
Sodium _____ 504 mg
Potassium ____ 455 mg

¾ cup sliced fresh shiitake
    or other mushrooms
1 tablespoon margarine *or*
    butter
1 teaspoon cornstarch
1 teaspoon Worcestershire
    sauce
½ teaspoon instant beef
    bouillon granules
1 tablespoon dry red *or*
    white wine

■ Meanwhile, for mushroom sauce, in a small saucepan cook the mushrooms in margarine or butter till tender. In a small bowl stir together the cornstarch, Worcestershire sauce, bouillon granules, and ⅓ cup *water.* Carefully add to the saucepan. Cook and stir till thickened and bubbly. Cook and stir for 1 minute more. Stir in wine. To serve, cut steak in half. Transfer steak halves to individual plates. Pour sauce over steak. Makes 2 servings.

EAST-WEST BARBECUED BEEF KABOBS

Chinese flavors from the East team up with American cooking techniques from the West to inspire these ginger- and pineapple-flavored beef kabobs.

8 ounces boneless beef sirloin steak, cut 1 inch thick

¼ cup orange *or* pineapple juice

2 tablespoons honey

1 tablespoon olive oil *or* cooking oil

1 teaspoon grated gingerroot *or* ⅛ teaspoon ground ginger

■ Cut steak into 1-inch cubes. Place cubes in a plastic bag set in a deep mixing bowl. For marinade, in a small bowl stir together the orange or pineapple juice, honey, olive oil or cooking oil, and gingerroot or ground ginger. Pour over steak in bag. Close bag and turn steak to coat well. Marinate at room temperature for 30 minutes or in the refrigerator for 2 hours, turning bag occasionally. Drain steak, reserving marinade.

1 medium sweet red *or* green pepper, cut into 1-inch squares

12 to 16 fresh pea pods

■ Meanwhile, in a medium saucepan cook the sweet red or green pepper squares and pea pods, covered, in a small amount of boiling water for 2 minutes. Drain.

1 8-ounce can pineapple chunks (juice pack), drained

■ Wrap a pea pod around each pineapple chunk. On 2 long or 4 short skewers alternately thread wrapped pineapple chunks, sweet red or green pepper squares, and steak cubes, leaving about ¼ inch between foods.

■ *To grill,* place kabobs on the rack of an uncovered grill. (See tip, page 27.) Grill directly over *medium-hot* coals for 6 to 8 minutes for medium doneness, turning and brushing with marinade frequently.

Or, to broil, place skewers on the unheated rack of a broiler pan. Broil 3 inches from the heat for 6 to 8 minutes for medium doneness, turning and brushing with marinade frequently. Makes 2 servings.

TIME ESTIMATE

Preparation ⎯ 20 min.
Marinating* ⎯ 30 min.
Grilling ⎯⎯⎯ 6 min.
Heat coals while marinating the meat.

MENU IDEA

Try Curried Rice (see recipe, page 187) as an accompaniment to the grilled meat.

PER SERVING

Calories ⎯⎯⎯ 407
Protein⎯⎯⎯ 28 g
Carbohydrate ⎯⎯ 46 g
Fat (total) ⎯⎯⎯ 13 g
   Saturated ⎯⎯⎯ 3 g
Cholesterol ⎯⎯ 76 mg
Sodium⎯⎯⎯ 63 mg
Potassium ⎯⎯ 719 mg

BEEF STROGANOFF

8 ounces boneless beef
    sirloin steak
½ cup dairy sour cream *or*
    plain yogurt
1 tablespoon all-purpose
    flour
1 tablespoon tomato paste
2 teaspoons Dijon-style
    mustard
2 teaspoons Worcestershire
    sauce
1 teaspoon instant beef
    bouillon granules
½ teaspoon caraway seed

■ Trim fat from beef. Partially freeze beef for 30 minutes. Thinly slice across the grain into bite-size strips. Set aside.

For sauce, in a bowl stir together the sour cream or yogurt, flour, tomato paste, mustard, Worcestershire sauce, bouillon granules, caraway seed, and ⅓ cup *water*. Set aside.

1 small onion, sliced and
    separated into rings
1 cup sliced fresh
    mushrooms
1 clove garlic, minced
1 tablespoon margarine *or*
    butter
3 cups hot cooked noodles

■ In a large skillet cook and stir the beef, onion, mushrooms, and garlic in hot margarine or butter till meat is of desired doneness and vegetables are tender. Add the sauce. Cook and stir over medium heat till thickened and bubbly. Cook and stir for 1 minute more. Serve over hot cooked noodles. Makes 2 servings.

TIME ESTIMATE

Start to finish — 50 min.

MENU IDEA

Select seasonal fruit for a refreshing side dish.

PER SERVING

Calories	716
Protein	42 g
Carbohydrate	74 g
Fat (total)	29 g
Saturated	12 g
Cholesterol	177 mg
Sodium	914 mg
Potassium	752 mg

HANDLING HOT CHILI PEPPERS

Take a few precautions when handling fresh or canned hot chili peppers to avoid burning your eyes or skin. Protect your hands by covering them with plastic bags or plastic or rubber gloves. If your bare hands touch the chili peppers, wash your hands and nails well with soap and water.

When using chili peppers, it's best to cook them with other foods rather than alone. Cook the peppers for just the time indicated in the recipe and avoid breathing directly over the pan as the peppers cook because of the powerful fumes.

BEEF STEAK FAJITAS

Substitute chicken for the beef, if you prefer. Use 8 ounces of boneless, skinless chicken breast halves and cook the chicken for 2 to 3 minutes or till no pink remains.

8 ounces beef top round *or* boneless sirloin steak
¼ cup water
1 tablespoon lemon *or* lime juice
½ teaspoon instant beef bouillon granules
¼ teaspoon dried oregano *or* thyme, crushed
⅛ teaspoon ground red pepper

■ Trim fat from beef. Partially freeze beef for 30 minutes. Thinly slice across the grain into bite-size strips.

For sauce, in a small bowl stir together the water, lemon or lime juice, bouillon granules, oregano or thyme, and ground red pepper. Set aside.

4 10-inch flour tortillas
1 tablespoon cooking oil
1 clove garlic, minced
1 small tomato, chopped

■ Wrap tortillas in foil. Heat in a 350° oven for 10 minutes to soften. Meanwhile, pour oil into a large skillet. Preheat over medium-high heat. Add the beef and garlic to the hot skillet. Cook and stir for 2 to 3 minutes or to desired doneness. Add the sauce and tomato. Cook and stir for 3 to 4 minutes or till most of the liquid has evaporated.

1 small avocado, halved, seeded, peeled, and sliced
½ cup chopped, peeled jicama *or* chopped celery
¼ cup plain yogurt *or* dairy sour cream
¼ cup salsa

■ To serve, in the center of each warmed tortilla place beef mixture, avocado slices, jicama or celery, yogurt or sour cream, and salsa. To fold the tortillas, bring up one edge of the tortilla to overlap the filling. Then, fold the two adjacent edges of the tortilla over the filling. Makes 2 servings.

TIME ESTIMATE
Start to finish — 55 min.

MENU IDEA
Mix margaritas to cool the heat from these Tex-Mex bundles.

PER SERVING
Calories _____ 736
Protein _____ 40 g
Carbohydrate _____ 79 g
Fat (total) _____ 34 g
  Saturated _____ 6 g
Cholesterol _____ 73 mg
Sodium _____ 945 mg
Potassium _____ 1,236 mg

13

ITALIAN PEPPER STEAK STIR-FRY

If you don't own a wok, stir-fry your pepper steak in a large skillet.

6 ounces boneless beef
   sirloin *or* top round
   steak
½ cup water
2 tablespoons dry white
   wine *or* water
2 teaspoons cornstarch
2 teaspoons instant beef
   bouillon granules
½ teaspoon dried Italian
   seasoning, crushed

■ Trim fat from beef. Partially freeze beef for 30 minutes. Thinly slice across the grain into bite-size strips.

   For sauce, in a small bowl stir together the water, white wine or water, cornstarch, bouillon granules, Italian seasoning, and ⅛ teaspoon *pepper*. Set aside.

TIME ESTIMATE
Start to finish — 55 min.

MENU IDEA
Toss mixed greens and a few vegetables together for side-dish salads.

PER SERVING
Calories _____ 466
Protein _____ 30 g
Carbohydrate _____ 54 g
Fat (total) _____ 14 g
  Saturated _____ 3 g
Cholesterol _____ 59 mg
Sodium _____ 1,032 mg
Potassium _____ 727 mg

1 tablespoon cooking oil
2 cloves garlic, minced
1 large yellow, green, *or*
   sweet red pepper, cut
   into thin strips
1 small onion, chopped
   (⅓ cup)
1 cup sliced fresh
   mushrooms

■ Pour cooking oil into a wok or large skillet. (Add more oil as necessary during cooking.) Preheat over medium-high heat. Stir-fry garlic in hot oil for 15 seconds. Add pepper strips and onion; stir-fry for 1 minute. Add mushrooms and stir-fry about 1 minute more or till vegetables are crisp-tender. Remove the vegetables from the wok.

1 medium tomato, seeded
   and chopped (¾ cup)
2 cups hot cooked spinach
   fettuccine, linguine, *or*
   other pasta
   Finely shredded *or*
   grated Parmesan cheese

■ Add the beef to the hot wok or skillet. Stir-fry for 2 to 3 minutes or to desired doneness. Push beef from the center of the wok. Stir sauce. Add sauce to the center of the wok or skillet. Cook and stir till thickened and bubbly. Return the vegetables to the wok or skillet. Add tomato. Stir ingredients together to coat with sauce. Cover and cook about 1 minute more or till heated through. Serve immediately over hot cooked pasta. Sprinkle with Parmesan cheese. Makes 2 servings.

ITALIAN PEPPER STEAK STIR-FRY

DILLED BEEF WITH NEW POTATOES AND ASPARAGUS

2 tablespoons all-purpose flour
¼ teaspoon salt
¼ teaspoon paprika
8 ounces beef top round *or* boneless sirloin steak, cut ¾ inch thick, *or* veal leg top round *or* boneless sirloin steak, cut ¾ inch thick
1 tablespoon olive oil *or* cooking oil

■ In a paper or plastic bag combine the flour, salt, and paprika. Trim fat from meat. Cut beef or veal into 4 equal pieces. Add the meat to the flour mixture in the bag, one piece at a time, shaking to coat well. Reserve the remaining flour mixture; set aside.

In a large skillet brown meat on both sides in hot oil. Drain off fat.

¾ cup water
1 tablespoon snipped fresh dillweed *or* 1 teaspoon dried dillweed
1 teaspoon instant beef bouillon granules
8 ounces whole tiny new potatoes, halved, *or* 1 medium potato, cut into bite-size pieces
8 ounces asparagus spears, cut into 2-inch pieces, *or* ½ of a 10-ounce package frozen cut asparagus

■ Add the water, dillweed, and bouillon granules to the skillet. Add the potatoes. Bring to boiling; reduce heat. Cover and simmer for 15 minutes. Add the asparagus; cover and simmer for 5 to 7 minutes more or till the meat and vegetables are tender. Transfer the meat and vegetables to individual plates; keep warm.

¼ cup water
1 teaspoon lemon juice
Fresh dillweed (optional)
Lemon wedges (optional)

■ For sauce, in the skillet stir together the reserved flour mixture and water. Cook and stir till thickened and bubbly. Cook and stir for 1 minute more. Stir in lemon juice; remove from heat. Spoon sauce over meat and vegetables. If desired, garnish with fresh dillweed and lemon wedges. Makes 2 servings.

TIME ESTIMATE
Start to finish — 40 min.

MENU IDEA
Spread French bread slices with Roasted Red Pepper Butter (see recipe, page 177). If desired, broil the buttered bread slices.

PER SERVING
Calories ———— 394
Protein ———— 35 g
Carbohydrate ——— 39 g
Fat (total) ———— 12 g
  Saturated ———— 2 g
Cholesterol ——— 71 mg
Sodium——— 801 mg
Potassium ——1,255 mg

BEEF ROAST WITH TOMATO-HERB SAUCE

1 **2-pound boneless beef chuck pot roast**
1 **tablespoon olive oil** *or* **cooking oil**

■ Trim separable fat from roast. Divide roast into 2 equal pieces. If desired, cut *one* piece of the roast into ¾-inch cubes to use for stew meat. Seal, label, and freeze stew meat or piece of roast for up to 3 months. Then use stew meat to prepare Beef Stew with Lentils (see recipe, page 167) or Hearty Beef and Squash Stew (see recipe, page 158).

In a Dutch oven or large skillet brown remaining roast on all sides in hot oil. Drain fat.

¾ **cup water**
¼ **cup sun-dried tomatoes*** **(see tip, page 157)**
½ **teaspoon dried thyme** *or* **basil, crushed**
1 **tablespoon tomato paste**
1 **teaspoon instant beef bouillon granules**
¼ **teaspoon dry mustard**
⅛ **teaspoon pepper**

■ For sauce, in a small bowl stir together the water, sun-dried tomatoes, thyme or basil, tomato paste, bouillon granules, dry mustard, and pepper. Pour sauce around roast in Dutch oven. Bring to boiling; reduce heat. Cover and simmer about 1¼ hours or till beef is tender. *Or,* bake, covered, in a 325° oven about 1¼ hours or till beef is tender. Remove beef from skillet, reserving juices.

1 **tablespoon cold water**
1 **teaspoon cornstarch**
2 **cups hot cooked noodles, orzo,** *or* **rice**

■ Stir together water and cornstarch. Add to juices in skillet. Cook and stir till thickened and bubbly. Cook and stir 2 minutes more.

To serve, slice beef. Transfer beef to individual plates with hot cooked noodles, orzo, or rice. Pour sauce over all. Makes 2 servings.

*If desired, for sauce, substitute one 7½-ounce can *tomatoes,* cut up, for the sun-dried tomatoes. Then reduce the water to ½ cup and omit the instant beef bouillon granules.

TIME ESTIMATE
Preparation ____ 20 min.
Cooking _____ 1¼ hrs.

MENU IDEA
Prepare a citrus fruit salad to complement the meat and noodles.

PER SERVING
Calories _____ 672
Protein _____ 57 g
Carbohydrate _____ 54 g
Fat (total) _____ 25 g
 Saturated _____ 6 g
Cholesterol _____ 193 mg
Sodium _____ 687 mg
Potassium ____ 1,048 mg

SAVORY ALMOND MEATBALLS

Create an eye-catching presentation for special occasions by using half spinach noodles and half plain noodles.

1 **egg white**
1 **tablespoon milk**
⅛ **teaspoon salt**
⅛ **teaspoon pepper**
¼ **cup finely chopped onion**
3 **tablespoons fine dry bread crumbs** *or* **finely crushed zwieback**
2 **tablespoons chopped toasted almonds** *or* **pecans**
2 **tablespoons snipped parsley**
6 **ounces ground beef** *or* **pork**
1 **tablespoon margarine** *or* **butter**

■ For meatballs, in a mixing bowl combine the egg white, milk, salt, and pepper. Stir in the onion, bread crumbs or zwieback, almonds or pecans, and parsley. Add the beef or pork; mix well. Shape into 12 meatballs.

In a large skillet cook meatballs in margarine or butter over medium heat about 10 minutes or till no pink remains, turning often. Remove meatballs from skillet, reserving *1 tablespoon* of the drippings in the skillet. Drain the meatballs on paper towels.

1 **tablespoon all-purpose flour**
1 **teaspoon instant beef bouillon granules**
Dash pepper
1 **cup milk**

■ For sauce, stir the flour, bouillon granules, and pepper into the reserved drippings. Add milk all at once. Cook and stir till thickened and bubbly. Cook and stir for 1 minute more. Return meatballs to skillet; heat through.

1½ **cups hot cooked spinach noodles** *or* **noodles**
Snipped parsley (optional)

■ To serve, divide hot cooked spinach noodles or noodles between 2 individual plates. Top with meatballs and sauce. If desired, garnish with parsley. Makes 2 servings.

TIME ESTIMATE

Start to finish _ 35 min.

MENU IDEA

Fill out your menu with hard rolls and buttered peas or baby carrots.

PER SERVING

Calories _____ 526
Protein _____ 31 g
Carbohydrate _____ 48 g
Fat (total) _____ 23 g
　Saturated _____ 7 g
Cholesterol _____ 65 mg
Sodium_____ 893 mg
Potassium _____ 620 mg

INDIAN BEEF PATTIES WITH CUCUMBER SAUCE

Cumin is used in many Indian and Mexican dishes. The seed, whether whole or ground, has a pungent, spicy, and slightly bitter flavor.

½ cup plain yogurt
⅓ cup chopped, seeded
    cucumber

¼ cup finely chopped onion
1 medium jalapeño pepper,
    seeded and chopped
    (see tip, page 12), *or 2*
    tablespoons canned
    diced green chili
    peppers
1 tablespoon snipped fresh
    mint leaves *or* 1
    teaspoon dried mint,
    crushed
1 clove garlic, minced, *or*
    ⅛ teaspoon garlic
    powder
½ teaspoon ground cumin
¼ teaspoon salt
8 ounces ground beef,
    pork, *or* raw turkey

■ For the sauce, in a small bowl stir together the yogurt and cucumber. Cover and chill in the refrigerator till ready to serve.

■ In a mixing bowl combine the onion, jalapeño pepper or green chili peppers, mint, garlic or garlic powder, cumin, and salt. Add beef, pork, or turkey; mix well. Shape mixture into two ¾-inch-thick patties.

■ *To broil,* place meat on the unheated rack of a broiler pan. Broil 3 to 4 inches from the heat for 12 to 14 minutes or till no pink remains, turning once.
    Or, to grill, place meat on the rack of an uncovered grill. (See tip, page 27.) Grill directly over *medium* coals for 12 to 14 minutes or till no pink remains, turning once.

■ To serve, transfer meat to individual plates. Spoon sauce over meat. Makes 2 servings.

TIME ESTIMATE
Start to finish — 30 min.

MENU IDEA
Tomato slices or wedges serve double duty as both a side dish and a colorful garnish.

PER SERVING
Calories _____ 216
Protein _____ 29 g
Carbohydrate _____ 8 g
Fat (total) _____ 8 g
    Saturated _____ 3 g
Cholesterol _____ 70 mg
Sodium _____ 426 mg
Potassium _____ 608 mg

GRILLED BACON-SAUCED MEAT LOAF

Stir the crispy, cooked bacon into a purchased barbecue sauce if you're especially short on time.

1 **slightly beaten egg white**
2 **tablespoons fine dry bread crumbs, quick-cooking rolled oats,** *or* **toasted wheat germ**
2 **tablespoons finely chopped onion**
2 **tablespoons vegetable juice cocktail, tomato juice,** *or* **milk**
1 **teaspoon prepared mustard, horseradish mustard,** *or* **Dijon-style mustard**
⅛ **teaspoon salt**
⅛ **teaspoon pepper**
8 **ounces lean ground beef** *or* **pork**

■ In a mixing bowl stir together the egg white; bread crumbs, oats, or wheat germ; onion; vegetable juice cocktail, tomato juice, or milk; mustard; salt; and pepper. Add beef or pork; mix well. On waxed paper shape mixture into a 4- to 5-inch round loaf.

To grill, in a covered grill arrange *medium-hot* coals around a drip pan. Test for *medium* heat above the pan. (See tip, page 27.) Carefully invert loaf onto the grill rack over the drip pan, but not over the coals. Peel off waxed paper. Lower the grill hood. Grill for 30 to 35 minutes or till no pink remains.

Or, to bake, place loaf in a shallow baking pan. Bake in a 350° oven for 30 to 35 minutes or till no pink remains.

TIME ESTIMATE

Start to finish _*40 min.
*Allow extra time
to heat coals.*

MENU IDEA

Serve corn on the cob slathered with butter with this all-American meat dish.

PER SERVING

Calories	291
Protein	30 g
Carbohydrate	21 g
Fat (total)	9 g
Saturated	3 g
Cholesterol	69 mg
Sodium	936 mg
Potassium	761 mg

1 **slice bacon, cut up**
¼ **cup finely chopped onion**
½ **of an 8-ounce can (½ cup) tomato sauce**
¼ **cup beer** *or* **water**
1 **tablespoon brown sugar**
1 **teaspoon lemon juice**
1 **teaspoon Worcestershire sauce**
¼ **teaspoon celery seed**
⅛ **teaspoon salt**
⅛ **teaspoon pepper**

■ Meanwhile, for sauce, in a small saucepan cook and stir bacon till crisp. Remove bacon from pan with a slotted spoon; drain on paper towels. Add onion to bacon drippings in saucepan. Cook over medium heat for 2 to 3 minutes or till onion is tender but not brown. Stir in bacon pieces, tomato sauce, beer or water, brown sugar, lemon juice, Worcestershire sauce, celery seed, salt, and pepper. Simmer sauce, uncovered, about 10 minutes or to desired consistency. To serve, spoon some of the sauce over the loaf. Pass the remaining sauce. Makes 2 servings.

VEAL CHOPS WITH VEGETABLE SAUCE

2 **veal top loin *or* pork loin chops, cut ½ to ¾ inch thick (8 to 12 ounces total)**

1 **tablespoon margarine *or* butter**

½ **of a 16-ounce package (2½ cups) loose-pack frozen broccoli, baby carrots, and water chestnuts**

¼ **cup water**

¼ **teaspoon instant chicken bouillon granules**

1 **small clove garlic, minced**

1 **tablespoon white wine Worcestershire *or* Worcestershire sauce**

1 **teaspoon cornstarch**

■ Trim fat from veal or pork. In a large skillet cook chops in hot margarine or butter over medium heat for 4 to 6 minutes for medium doneness, turning once. Transfer to individual plates, reserving drippings in skillet. Cover veal or pork to keep warm.

■ Stir the vegetables, water, bouillon granules, and garlic into the skillet drippings. Bring to boiling; reduce heat. Cover and simmer for 2 minutes.

Stir together white wine Worcestershire or Worcestershire sauce and cornstarch; add to skillet. Cook and stir till thickened and bubbly. Cook and stir for 2 minutes more. Spoon sauce over the chops. Makes 2 servings.

TIME ESTIMATE
Start to finish — 20 min.

MENU IDEA
Crusty French bread or rolls lend a contrasting texture to the veal and sauce.

PER SERVING

Calories	212
Protein	19 g
Carbohydrate	13 g
Fat (total)	9 g
Saturated	2 g
Cholesterol	86 mg
Sodium	331 mg
Potassium	221 mg

ROASTING FRESH PEPPERS

When a recipe calls for roasted sweet red peppers, you may purchase them roasted or roast your own. Roasting mellows and sweetens the flavor of sweet red or other fresh peppers, and makes removing their skins easier.

To roast fresh peppers, halve the peppers; remove stems, seeds, and membranes. Place peppers, cut sides down, on a foil-lined baking sheet. Bake in a 425° oven for 20 to 25 minutes or till skin is bubbly and browned. Place peppers in a *new* brown paper bag; seal and let stand for 20 to 30 minutes or till peppers are cool enough to handle. Using a paring knife, start at the stem end and pull the skin off gently and slowly. Slice or chop the peppers as directed in the recipe.

VEAL WITH ARTICHOKES AND HOLLANDAISE SAUCE

Another time, choose this easy-to-fix hollandaise sauce to perk up plain cooked vegetables.

8 ounces veal leg top round
  or boneless sirloin
  steak *or* pork
  tenderloin
¼ cup all-purpose flour
½ teaspoon salt
  Hollandaise Sauce

■ Trim fat from veal or pork. Cut the meat into 4 equal portions. Place each piece of meat between 2 pieces of plastic wrap. Working from the center to the edges, pound meat lightly with the flat side of a meat mallet to ⅛-inch thickness. Remove plastic wrap.

In a paper or plastic bag combine flour and salt. Add meat to the bag, one piece at a time, shaking to coat. Set meat aside.

Prepare Hollandaise Sauce.

1 tablespoon lemon juice
1 4-ounce can artichoke
  hearts, drained and cut
  in half, *or* 4 or 5
  frozen artichoke hearts,
  thawed and cut in half
1 tablespoon margarine,
  olive oil, *or* cooking oil

■ In a large skillet sprinkle lemon juice over artichoke hearts. Cook artichoke hearts in hot margarine or oil for 2 minutes. Add pounded veal or pork to the skillet. Cook over medium-high heat for 1 to 2 minutes per side or till meat and artichokes are tender.

Transfer veal and artichokes to individual plates. Spoon hollandaise sauce over veal and artichokes. Makes 2 servings.

HOLLANDAISE SAUCE

2 teaspoons margarine *or*
  butter
1½ teaspoons all-purpose
  flour
  Dash salt
  Dash white *or* black
  pepper
½ cup milk, half-and-half,
  or light cream
1 beaten egg yolk
1 teaspoon lemon juice

■ In a small saucepan melt margarine or butter. Stir in flour, salt, and white or black pepper. Add milk, half-and-half, or light cream all at once. Cook and stir over medium heat till thickened and bubbly. Cook and stir for 1 minute more. Gradually stir the hot mixture into the beaten egg yolk. Return the egg mixture to the saucepan. Bring to a gentle boil. Cook and stir 1 minute more. Stir in lemon juice. Keep warm over low heat.

TIME ESTIMATE
Start to finish — 25 min.

MENU IDEA
Savor the citrus flavor of Poppyseed and Orange Pasta (see recipe, page 184) with the meat and vegetables.

PER SERVING
Calories _____ 364
Protein _____ 32 g
Carbohydrate _____ 23 g
Fat (total) _____ 17 g
  Saturated _____ 5 g
Cholesterol ____ 200 mg
Sodium_____ 831 mg
Potassium _____ 623 mg

MUSHROOM-AND-BLUE-CHEESE-STUFFED PORK CHOPS

Brushing the chops with fruit juice gives them a golden finish as they cook.

2 pork loin rib chops, cut 1¼ inches thick (about 1 pound total)

■ Trim fat from chops. Make a pocket in each chop by cutting a horizontal slit from the fat side of the chop almost to the bone. Set aside.

½ cup sliced fresh mushrooms
1 green onion, finely chopped (2 tablespoons)
1 tablespoon chopped pecans *or* walnuts
1 tablespoon margarine *or* butter
2 tablespoons crumbled blue cheese

■ For stuffing, in a small saucepan cook mushrooms, onion, and pecans or walnuts in margarine or butter till mushrooms and onion are tender. Remove from heat. Stir in blue cheese.

1 tablespoon apple, orange, *or* pineapple juice

■ Spoon *half* of the stuffing into *each* pork chop pocket. If necessary, fasten the pockets with wooden toothpicks. Brush chops with apple, orange, or pineapple juice.

To bake, place stuffed chops on a rack in a shallow roasting pan. Bake chops, uncovered, in a 375° oven for 35 to 40 minutes or till pork is slightly pink and juices run clear.

Or, to grill, in a covered grill arrange *medium-hot* coals around a drip pan. Test for *medium* heat above the pan. (See tip, page 27.) Place chops on the rack over drip pan, but not over the coals. Lower the grill hood. Grill for 35 to 45 minutes or till pork is slightly pink and juices run clear. Makes 2 servings.

TIME ESTIMATE

Preparation ____ 20 min.
Baking _____ 35 min.

MENU IDEA

Chilled fresh or canned fruit complements the blue cheese stuffing.

PER SERVING

Calories _____ 323
Protein _____ 35 g
Carbohydrate _____ 3 g
Fat (total) _____ 20 g
  Saturated _____ 7 g
Cholesterol _____ 88 mg
Sodium _____ 335 mg
Potassium _____ 510 mg

23

PORK CHOPS WITH CURRANT-NUT STUFFING

2 **pork loin rib chops, cut
1¼ inches thick (about
1 pound total)**

■ Trim fat from chops. Make a pocket in each chop by cutting a horizontal slit from the fat side of the chop almost to the bone. Set aside.

1½ **cups corn bread stuffing
mix**
2 **tablespoons chopped
hazelnuts *or* pecans,
toasted (see tip, page
201)**
2 **tablespoons dried
currants *or* snipped
raisins**
1 **tablespoon thinly sliced
green onion**
1 **tablespoon margarine *or*
butter, melted**
⅓ **cup water**
¼ **teaspoon instant chicken
bouillon granules**

■ For stuffing, in a mixing bowl stir together the stuffing mix, hazelnuts or pecans, currants or raisins, green onion, and margarine or butter. In another bowl, stir together the water and bouillon granules. Toss stuffing mixture with *3 tablespoons* of the water mixture. Spoon *2 tablespoons* of the stuffing into *each* pork chop pocket. If necessary, fasten pockets with wooden toothpicks. Stir the remaining water mixture into the remaining stuffing.

Place stuffed chops on a rack in a shallow roasting pan. Place remaining stuffing in a small greased casserole; cover and refrigerate till ready to bake.

3 **tablespoons currant, crab
apple, *or* cherry jelly**
1½ **teaspoons lemon juice *or*
white wine vinegar**
¼ **teaspoon ground ginger**

■ For glaze, in a small saucepan cook and stir the jelly, lemon juice or wine vinegar, and ginger till jelly is melted. Brush tops of chops with glaze.

**Fresh raspberries
(optional)
Fresh sage (optional)**

■ Bake chops, uncovered, in a 375° oven for 25 minutes. Brush again with glaze. Place casserole with stuffing in oven beside the pork chops. Bake about 15 minutes more or till pork is slightly pink, juices run clear, and stuffing is heated through.

To serve, brush chops with remaining glaze. Transfer chops to individual plates. Spoon stuffing from casserole onto plates. If desired, garnish with raspberries and sage leaves. Makes 2 servings.

TIME ESTIMATE
Preparation —— 20 min.
Baking ———— 40 min.

MENU IDEA
Serve piping hot baked acorn squash wedges with the stuffed chops for an elegant autumn meal.

PER SERVING
Calories ———————551
Protein ——————37 g
Carbohydrate ——61 g
Fat (total) ————19 g
 Saturated ———— 4 g
Cholesterol —— 77 mg
Sodium———— 739 mg
Potassium —— 520 mg

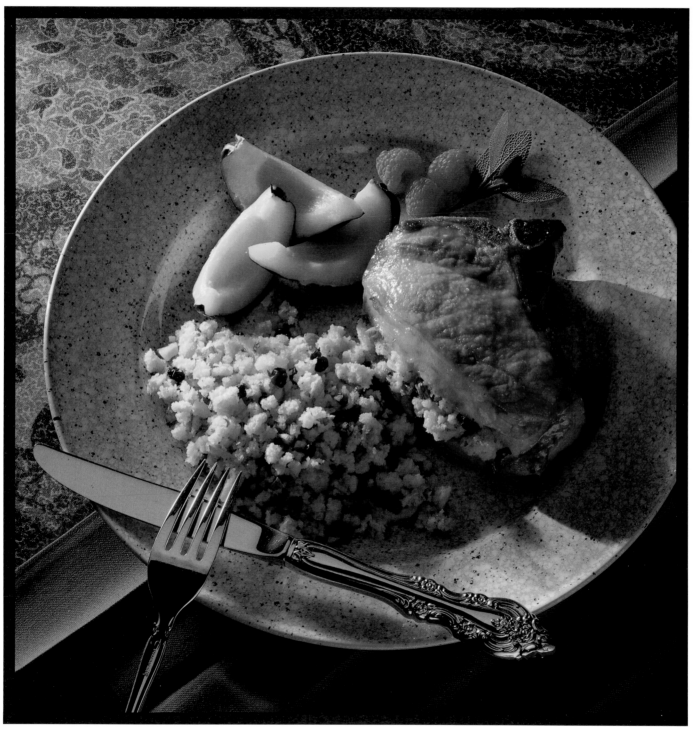

PORK CHOPS WITH CURRANT-NUT STUFFING

PORK CHOPS WITH PEANUT AND GINGER SAUCE

Check the Oriental section of your supermarket for rice sticks, which are also known as rice noodles.

2 ounces rice sticks *or* 1½ cups hot cooked fine egg noodles

■ If using rice sticks, in a medium or large saucepan cook rice sticks in boiling water for 1 to 2 minutes or just till tender. Drain and keep warm.

2 pork loin *or* loin rib chops, cut ¾ inch thick (about 12 ounces total)
1 tablespoon cooking oil

■ Meanwhile, in a large skillet cook pork chops in hot oil over medium heat for 10 to 12 minutes or till pork is slightly pink and juices run clear, turning once. Remove pork chops from skillet. Cover chops with foil to keep warm. Drain off fat in the skillet.

¼ cup water
1 green onion, thinly sliced (2 tablespoons)
1 tablespoon peanut butter
1 teaspoon lemon juice
2 cloves garlic, minced, *or* ¼ teaspoon garlic powder
¼ teaspoon instant chicken bouillon granules
¼ teaspoon ground ginger

■ For sauce, in the same skillet stir together the water, green onion, peanut butter, lemon juice, garlic or garlic powder, bouillon granules, and ginger. Cook and stir over medium heat about 30 seconds or till slightly thickened. (Sauce should be smooth.)

2 tablespoons chopped peanuts

■ Serve chops atop hot cooked rice sticks or fine egg noodles. Spoon sauce over chops. Top with peanuts. Makes 2 servings.

TIME ESTIMATE
Start to finish — 30 min.

MENU IDEA
Feature a fruit salad with the Oriental-style meal.

PER SERVING
Calories	492
Protein	38 g
Carbohydrate	35 g
Fat (total)	24 g
Saturated	6 g
Cholesterol	105 mg
Sodium	266 mg
Potassium	545 mg

HERB-RUBBED PORK CHOPS

2 boneless pork loin chops, cut ¾ inch thick (about 8 ounces total)

2 teaspoons lemon juice

■ Trim fat from chops. Brush both sides of chops with lemon juice.

TIME ESTIMATE
Start to finish — 15 min.

¼ teaspoon dried thyme *or* savory, crushed

¼ teaspoon dried marjoram *or* basil, crushed

⅛ teaspoon ground ginger

■ In a small bowl stir together thyme or savory, marjoram or basil, and ginger. Rub herb mixture onto both sides of chops.

Place chops on the unheated rack of a broiler pan. Broil 3 inches from heat for 4 minutes. Turn and broil for 4 to 6 minutes more or till pork is slightly pink and juices run clear. Makes 2 servings.

PER SERVING
Calories	162
Protein	26 g
Carbohydrate	1 g
Fat (total)	6 g
Saturated	2 g
Cholesterol	66 mg
Sodium	59 mg
Potassium	322 mg

GRILLING BASICS

For a sizzling, not fizzling, fire, follow these barbecue tips.

■ Pile briquettes in a mound in the center of the grill. Drizzle liquid lighter or jelly fire starter over entire charcoal surface. Wait 1 minute, then ignite with a match. Charcoal is ready when it's glowing or gray and has no black showing. This usually takes 20 to 30 minutes.

■ When the coals are ready, spread them according to the appropriate recipe directions. *For direct cooking,* use long-handled tongs to spread the hot coals in a single layer. For more even heat and fewer flare-ups, arrange the coals ½ inch apart. *For indirect cooking,* move coals from the center of the grill with long-handled tongs. Place a disposable foil drip pan in the center of the grill; arrange coals in a circle around the pan.

■ Determine the temperature of the coals by holding your hand, palm side down, above the coals at the height your food will be cooked. Start counting seconds, "one thousand one, one thousand two. . . ." If you need to withdraw your hand after 2 seconds the coals are *hot;* after 3 seconds, *medium-hot;* after 4 seconds, *medium;* after 5 seconds, *medium-slow;* and after 6 seconds, *slow.*

PICATTA-STYLE PORK

Add zest and zing to a pork tenderloin with a tangy lemon sauce.

8 ounces pork tenderloin, sliced ½ inch thick

■ Place each pork slice between 2 pieces of plastic wrap. Working from the center to the edges, pound pork lightly with the flat side of a meat mallet to ⅛-inch thickness. Remove plastic wrap.

2 tablespoons water
¼ teaspoon instant beef *or* chicken bouillon granules
Nonstick spray coating

■ Combine water and bouillon granules; set aside. Spray the unheated rack of a broiler pan generously with nonstick spray coating. Arrange pork slices on broiler pan; brush generously with bouillon mixture. Broil pork 3 to 4 inches from the heat about 2 minutes per side or till pork is slightly pink and juices run clear, brushing pork frequently with bouillon mixture to keep moist.

2 tablespoons lemon juice
2 tablespoons margarine or butter
½ teaspoon Dijon-style mustard
Dash pepper

■ Meanwhile, for sauce, in a small saucepan combine the lemon juice, margarine or butter, mustard, and pepper. Heat through over low heat, using a fork to mix well.

2 lemon peel strips (optional)

■ To serve, transfer pork slices to individual plates. Spoon sauce over pork. If desired, garnish each serving with a lemon peel strip. Makes 2 servings.

TIME ESTIMATE

Start to finish — 25 min.

MENU IDEA

Offer broccoli spears and pasta drizzled with some of the sauce.

PER SERVING

Calories ———— 245
Protein ———— 25 g
Carbohydrate ——— 2 g
Fat (total) ——— 16 g
Saturated ——— 4 g
Cholesterol ——— 67 mg
Sodium ——— 346 mg
Potassium ——— 483 mg

CHINESE-STYLE PORK AND VEGETABLES

Hoisin sauce with its sweet, piquant taste is a thick and reddish-brown Oriental ingredient similar to Americans' beloved catsup. You also can try hoisin sauce as a jazzy condiment for burgers or chicken.

6 ounces fresh refrigerated *or* 4 ounces packaged spaghetti, linguine, *or* fettuccine

■ Cook pasta (see chart, page 185). Drain immediately.

½ cup water
2 tablespoons soy sauce
1 tablespoon hoisin sauce, catsup, *or* teriyaki sauce
1 teaspoon cornstarch
½ teaspoon instant chicken bouillon granules

■ Meanwhile, for sauce, in a small bowl stir together the water; soy sauce; hoisin sauce, catsup, or teriyaki sauce; cornstarch; and bouillon granules. Set aside.

1 tablespoon cooking oil
1 clove garlic, minced
3 medium carrots, thinly bias-sliced (1½ cups)
6 green onions, bias-sliced into 1-inch pieces
8 ounces lean boneless pork, chicken, *or* turkey, cut into ½-inch cubes

■ Pour cooking oil into a wok or large skillet. (Add more oil as necessary during cooking.) Preheat over medium-high heat. Stir-fry garlic in hot oil for 15 seconds. Add carrots; stir-fry for 2 minutes. Add green onions; stir-fry about 2 minutes more or till vegetables are crisp-tender. Remove vegetables from the wok or skillet.

Add pork, chicken, or turkey to the hot wok or skillet. Stir-fry for 2 to 3 minutes or till no pink remains. Push meat from the center of the wok or skillet. Stir sauce. Add the sauce to the center of the wok or skillet. Cook and stir till thickened and bubbly.

■ Return vegetables to the wok. Stir all ingredients together to coat with sauce. Cook and stir about 1 minute more or till heated through. Serve immediately over the hot cooked pasta. Makes 2 servings.

TIME ESTIMATE
Start to finish — 25 min.

MENU IDEA
Create a simple dessert by sprinkling crushed cookies over ice cream.

PER SERVING
Calories	518
Protein	37 g
Carbohydrate	62 g
Fat (total)	15 g
Saturated	3 g
Cholesterol	66 mg
Sodium	1,539 mg
Potassium	880 mg

CORIANDER-AND-HONEY-GLAZED PORK RIBS

Pick a sunny backyard location and gather the gang for a rib-eating feast. You can easily increase this recipe to feed as many people as you like.

⅓ cup catsup
2 tablespoons honey
½ teaspoon ground coriander *or* curry powder
¼ teaspoon garlic powder

■ For glaze, in a small bowl stir together the catsup, honey, coriander or curry powder, and garlic powder. Set aside.

1 to 1½ pounds pork country-style ribs *or* 8 to 10 ounces boneless pork country-style ribs

■ *To roast,* place the ribs on a rack in a shallow roasting pan. If using ribs with bones, place bone side down on rack. Roast in a 350° oven for 1 hour. Drain fat from pan.

■ Brush the ribs with some of the glaze. Roast for 30 to 45 minutes more or till pork is tender and no pink remains, brushing occasionally with glaze.

■ *Or, to grill,* in a covered grill arrange *medium-hot* coals around a drip pan. Test for *medium* heat above the pan. (See tip, page 27.) Place ribs on the grill rack over the drip pan, but not over the coals. Lower the grill hood. Grill for 1 hour. Brush ribs with glaze. Grill ribs for 15 to 30 minutes more or till pork is tender and no pink remains, brushing occasionally with glaze. Makes 2 servings.

TIME ESTIMATE
Start to finish —1¾ hrs.

MENU IDEA
Enjoy summer's bounty of fresh tomatoes— serve them sliced with a sprinkling of salt and pepper or with snipped fresh basil or cilantro.

PER SERVING
Calories _____ 295
Protein _____ 31 g
Carbohydrate _____ 29 g
Fat (total) _____ 8 g
  Saturated _____ 3 g
Cholesterol _____ 77 mg
Sodium _____ 550 mg
Potassium _____ 587 mg

HAM WITH CHUNKY CRANBERRY SAUCE

1 **small apple, cored and chopped (½ cup)**

1 **stalk celery, sliced (½ cup)**

1 **tablespoon margarine *or* butter**

½ **cup cranberry-orange sauce**

2 **tablespoons vinegar**

⅛ **teaspoon ground allspice**

■ For sauce, in a large skillet cook the apple and celery in hot margarine or butter till tender. Stir in the cranberry-orange sauce, vinegar, and allspice. Cook and stir till heated through. Remove from skillet; keep warm.

8 **ounces fully cooked ham, sliced ⅛ inch thick**

■ In the same skillet cook ham over medium heat about 5 minutes or till heated through, turning once. (Overlap the slices in the skillet, if necessary.)

To serve, transfer ham slices to individual plates. Spoon sauce over ham. Serves 2.

TIME ESTIMATE

Start to finish _ 20 min.

MENU IDEA

Turn this into a traditional holiday dinner for two by serving Creamy Mashed Sweet Potatoes (see recipe, page 179) with the ham.

PER SERVING

Calories	390
Protein	29 g
Carbohydrate	42 g
Fat (total)	12 g
Saturated	3 g
Cholesterol	62 mg
Sodium	1,620 mg
Potassium	553 mg

PORK UPDATE

Today's pork is leaner and lower in fat and calories than ever before. And because there is so little fat in today's pork, it is essential to carefully watch the time and temperature in each recipe to ensure that you serve flavorful, tender, and juicy meat.

To achieve the best flavor, the latest recommendations for cooking pork now offer a choice of doneness for selected pork cuts. Roasts and chops from the loin and rib sections can be cooked to an internal temperature of 160° (medium well) or 170° (well-done). The meat will be slightly pink at 160°, but when a small cut is made in the meat, the juices should run clear.

Ground pork and the less-tender cuts of pork, such as sirloin or loin blade roasts and chops, should be cooked to 170° (well-done) or till no pink remains.

BEANS AND BRATS WITH MUSTARD BISCUITS

Mustard Biscuits
¼ **cup chopped onion**
3 **tablespoons water**
1 **clove garlic, minced**

■ Prepare and bake Mustard Biscuits. Set aside. Meanwhile, in a medium saucepan combine the onion, water, and garlic. Bring to boiling; reduce heat. Cover and simmer 5 minutes or till onion is tender. *Do not drain.*

TIME ESTIMATE
Start to finish — 45 min.

MENU IDEA
Choose cool vegetable relishes or wedges of lettuce drizzled with Italian salad dressing.

1 **15-ounce can navy** *or*
   great northern beans,
   drained
¼ **cup catsup**
2 **tablespoons honey** *or*
   maple-flavored syrup
1½ **teaspoons cider vinegar**
   Dash pepper
6 **ounces fully cooked**
   smoked bratwurst, cut
   into ½-inch slices, *or* **6-**
   ounces cocktail weiners

■ Stir in the navy or great northern beans, catsup, honey or syrup, vinegar, and pepper. Stir in the bratwurst or cocktail weiners. Bring to boiling; reduce heat. Cover and simmer for 5 minutes. Uncover and simmer about 5 minutes more or till the mixture is of desired consistency.

PER SERVING
Calories _____ 804
Protein _____ 29 g
Carbohydrate ___ 93 g
Fat (total) _____ 37 g
  Saturated _____ 11 g
Cholesterol ____ 55 mg
Sodium _____ 1,575 mg
Potassium ____ 1,087 mg

1 **small apple, cored and**
   chopped (½ cup)

■ Stir in the apple. Cover and cook for 2 to 3 minutes more or till apple is just tender. To serve, ladle bean mixture into bowls. Top with warm Mustard Biscuits. Serves 2.

MUSTARD BISCUITS

⅓ **cup all-purpose flour**
½ **teaspoon baking powder**
¼ **teaspoon sugar**
2 **tablespoons margarine**
   or **butter**
2 **tablespoons milk**
1½ **teaspoons prepared**
   mustard

■ In a medium mixing bowl stir together the flour, baking powder, and sugar. Using a pastry blender or fork, cut in the margarine or butter till mixture resembles coarse crumbs. Make a well in the center. Stir together the milk and mustard; add to dry ingredients all at once. Stir just till dough clings together. Drop dough from a tablespoon into 4 mounds on a greased baking sheet. Bake in a 400° oven for 10 to 12 minutes or till bottoms are golden brown. Serve warm.

CHEESY BRATWURSTS AND CABBAGE

2 fully cooked smoked bratwursts, knockwursts *or* Polish sausage links
3 cups shredded cabbage
½ cup water
¼ cup chopped onion
¼ cup shredded carrot
½ teaspoon caraway seed
⅛ teaspoon pepper

■ Make slits in bratwursts, knockwursts, or Polish sausages at 1-inch intervals, cutting to, *but not through,* the opposite side. Set aside.

In a large skillet stir together the cabbage, water, onion, carrot, caraway seed, pepper, and dash *salt.* Arrange sausages atop. Bring to boiling; reduce heat. Cover and simmer for 10 to 15 minutes or till cabbage is tender and bratwursts are heated through.

2 ounces process Swiss cheese, torn

■ Remove sausages from skillet; keep warm. Drain cabbage mixture. Add Swiss cheese to cabbage. Cook and stir over low heat till cheese is melted.

To serve, transfer cabbage mixture and sausages to individual plates. Serves 2.

TIME ESTIMATE
Start to finish — 30 min.

MENU IDEA
Wrap up the menu with rye crackers or rolls, and don't forget to pass the mustard!

PER SERVING

Calories	361
Protein	19 g
Carbohydrate	12 g
Fat (total)	27 g
Saturated	12 g
Cholesterol	68 mg
Sodium	1,253 mg
Potassium	601 mg

MEAL PLANNING

Spending a little time each week planning meals can make the challenge of preparing fresh-tasting and satisfying meals for two easier. Add interest to each meal by using a variety of colors, shapes, flavors, textures, and temperatures. To plan daily menus, think of all the meals for the day. Then use these guidelines to help you.

■ Start by choosing the main dish.

■ Add a bread or cereal, such as rolls, rice, or pasta, if one is not part of the main dish.

■ Choose a hot or cold vegetable and/or a fruit or vegetable salad.

■ Select a beverage such as low-fat or skim milk, fruit juice, or water.

■ If desired, add a dessert. Fruit and milk-based desserts, such as pudding, are nutritious choices while desserts such as cake or candy mostly just add calories to your meal.

ROAST PORK WITH WARM FRUIT SAUCE

You may find this cut of pork at your supermarket labeled "Chef's Prime." If you prefer to cook the whole roast at once, allow 1 to 1¼ hours.

1 2-pound boneless rib-end pork loin roast

■ Trim separable fat from roast. Cut roast in half crosswise. If desired, slice one half of the roast into 4 pork chops. Seal, label, and freeze the 4 pork chops or half of roast for up to 3 months. Use 2 of the chops for Herb-Rubbed Pork Chops on page 27. Broil or grill remaining chops (see charts, pages 38 and 39).

Place remaining half of roast, fat side up, on a rack in a shallow baking pan. Insert meat thermometer. Roast pork in a 325° oven for 45 to 60 minutes or till meat thermometer registers 160°. (Pork will be slightly pink and juices will run clear.) Let pork stand, covered, for 10 minutes.

½ of an 8-ounce package (¾ cup) mixed dried fruit
1 cup apple juice, apricot nectar, *or* orange juice
1 tablespoon orange liqueur (optional)
Dash ground nutmeg, allspice, *or* cinnamon
1 tablespoon water
2 teaspoons cornstarch

■ Meanwhile, for sauce, if desired, cut up any large pieces of dried fruit. In a small saucepan stir together dried fruit; apple juice, apricot nectar, or orange juice; orange liqueur (if desired); and nutmeg, allspice, or cinnamon. Bring to boiling; reduce heat. Cover and simmer for 5 minutes. Stir together the water and cornstarch; stir into fruit mixture. Cook and stir till thickened and bubbly. Cook and stir for 2 minutes more.

Fresh thyme (optional)

■ To serve, slice the pork roast. Arrange *half* of the slices on individual plates. Spoon sauce over and around pork. If desired, garnish with fresh thyme.

Cover and chill remaining sliced cooked pork for up to 2 days. If desired, use chilled cooked pork for Pork and Pear Spinach Salad (see recipe, page 129). Makes 2 servings.

TIME ESTIMATE
Preparation _____ 5 min.
Roasting _____ 45 min.
Standing _____ 10 min.

MENU IDEA
Bring a touch of spring to the meal with fresh asparagus spears.

PER SERVING
Calories _____ 364
Protein _____ 28 g
Carbohydrate _____ 53 g
Fat (total) _____ 7 g
  Saturated _____ 2 g
Cholesterol _____ 66 mg
Sodium _____ 73 mg
Potassium _____ 911 mg

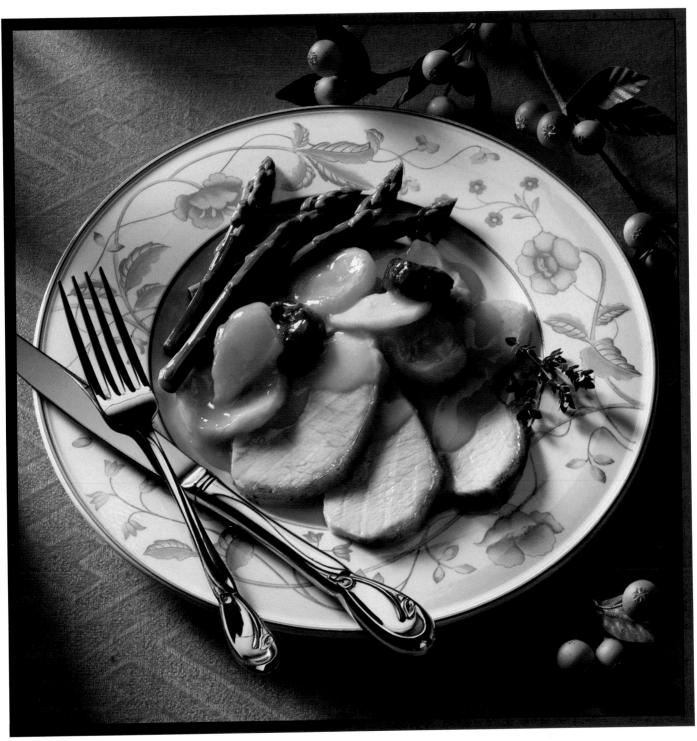

ROAST PORK WITH WARM FRUIT SAUCE

LAMB CHOPS WITH LEEK SAUCE

Leeks, a member of the onion family, lend a sweet, subtle onion flavor to the sauce. To prepare them, wash well and cut slices from the white base up to about 1 inch into the green stalk.

4 lamb loin chops, cut 1
   inch thick (about 1
   pound total)
1 tablespoon olive oil *or*
   cooking oil

■ Trim fat from chops. In an 8-inch skillet cook chops in hot oil over medium heat to desired doneness, turning once. (Allow 7 to 9 minutes for medium and 10 to 13 minutes for well-done.) Transfer chops to individual plates and keep warm. Drain fat from skillet.

2 tablespoons water
2 medium leeks, sliced
   (⅔ cup), *or* 2 green
   onions, sliced (¼ cup)
1 teaspoon snipped fresh
   tarragon *or* ¼ teaspoon
   dried tarragon, crushed

■ For sauce, add the water to the skillet; scrape up crusty bits from the bottom of the skillet. Add leeks or green onions and tarragon. Simmer, uncovered, for 1 to 2 minutes or till the leeks or green onions are almost tender.

⅓ cup whipping cream, half-
   and-half, *or* light cream

■ Stir in the whipping cream, half-and-half, or light cream. Bring to boiling; reduce heat. Simmer, uncovered, for 1 to 2 minutes or till the sauce is of desired consistency, stirring once. Spoon the sauce over the chops. Makes 2 servings.

TIME ESTIMATE
Start to finish — 25 min.

MENU IDEA
Buttered Pasta (see recipe, page 184) and cooked baby carrots are two side dishes you can put together in no time.

PER SERVING
Calories _____ 411
Protein _____ 29 g
Carbohydrate _____ 6 g
Fat (total) _____ 31 g
   Saturated _____ 14 g
Cholesterol _____ 139 mg
Sodium _____ 98 mg
Potassium _____ 437 mg

LAMB CHOPS TERIYAKI

For even more flavor, turn the sauce into a marinade. Just double the ingredients, marinate the chops for 2 to 24 hours in the refrigerator, then cook as directed.

1 tablespoon brown sugar
1 tablespoon soy sauce
2 teaspoons catsup
1 teaspoon lemon juice
½ teaspoon grated
    gingerroot *or* ⅛
    teaspoon ground ginger
⅛ teaspoon salt
    Dash garlic powder
    Dash pepper

2 lamb leg sirloin chops *or*
    4 lamb rib chops, cut 1
    inch thick (about 12
    ounces total)
1 tablespoon snipped
    parsley (optional)

■ For sauce, in a small bowl stir together the brown sugar, soy sauce, catsup, lemon juice, gingerroot or ground ginger, salt, garlic powder, and pepper. Set aside.

■ Trim fat from meat. *To broil,* place chops on the unheated rack of a broiler pan. Broil 3 inches from the heat to desired doneness, turning once and brushing with sauce the last 2 to 3 minutes of cooking. (Allow 8 to 10 minutes for rare and 10 to 12 minutes for medium.)

Or, to grill, place chops on the rack of an uncovered grill. (See tip, page 27.) Grill directly over *medium* coals to desired doneness, turning once and brushing with sauce the last 2 to 3 minutes of cooking. (Allow 10 to 14 minutes for rare and 14 to 16 minutes for medium.)

If desired, garnish each chop with parsley. Makes 2 servings.

TIME ESTIMATE

Start to finish _ 20 min.

MENU IDEA

Carry out an Oriental theme for the meal with pea pods and Hot Cooked Rice (see recipe, page 187.)

PER SERVING

Calories	192
Protein	22 g
Carbohydrate	9 g
Fat (total)	7 g
Saturated	2 g
Cholesterol	69 mg
Sodium	765 mg
Potassium	331 mg

BROILING MEAT

Place meat on the unheated rack of a broiler pan. For cuts less than 1¼ inches thick, broil 3 inches from the heat. For cuts 1¼ inches thick or thicker, broil 4 to 5 inches from the heat. Broil for the time given or till done, turning meat over after half of the broiling time.

CUT	THICKNESS (INCHES)	DONENESS	TIME (MINUTES)
Beef Steak (top loin, tenderloin, T-bone*, porterhouse*, sirloin*, rib, rib eye)	1	Rare Medium Well-done	8 to 12 13 to 17 18 to 22
Steak (chuck, top round)*	1	Rare Medium Well-done	16 to 20 22 to 24 26 to 28
Veal Chop	1	Medium to well-done	12 to 15
Lamb Chop	1	Rare Medium	8 to 10 10 to 12
Pork Chop (boneless)	1 1½	Medium Well-done Medium Well-done	11 to 13 13 to 15 16 to 18 18 to 20
Chop (with bone)	¾ 1¼ to 1½	Medium to well-done Medium to well-done	8 to 14 18 to 25
Canadian-style bacon	¼	Heated	3 to 5
Miscellaneous Fresh link sausage (bratwurst or Italian or Polish sausage)		Well-done	10 to 12
Ground-meat patties (beef, lamb, pork**)	¾ (4 per pound)	Medium to well-done	14 to 18

*Some of these cuts may provide more than two 4-ounce portions of meat. **Pork should be cooked till no pink remains.*

GRILLING MEAT

Test for the desired temperature of the coals (see tip, page 27). Place meat on grill rack directly over preheated coals. Grill the meat, uncovered, for the time given or till done, turning the meat over after half of the grilling time.

CUT	THICKNESS (INCHES)	COAL TEMPERATURE	DONENESS	TIME (MINUTES)
Beef Flank steak*	¾	Medium	Medium	12 to 14
Steak (top loin, tenderloin, T-bone*, porterhouse*, sirloin*, rib, rib eye)	1	Medium-hot	Rare Medium Well-done	8 to 12 12 to 15 16 to 20
Steak (chuck, top round)*	1	Medium	Rare Medium Well-done	14 to 16 18 to 20 22 to 24
Veal Chop	1	Medium	Medium to well-done	19 to 23
Lamb Chop	1	Medium	Rare Medium-well	10 to 14 14 to 16
Pork Chop (with bone)	¾	Medium-hot	Medium to well-done	12 to 14
	1¼ to 1½	Medium	Medium to well-done	30 to 40
Candian-style bacon	¼	Medium-hot	Heated	3 to 5
Miscellaneous Fresh link sausage (bratwurst or Italian or Polish sausage)		Medium-hot	Well-done	12 to 14
Ground-meat patties (beef, lamb, pork**)	¾ (4 per pound)	Medium	Medium to well-done	14 to 18

*Some of these cuts may provide more than two 4-ounce portions of meat. **Pork should be cooked till no pink remains.*

EAT TWO/FREEZE TWO

STEAK PINWHEELS STUFFED WITH SPINACH AND BACON

8 slices bacon
1 1- to 1½-pound beef flank
   steak *or* beef top round
   steak
½ teaspoon lemon-pepper
   seasoning
¼ teaspoon salt

■ In a large skillet cook bacon just till done but not crisp. Drain on paper towels. Score steak by making shallow cuts at 1-inch intervals diagonally across steak in a diamond pattern. Repeat on second side. Place steak between 2 pieces of plastic wrap. Working from the center to the edges, pound meat lightly with the flat side of a meat mallet to form a 12x8-inch rectangle. Remove plastic wrap. Sprinkle the lemon-pepper seasoning and salt over top. Arrange the bacon lengthwise on the steak.

1 10-ounce package frozen
   chopped spinach,
   thawed and well
   drained
2 tablespoons fine dry
   bread crumbs
½ teaspoon dried thyme,
   crushed
¼ teaspoon lemon-pepper
   seasoning
   Dash salt

■ In a mixing bowl stir together the spinach, bread crumbs, thyme, lemon-pepper seasoning, and salt. Spread the spinach mixture over the bacon. Roll up meat from a short side. Secure with wooden toothpicks at 1-inch intervals, starting ½ inch from one end. Cut between toothpicks into eight 1-inch slices. Cook 4 of the pinwheels immediately and freeze the remaining pinwheels as directed. Makes 4 servings.

TIME ESTIMATE
Preparation ___ 30 min.
Grilling _____ *12 min.
Allow extra time to heat coals.

MENU IDEA
Dress up steamed asparagus by tying several spears together with a strip of lemon or orange peel. Add cooked orzo and your meal's complete.

PER SERVING
Calories _____ 281
Protein _____ 31 g
Carbohydrate _____ 6 g
Fat (total) _____ 15 g
  Saturated _____ 6 g
Cholesterol _____ 68 mg
Sodium _____ 671 mg
Potassium _____ 622 mg

TO EAT TWO: *To grill,* horizontally thread *two* pinwheels onto *each* of 2 long skewers. Remove wooden toothpicks. Place pinwheels on the rack of an uncovered grill. (See tip, page 27.) Grill directly over *medium* coals 12 to 14 minutes or to desired doneness, turning once.

  Or, to broil, place pinwheels, cut side down, on the unheated rack of a broiler pan. Broil 3 to 4 inches from the heat for 12 to 14 minutes or to desired doneness, turning once. Remove toothpicks.

TO FREEZE TWO: Place *two* pinwheels into *each* of 2 individual freezer containers. Seal, label, and freeze for up to 3 months. *To serve,* thaw 2 or 4 of the pinwheels overnight in the refrigerator. Cook according to the directions above.

STEAK PINWHEELS STUFFED WITH SPINACH AND BACON

WELLINGTON-STYLE BEEF TENDERLOIN

½ of a 17½-ounce package
   (1 sheet) frozen puff
   pastry
4 4- to 5-ounce beef
   tenderloin steaks, cut ¾
   inch thick, *or* two 8-
   ounce beef top loin
   steaks, cut ¾ inch thick
1 tablespoon cooking oil

2 cups fresh mushrooms,
   finely chopped
3 green onions, thinly
   sliced (⅓ cup)
2 tablespoons margarine
   or butter
2 tablespoons dry white
   wine (optional)
⅛ teaspoon dried thyme,
   crushed
⅛ teaspoon pepper

■ To thaw pastry, let stand at room temperature for 20 minutes. Or, thaw overnight in the refrigerator.

Meanwhile, if using the top loin steaks, cut each steak in half crosswise. In a large skillet brown tenderloin or top loin steaks in hot oil over medium-high heat for 1 minute on each side. Drain on paper towels. Set aside.

■ In the same skillet cook mushrooms and onions in hot margarine or butter and, if desired, wine for 5 to 6 minutes or till tender and liquid has evaporated. Remove skillet from the heat. Stir in thyme and pepper.

Unfold pastry and place on a lightly floured surface. Roll into an 11-inch square. Cut into four 5½-inch squares. Place some of the mushroom mixture in the center of each square. Place a steak on top. Fold pastry over meat. If necessary, trim pastry to within ½ inch of edge of meat. (See photo, right.) Reserve pastry trimmings. Turn bundles over. If desired, cut small shapes from trimmings; moisten with water and place on top of bundles. Bake 2 bundles immediately; freeze remaining bundles as directed. Serves 4.

TIME ESTIMATE
Preparation ____ 35 min.
Baking _____ 18 min.

MENU IDEA
Pour a little melted butter with a squeeze of lemon juice over cooked artichoke hearts or brussels sprouts.

PER SERVING
Calories _____ 527
Protein _____ 29 g
Carbohydrate _____ 24 g
Fat (total) _____ 35 g
  Saturated _____ 5 g
Cholesterol _____ 72 mg
Sodium _____ 414 mg
Potassium _____ 513 mg

TO EAT TWO: Place 2 bundles, pastry side up, on a rack in a shallow baking pan. Bake, uncovered, in a 425° oven for 18 minutes. (Meat will be medium-rare.)

TO FREEZE TWO: Seal, label, and freeze 2 bundles for up to 3 months. *To serve,* unwrap 1 or 2 frozen bundles. Place, pastry side up, on a rack in a shallow baking pan. Bake, uncovered, in a 425° oven for 30 minutes. (Meat will be medium-rare.) If necessary, cover pastry loosely with foil during the last 5 minutes to prevent overbrowning.

LEMON-DILL MEATBALLS IN CREAMY TOMATO SAUCE

¾ cup chopped onion
2 cloves garlic, minced
2 tablespoons margarine
2 14½-ounce cans Italian-style stewed tomatoes *or* stewed tomatoes
1 tablespoon snipped fresh dillweed *or* 1 teaspoon dried dillweed
½ teaspoon sugar

1 beaten egg
½ cup soft bread crumbs
2 tablespoons finely chopped onion
1½ teaspoons finely shredded lemon peel
12 ounces ground beef, pork, *or* raw turkey
2 tablespoons cooking oil

■ For sauce, in a medium saucepan cook the onion and garlic in hot margarine till onion is tender but not brown.

Carefully stir in the *undrained* tomatoes, dillweed, sugar, ¼ teaspoon *salt,* and ⅛ teaspoon *pepper.* Bring to boiling; reduce heat. Simmer, uncovered, for 30 to 35 minutes or to desired consistency, stirring occasionally.

■ Meanwhile, combine egg, bread crumbs, onion, and lemon peel. Add meat; mix well. Shape meat mixture into a 6x4-inch rectangle. Using a long knife, cut into twenty-four 1-inch squares (see photo, right). Roll each square into a ball. In a large skillet cook meatballs in hot oil for 8 to 10 minutes or till no pink remains. Drain well. Stir meatballs into sauce. Transfer *half* of the sauce-meatball mixture to 1 or 2 individual freezer containers and freeze as directed. Cook the remaining sauce-meatball mixture in the saucepan immediately. Makes 4 servings.

TIME ESTIMATE
Start to finish __ 50 min.

PER SERVING
Calories _____ 509
Protein _____ 23 g
Carbohydrate ____ 42 g
Fat (total) _____ 28 g
　Saturated _____ 9 g
Cholesterol ____ 121 mg
Sodium _____ 881 mg
Potassium _____ 901 mg

TO EAT TWO: Slowly add ¼ cup **whipping cream** *or* **half-and-half** to sauce-meatball mixture in the saucepan, stirring constantly. Cook and stir about 2 minutes or till heated through. Serve over 2 cups hot cooked **spaghetti, linguine,** *or* **other pasta.**

TO FREEZE TWO: Seal, label and freeze the freezer containers for up to 3 months. *To serve,* place 1 or 2 of the frozen servings in a saucepan. Cook, covered, over medium-low heat about 25 minutes or till hot, stirring occasionally. For *each* serving, slowly add 2 tablespoons **whipping cream** *or* **half-and-half** to sauce-meatball mixture, stirring constantly. Cook and stir about 2 minutes more or till hot. Spoon each serving over 1 cup hot cooked **spaghetti, linguine,** *or* **other pasta.**

VEAL RAGOUT WITH PEAS AND PASTA

12 ounces boneless veal shoulder roast *or* beef chuck pot roast
1 clove garlic, minced
1 tablespoon olive oil *or* cooking oil
1 14½-ounce can whole Italian-style tomatoes, cut up
1 8-ounce can tomato sauce
1 cup chopped celery
½ cup chopped carrot
½ cup chopped onion
2 tablespoons dry red wine, dry sherry, *or* water
¼ teaspoon dried sage *or* basil, crushed
⅛ teaspoon crushed red pepper
1 bay leaf

■ Trim separable fat from veal or beef. Cut meat into 1-inch pieces. In a large skillet brown the veal or beef with the garlic in hot oil over medium-high heat. Drain off fat.

Stir in the *undrained* tomatoes; tomato sauce; celery; carrot; onion; wine, dry sherry, or water; sage or basil; crushed red pepper; bay leaf; ¼ teaspoon *salt;* and ⅛ teaspoon *pepper*. Bring to boiling; reduce heat. Cover and simmer for 45 to 50 minutes for the veal or 1 to 1¼ hours for the beef or till meat is tender. Discard bay leaf.

TIME ESTIMATE
Start to finish —1¼ hrs.

MENU IDEA
Finish your meal in style with chocolate-dipped strawberries or dried apricots and cups of steaming, freshly brewed coffee.

PER SERVING
Calories _____ 354
Protein _____ 27 g
Carbohydrate _____ 39 g
Fat (total) _____ 10 g
  Saturated _____ 3 g
Cholesterol ____ 102 mg
Sodium _____ 829 mg
Potassium _____ 942 mg

1 cup loose-pack frozen peas
2 ounces prosciutto *or* fully cooked ham, cut into thin strips

■ Stir in the peas and prosciutto or ham. Pour *half* of the veal mixture into 1 or 2 individual freezer containers and freeze as directed. Leave remaining mixture in the skillet and cook immediately. Makes 4 servings.

TO EAT TWO: Cook the remaining 2 servings in the skillet till peas are tender and mixture is heated through. Serve over 2 cups hot cooked **fettuccine, noodles,** *or* **other pasta.**

TO FREEZE TWO: Seal, label, and freeze the freezer containers for up to 3 months. *To serve,* transfer 1 or 2 frozen portions to a medium saucepan. Cover and cook over medium-low heat about 20 minutes or till heated through, stirring occasionally. For *each* serving, serve over 1 cup hot cooked **fettuccine, noodles,** *or* **other pasta.**

PORK AND CRANBERRY PIES

½ of a 15-ounce package (1 crust) folded refrigerated unbaked piecrusts

■ On a lightly floured surface unfold unbaked piecrust and roll into a 12-inch circle. Cut four 5-inch circles from pastry. Cover and set aside.

TIME ESTIMATE
Preparation ____ 30 min.
Baking _____ 10 min.

1 cup cranberries
2 stalks celery, sliced (1 cup)
1 cup apple juice *or* apple cider
1 medium onion, chopped (½ cup)
¼ cup water
2 tablespoons brown sugar
1½ teaspoons instant beef bouillon granules
½ teaspoon dried thyme *or* basil, crushed

■ In a large saucepan combine the cranberries, celery, apple juice or apple cider, onion, water, brown sugar, bouillon granules, and thyme or basil. Bring to boiling; reduce heat. Cover and boil gently for 3 to 4 minutes or till cranberry skins pop.

MENU IDEA

Compose a fresh fruit plate to pass with the pies and serve small scoops of sherbet for dessert.

PER SERVING

Calories	528
Protein	33 g
Carbohydrate	50 g
Fat (total)	22 g
Saturated	18 g
Cholesterol	73 mg
Sodium	656 mg
Potassium	617 mg

½ cup water
¼ cup all-purpose flour
2½ cups cubed cooked pork, chicken, *or* turkey

■ In a small bowl stir together water and flour; stir into saucepan. Cook and stir till thickened and bubbly. Stir in pork, chicken, or turkey; heat till bubbly.

Pour meat mixture into four 10-ounce round casseroles. Place 1 pastry circle atop each casserole. If desired, flute edges of pastry. Cut slits in the top to allow steam to escape. Bake 2 casseroles immediately; freeze remaining casseroles as directed. Serves 4.

TO EAT TWO: Place 2 of the casseroles in a shallow baking pan. Bake, uncovered, in a 450° oven for 10 to 12 minutes or till pork mixture is bubbly and pastry is golden brown.

TO FREEZE TWO: Seal, label, and freeze 2 of the casseroles for up to 3 months. *To serve,* place 1 or 2 of the frozen casseroles in a shallow baking pan. Bake, uncovered, in a 400° oven for 40 to 45 minutes or till pork mixture is bubbly and pastry is golden brown.

EAT TWO/FREEZE TWO

SPICY SAUSAGE PIZZA IN POTATO CRUST

¼ cup margarine *or* butter
1½ cups all-purpose flour
1½ cups packaged instant
    mashed potatoes
1 cup milk
12 ounces bulk Italian *or*
    pork sausage
⅓ cup chopped onion
1 8-ounce can tomato sauce
1 2¼-ounce can sliced
    pitted ripe olives
½ teaspoon dried Italian
    seasoning, crushed
⅛ teaspoon garlic powder

¾ cup shredded mozzarella
    cheese (3 ounces)
2 tablespoons margarine
    or butter, melted

■ For crust, melt margarine or butter. In a mixing bowl stir together the margarine or butter, flour, instant mashed potatoes, and milk. Set mixture aside.

For filling, in a large skillet cook the sausage and onion till sausage is brown and onion is tender. Drain off fat. Stir in the tomato sauce, olives, Italian seasoning, garlic powder, and ⅛ teaspoon *pepper*.

■ Meanwhile, divide crust into 8 equal portions; form into balls. Press 1 ball each into bottom and up sides of 4 greased 10-ounce round casseroles. Divide filling among casseroles. Sprinkle with cheese.

Between 2 sheets of floured waxed paper roll each remaining ball into a 5-inch circle. Remove top sheet of waxed paper. Invert circle over filling in casserole. Peel off second sheet of paper. Turn edges under; press onto bottom crust to seal. Cut slits in top crust to allow steam to escape. Brush tops with melted margarine. Bake 2 casseroles immediately and freeze others as directed. Serves 4.

TO EAT TWO: Bake 2 of the casseroles, covered, in a 425° oven for 20 minutes. Uncover and bake for 10 to 15 minutes more or till filling is hot and crusts are golden brown.

TO FREEZE TWO: Seal, label, and freeze 2 casseroles up to 3 months. *To serve,* bake 1 or 2 frozen casseroles, covered, in a 425° oven 45 minutes. Uncover; bake 10 to 15 minutes or till hot and golden.

TIME ESTIMATE
Preparation ___ 40 min.
Baking ___ 30 min.

MENU IDEA
Team refreshing tossed salads or vegetable relishes with the pizza.

PER SERVING
Calories ___ 689
Protein ___ 26 g
Carbohydrate ___ 60 g
Fat (total) ___ 38 g
   Saturated ___ 12 g
Cholesterol ___ 62 mg
Sodium ___ 1,339 mg
Potassium ___ 764 mg

BLACK BEAN AND SAUSAGE BURRITOS

12 ounces bulk chorizo *or* Italian sausage
¾ cup chopped onion
½ cup chopped green pepper
1 clove garlic, minced
1 cup ricotta cheese
¾ cup shredded Monterey Jack cheese with jalapeño peppers *or* cheddar cheese
1 4-ounce can diced green chili peppers, drained

8 10-inch flour tortillas
1 15-ounce can black beans, rinsed and drained

■ For the filling, in a large skillet cook the chorizo or Italian sausage, onion, green pepper, and garlic till meat is brown and onion is tender. Drain off fat. Stir in the ricotta cheese, Monterey Jack cheese with jalapeño peppers or cheddar cheese, and chili peppers. Set aside.

■ Meanwhile, stack tortillas; wrap tightly in foil. Heat in a 350° oven for 10 minutes to soften. Use a fork to mash the black beans till they form a paste. Spread about *2 tablespoons* black beans in the center of *each* tortilla to within 2 inches of the edge. Spoon a scant *½ cup* filling onto *each* tortilla just below the center. Fold bottom edge of tortilla up and over filling, just till mixture is covered. Fold in opposite sides of tortilla, just till they meet. Roll up tortilla from the bottom. Secure with wooden toothpicks. Bake 4 burritos immediately; freeze others as directed. Serves 4.

TO EAT TWO: Arrange 4 of the burritos on a baking sheet. Bake in a 350° oven 10 to 12 minutes or till hot. Remove toothpicks. If desired, serve on shredded **lettuce**. Top with **salsa** and shredded **cheese**.

TO FREEZE TWO: Wrap 4 burritos individually in heavy-duty foil. Label and freeze burritos for up to 3 months. *To serve,* bake 2 or 4 frozen foil-wrapped burritos in a 375° oven about 45 minutes or till hot. (*Or,* thaw burritos overnight in the refrigerator. Bake about 15 minutes or till hot.) Remove toothpicks. If desired, serve as directed.

TIME ESTIMATE
Preparation —— 25 min.
Baking ———— 10 min.

MENU IDEA
Mix some torn greens with orange, avocado, and onion slices and toss them with Lemon-Nut Vinaigrette (see recipe, page 136.)

PER SERVING
Calories ————— 823
Protein ————— 39 g
Carbohydrate —— 87 g
Fat (total) ———— 38 g
    Saturated ——— 16 g
Cholesterol ——— 94 mg
Sodium ——— 1,412 mg
Potassium ——— 747 mg

POULTRY

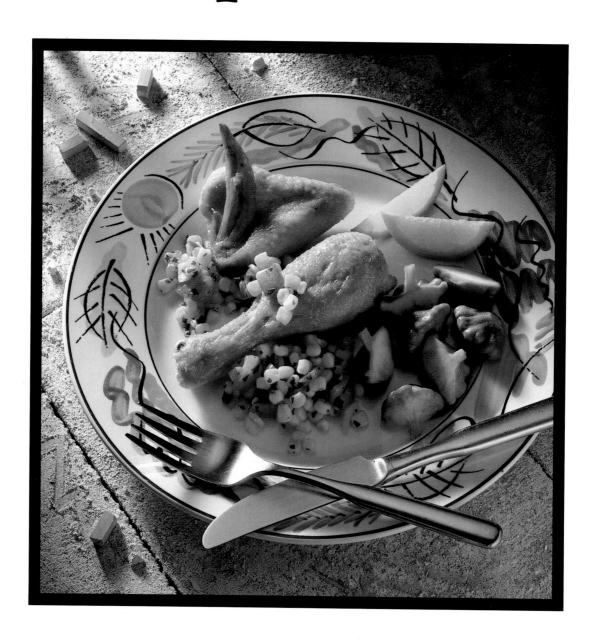

CORN SALSA OVER CHICKEN

CORN SALSA OVER CHICKEN

To ease last-minute work, make the salsa up to three days in advance and store it covered in the refrigerator.

⅓ cup loose-pack frozen
corn
1 small tomato, peeled and
chopped (about ½ cup)
1 jalapeño pepper, finely
chopped (see tip, page
12), *or* 2 tablespoons
canned diced green
chili peppers, drained
1 tablespoon finely
chopped onion
1 tablespoon snipped
cilantro *or* parsley
1 tablespoon lemon *or*
lime juice
1 tablespoon olive oil *or*
cooking oil
1 clove garlic, minced

■ Cook the corn according to package directions. Drain well.

For salsa, in a medium mixing bowl stir together the corn, tomato, jalapeño pepper or green chili peppers, onion, cilantro or parsley, lemon or lime juice, olive oil or cooking oil, and garlic. Cover and chill for at least 1 hour.

TIME ESTIMATE

Preparation ____ 10 min.
Chilling _____ 1 hr.
Cooking _____ 45 min.

MENU IDEA

Patty pan squash, orange wedges, and crusty hard rolls are great accompaniments to the salsa-topped chicken.

PER SERVING

Calories _____ 369
Protein _____ 24 g
Carbohydrate _____ 9 g
Fat (total) _____ 26 g
  Saturated _____ 5 g
Cholesterol _____ 77 mg
Sodium_____ 143 mg
Potassium _____ 350 mg

2 chicken drumsticks and 2
chicken wings, *or* 2
chicken legs, *or* 1
whole medium chicken
breast, halved
lengthwise (about 12
ounces total)
1 tablespoon olive oil *or*
cooking oil

■ Rinse chicken; pat dry. In a medium skillet cook chicken, uncovered, in hot olive oil or cooking oil over medium heat for 15 minutes, turning to brown evenly. Reduce heat; cover tightly. Cook for 25 minutes. Uncover; cook for 5 to 10 minutes more or till the chicken is tender and no pink remains. Drain on paper towels.

Or, to grill, omit olive oil. Place chicken pieces, skin side down, on the rack of an uncovered grill. (See tip, page 27.) Grill directly over *medium* coals for 20 minutes. Turn chicken and grill 15 to 25 minutes more or till the chicken is tender and no pink remains.

To serve, transfer chicken to individual plates. Spoon salsa over chicken. Serves 2.

49

LEMON-HERB CHICKEN AND VEGETABLE KABOBS

6 **whole tiny new potatoes**
1 **small zucchini *or* yellow summer squash, diagonally cut into 1-inch slices**

■ Remove a narrow strip of peel from the center of each potato. Cook potatoes, covered, in a small amount of boiling water for 12 minutes. Add zucchini and cook, covered, for 1 to 2 minutes more or till vegetables are *nearly* tender. Drain and cool.

2 **large boneless, skinless chicken breast halves (8 ounces total)**

■ Rinse chicken and pat dry. Cut *each* breast half into 4 lengthwise strips. Place chicken in a plastic bag set in a mixing bowl. Set aside.

¼ **cup lemon *or* lime juice**
1 **tablespoon olive oil *or* cooking oil**
1 **tablespoon water**
2 **cloves garlic, minced**
½ **teaspoon dried basil *or* oregano, crushed**
¼ **teaspoon dried thyme *or* rosemary, crushed**
⅛ **teaspoon pepper**

■ For marinade, in a bowl combine the lemon juice, olive oil, water, garlic, basil, thyme, pepper, and ⅛ teaspoon *salt.* Add potatoes and zucchini to the plastic bag with the chicken. Pour the marinade over chicken and vegetables in the bag. Close bag and turn to coat well. Marinate at room temperature for 30 minutes or in the refrigerator for 2 hours, turning bag occasionally. Drain the chicken and vegetables, reserving marinade.

■ On 2 long or 4 short skewers, alternately thread the chicken, accordion style, with potatoes and zucchini.

To grill, place kabobs on the rack of an uncovered grill. (See tip, page 27.) Grill directly over *medium-hot* coals 8 to 10 minutes or till chicken is tender and no pink remains, turning and brushing with marinade often.

Or, to broil, place skewers on the unheated rack of a broiler pan. Broil 4 to 5 inches from heat for 5 minutes, brushing with marinade frequently. Turn and broil for 3 to 5 minutes more or till chicken is tender and no pink remains, brushing with marinade often. Makes 2 servings.

TIME ESTIMATE

Preparation ___ 20 min.
Marinating* ___ 30 min.
Grilling ___ 10 min.
Heat the coals while marinating the chicken.

MENU IDEA

Team these hearty kabobs with a crisp lettuce salad and icy cold glasses of lemonade.

PER SERVING

Calories ___ 352
Protein ___ 30 g
Carbohydrate ___ 34 g
Fat (total) ___ 11 g
  Saturated ___ 2 g
Cholesterol ___ 72 mg
Sodium ___ 78 mg
Potassium ___ 993 mg

INGREDIENTS TO KEEP ON HAND

Do you ever get ready to cook, then go to your cupboard and find you're missing a needed ingredient? Or, do you have several ingredients on hand, but get tired of making the same recipes?

Now there's a solution. We've compiled a list of ingredients to help make your cooking more creative and fun. Just keep on hand staples, such as milk, eggs, margarine or butter, salt, sugar, and all-purpose flour. Then, shop from the list of ingredients below and you'll be able to prepare a variety of recipes in this book. To ensure freshness of the ingredients, store them no longer than indicated.

Refrigerator	Freezer	Cupboard

(store for up to 1 week)
lettuce
green *or* sweet red peppers
green onions
jalapeño peppers
ricotta cheese
	(store for up to 3 months)
	fish steaks *or* fillets
	ground beef, pork, chicken, *or*
	   turkey
	pork chops
		(store for up to 6 months)
		olive oil *or* cooking oil
		brown rice
		instant chicken *or* beef bouillon
		   granules

(store for up to 2 weeks)
half-and-half *or* light cream
grated Parmesan cheese
soft-style cream cheese
dairy sour cream
lemons
apples
shredded Monterey Jack,
   cheddar, *or* mozzarella
cheese
garlic
gingerroot
	(store for up to 6 months)
	boneless chicken breast halves
	   or pieces
	chicken pieces
	turkey tenderloin steaks
	beef steaks
	nuts
	dried fruits
		(store for up to 1 year)
		dried herbs
		spices
		wine vinegar *or* vinegar
		canned tomatoes
		assorted pastas
		long grain rice

(store for up to 6 months) Dijon-style mustard catsup Worcestershire sauce chutney sun-dried tomatoes (oil pack)		

CHICKEN WITH SWEET POTATOES

Savor the flavor of tender chicken and pan-fried sweet potatoes drizzled with a luscious mellow wine sauce.

¼ **cup dry white wine**
¼ **cup water**
½ **teaspoon instant chicken bouillon granules**
¼ **teaspoon dried thyme, marjoram, *or* basil, crushed**

2 **large boneless, skinless chicken breast halves *or* turkey tenderloin steaks (8 ounces total)**
1 **medium sweet potato, peeled and cut into ½-inch-thick slices**
2 **tablespoons olive oil *or* cooking oil**

■ For sauce, in a small bowl stir together the white wine, water, chicken bouillon granules, and thyme, marjoram, or basil. Set aside.

■ Rinse the chicken or turkey and pat dry. Set aside.

In a large skillet cook the sweet potato slices in hot olive oil or cooking oil, covered, over medium heat for 4 minutes, turning once. Add the chicken or turkey. Cook, uncovered, for 8 to 10 minutes more or till the chicken or turkey is tender and no pink remains and the potatoes are tender; turn the chicken or turkey once and the potatoes occasionally. Transfer the chicken or turkey and sweet potatoes to individual plates, reserving drippings in skillet. Cover to keep chicken or turkey and sweet potatoes warm.

■ Carefully add the sauce to the hot skillet. Stir and scrape any crusty browned bits off the bottom. Simmer gently about 2 minutes or till the sauce is reduced by half. Pour the sauce over the chicken or turkey and sweet potatoes. Makes 2 servings.

TIME ESTIMATE

Start to finish — 25 min.

MENU IDEA

Serve this festive entrée with your favorite cranberry relish and piping hot Dinner Rolls (see recipe, page 207).

PER SERVING

Calories —————— 368
Protein ————— 28 g
Carbohydrate ——— 19 g
Fat (total) ———— 18 g
 Saturated ———— 3 g
Cholesterol ——— 72 mg
Sodium————— 302 mg
Potassium ——— 368 mg

PAELLA-STYLE BROWN RICE AND CHICKEN

4 chicken drumsticks *or*
  thighs, *or* 2 chicken
  legs, *or* 1 whole
  medium chicken breast,
  halved lengthwise
  (about 12 ounces total)
1 tablespoon olive oil *or*
  cooking oil

■ If desired, remove the skin from the chicken. Rinse the chicken and pat dry.

In a medium skillet cook the chicken, uncovered, in hot olive oil or cooking oil over medium heat for 15 minutes, turning to brown evenly. Remove the chicken from the skillet, reserving the drippings in the skillet.

1 small onion, cut into thin
  wedges (½ cup)
¼ cup sweet red, yellow, *or*
  green pepper cut into
  ½-inch squares
1 clove garlic, minced

■ Add the onion, pepper, and garlic to the drippings in the skillet. Cook and stir till the vegetables are tender but not brown. (Add more oil, if necessary.) Drain excess fat from the skillet.

1 8-ounce can stewed
  tomatoes
¾ cup water
⅔ cup quick-cooking brown
  rice
1 teaspoon instant chicken
  bouillon granules
1 teaspoon chili powder

■ Add the *undrained* tomatoes, water, rice, bouillon granules, and chili powder to the vegetables in the skillet. Bring to boiling, scraping up any browned bits. Add chicken pieces. Reduce heat; cover and simmer for 20 to 25 minutes or till chicken is *nearly* done.

1 cup loose-pack frozen
  peas, thawed
¼ cup plain yogurt *or* dairy
  sour cream

■ Sprinkle the peas over the rice-chicken mixture. Cover and cook about 5 minutes more or till chicken is tender and no pink remains and rice is tender. Dollop with yogurt or sour cream. Makes 2 servings.

TIME ESTIMATE
Start to finish ——1 hr.

MENU IDEA
Complement this colorful rice and chicken dish with crusty French rolls and sliced fresh strawberries or peaches.

PER SERVING
Calories ——————— 645
Protein ——————40 g
Carbohydrate ———73 g
Fat (total) ————22 g
  Saturated ————5 g
Cholesterol ———98 mg
Sodium———————936 mg
Potassium ———958 mg

GLAZED CHICKEN AND GRAPES

2 large boneless, skinless chicken breast halves *or* turkey tenderloin steaks (8 ounces total)
1 tablespoon margarine *or* butter

■ Rinse chicken or turkey and pat dry. In a medium skillet cook chicken or turkey in hot margarine over medium heat for 8 to 10 minutes or till tender and no pink remains, turning once. Transfer the chicken or turkey to individual plates, reserving drippings in skillet. Cover chicken or turkey to keep warm.

½ cup seedless grapes
¼ cup apple *or* currant jelly
1 tablespoon dry sherry *or* dry white wine
1 teaspoon lemon juice
1 tablespoon snipped parsley

■ Cut the grapes in half. Set aside.

For glaze, add the apple or currant jelly, dry sherry or white wine, lemon juice, and ⅛ teaspoon *salt* to the skillet. Cook and stir till the jelly is melted. Stir in grapes and parsley. Heat through. To serve, spoon glaze over chicken or turkey. Makes 2 servings.

TIME ESTIMATE
Start to finish _ 20 min.

MENU IDEA
Serve flowering kale and Hot Cooked Rice (see recipe, page 187).

PER SERVING
Calories	335
Protein	27 g
Carbohydrate	33 g
Fat (total)	10 g
Saturated	2 g
Cholesterol	72 mg
Sodium	143 mg
Potassium	337 mg

SPECIAL DINNERS

Sometimes it's fun to make a meal special by jazzing up your tabletop. With a few simple notions you can create moods that range from picnic casual to black-tie formal.

To help get your wheels turning, here's a list of some easy decorating ideas.

■ For place mats, use rectangles of colored tissue paper. (To add texture, slightly crumple and then reshape.)

■ Use plain or printed wrapping paper as a table runner.

■ Light tapered candles in candlesticks and/or votive candles for a centerpiece.

■ Tie ribbons around your silverware or stemmed glassware.

■ Use ceramic tile as art deco coasters or place mats.

■ Place fresh cut flowers in vases or jars of various sizes, shapes, and colors.

■ Use baskets lined with waxed paper to serve burgers or fajitas.

■ For fall, decorate your table with leaves and various squash. Or, for Christmas, use holly, candles, and tree ornaments.

GLAZED CHICKEN AND GRAPES

SAUCY ITALIAN CHICKEN AND ARTICHOKES

4 chicken thighs, *or* 2 chicken legs, *or* 1 whole medium chicken breast, halved lengthwise (about 12 ounces total)
3 tablespoons all-purpose flour
⅛ teaspoon salt
1 tablespoon olive oil *or* cooking oil

■ If desired, remove the skin from the chicken. Rinse the chicken and pat dry.

In a plastic bag combine the flour, salt, and ⅛ teaspoon *pepper*. Add the chicken pieces to the bag, 1 or 2 at a time, shaking to coat well.

In a large skillet cook the chicken in hot olive oil or cooking oil over medium heat for 15 minutes, turning to brown evenly. Remove the chicken from the skillet. Set aside.

1 medium onion, chopped (½ cup)
¼ cup coarsely chopped carrot
1 clove garlic, minced

■ Drain the fat from the skillet, reserving *1 tablespoon* of the drippings. Add the onion, carrot, and garlic to the drippings in the skillet. Cook and stir till the vegetables are tender but not brown.

1 7¼-ounce can artichoke hearts, drained, *or* ½ of a 9-ounce package frozen artichoke hearts
1 14½-ounce can whole Italian-style tomatoes, cut up
½ of a 6-ounce can (⅓ cup) tomato paste
¼ cup dry white wine *or* water
½ teaspoon dried basil *or* oregano, crushed

■ If using frozen artichoke hearts, run water over artichokes in a colander till separated. Carefully add the artichoke hearts, *undrained* tomatoes, tomato paste, white wine or water, and basil or oregano to the skillet. Return the chicken to the skillet. Bring to boiling; reduce heat. Cover and simmer for 35 to 40 minutes or till the chicken is tender and no pink remains, stirring once or twice.

2 cups hot cooked fettuccine, linguine, *or* fusilli

■ To serve, transfer chicken to individual plates; cover to keep warm. Gently boil the sauce, uncovered, about 5 minutes or to desired consistency. Spoon the sauce over the chicken and cooked pasta. Makes 2 servings.

TIME ESTIMATE
Start to finish —1¼ hrs.

MENU IDEA
Complete your meal by adding breadsticks and glasses of dry red or white wine.

PER SERVING
Calories _____ 755
Protein _____ 45 g
Carbohydrate _____ 77 g
Fat (total) _____ 28 g
 Saturated _____ 7 g
Cholesterol ___ 116 mg
Sodium _____ 956 mg
Potassium ___ 1,498 mg

BUTTERMILK FRIED CHICKEN

Home-style cooking at its best—buttermilk-dipped chicken pan-fried to golden perfection.

4 chicken drumsticks *or* thighs, *or* 2 chicken legs, *or* 1 whole medium chicken breast, halved lengthwise (about 12 ounces total)
⅓ cup all-purpose flour
½ teaspoon dried basil *or* thyme, crushed
¼ teaspoon salt
¼ teaspoon onion powder
⅛ teaspoon pepper
¼ cup buttermilk

■ If desired, remove the skin from the chicken. Rinse the chicken and pat dry.

In a plastic bag combine the flour, basil or thyme, salt, onion powder, and pepper. Add the chicken pieces to the bag, 1 or 2 at a time, shaking to coat well.

Then, dip the chicken pieces, 1 at a time, into the buttermilk. Add the pieces again to the plastic bag, shaking to coat well.

1 tablespoon cooking oil

■ In a medium skillet cook the chicken, uncovered, in hot cooking oil over medium heat for 15 minutes, turning to brown evenly. Reduce heat to medium-low and cook, uncovered, for 35 to 40 minutes more or till the chicken is tender and no pink remains, turning occasionally. Remove the chicken from the skillet; drain on paper towels. Reserve the drippings in the skillet. Transfer the chicken to individual plates. Cover to keep warm.

2 teaspoons all-purpose flour
½ teaspoon instant chicken bouillon granules
¾ cup milk
Creamy Mashed Potatoes (see recipe, page 179) (optional)

■ For gravy, stir the flour, bouillon granules, and dash *pepper* into the drippings in the skillet, scraping up any browned bits. Add the milk all at once. Cook and stir over medium heat till thickened and bubbly. Cook and stir for 1 minute more. Serve the gravy over chicken and, if desired, over the Creamy Mashed Potatoes. Makes 2 servings.

TIME ESTIMATE
Start to finish _ 65 min.

MENU IDEA
Complement this entrée with fresh green beans and mixed green salads topped with Pepper Vinaigrette (see recipe, page 137).

PER SERVING
Calories _____ 430
Protein _____ 35 g
Carbohydrate _____ 24 g
Fat (total) _____ 21 g
  Saturated _____ 5 g
Cholesterol ____ 105 mg
Sodium_____ 664 mg
Potassium _____ 468 mg

CHICKEN WITH BRANDIED CHERRY SAUCE

Brandy adds a bit of welcome warmth to this sweet cherry sauce.

1 8¾-ounce can pitted dark
  sweet cherries
1 green onion, thinly
  sliced (2 tablespoons)
1 teaspoon cornstarch
½ teaspoon instant chicken
  bouillon granules
  Dash pepper

■ Drain the cherries, reserving ⅓ cup of the juice. Add enough water to the juice to equal ½ *cup*. Set cherries aside.

For sauce, in a small mixing bowl stir together the cherry juice mixture, green onion, cornstarch, bouillon granules, and pepper. Set aside.

2 large boneless, skinless
  chicken breast halves
  or 4 turkey breast slices
  (8 ounces total)

■ Rinse chicken or turkey and pat dry. If using chicken, place each breast half between 2 pieces of plastic wrap. Working from the center to the edges, pound chicken lightly with the flat side of a meat mallet to ¼- to ⅛-inch thickness. Remove plastic wrap. Lightly season chicken or turkey with salt and pepper.

1 tablespoon margarine *or*
  cooking oil

■ In a large skillet cook the chicken or turkey in hot margarine or cooking oil over medium heat for 6 to 8 minutes or till chicken or turkey is tender and no pink remains, turning once. Remove the skillet from heat. Transfer the chicken or turkey to individual plates, reserving the drippings in the skillet. Cover the chicken or turkey to keep warm.

1 tablespoon brandy
  (optional)

■ Stir sauce. Add sauce to skillet. Return to heat. Cook and stir till thickened and bubbly. Cook and stir 1 minute more. Stir in cherries and, if desired, brandy. Heat through.

To serve, spoon *some* of the sauce over the chicken or turkey. Pass the remaining sauce. Makes 2 servings.

TIME ESTIMATE
Start to finish — 20 min.

MENU IDEA
As accompaniments, serve wild rice and buttered asparagus.

PER SERVING
Calories _____ 308
Protein _____ 27 g
Carbohydrate _____ 28 g
Fat (total) _____ 10 g
  Saturated _____ 2 g
Cholesterol _____ 72 mg
Sodium _____ 362 mg
Potassium _____ 411 mg

CHICKEN SPIRALS WITH BASIL ALFREDO FETTUCCINE

2 large boneless, skinless chicken breast halves (8 ounces total)
1 tablespoon snipped fresh basil *or* 1 teaspoon dried basil, crushed
¼ teaspoon finely shredded lemon peel

■ Rinse the chicken and pat dry. Place each breast half between 2 pieces of plastic wrap. Working from the center to the edges, pound lightly with the flat side of a meat mallet to form ⅛-inch-thick rectangles. Remove plastic wrap.

In a small bowl stir together the basil and lemon peel.

2 thin slices prosciutto *or* fully cooked ham
2 thin slices provolone *or* mozzarella cheese
2 tablespoons margarine *or* butter

■ For each roll, place 1 slice of prosciutto or ham on a chicken piece, folding, if necessary, to fit. Place 1 slice of cheese atop prosciutto near one edge. Sprinkle half of the basil mixture atop. Fold in long sides of chicken and roll up jelly-roll style, starting from the edge with cheese. Secure with wooden toothpicks.

In a medium skillet cook the chicken rolls, uncovered, in hot margarine or butter over medium-low heat for 25 to 30 minutes or till chicken is tender and no pink remains, turning to brown evenly. Remove toothpicks.

6 ounces fresh refrigerated *or* 4 ounces packaged fettuccine *or* linguine
1 tablespoon margarine *or* butter
1 tablespoon snipped fresh basil *or* 1 teaspoon dried basil, crushed
¼ teaspoon finely shredded lemon peel
½ cup half-and-half *or* light cream
⅓ cup grated Parmesan cheese

■ Meanwhile, cook pasta (see chart, page 185). Drain immediately. Keep warm. In the same saucepan melt margarine or butter. Stir in basil and lemon peel. Add half-and-half or light cream and Parmesan cheese. Cook and stir till the sauce bubbles and thickens slightly (sauce may appear curdled). Add pasta. Toss till pasta is coated.

To serve, transfer pasta to individual plates. Cut chicken rolls into ½-inch-thick slices. Arrange the slices decoratively over the pasta. Makes 2 servings.

TIME ESTIMATE
Start to finish _ 45 min.

MENU IDEA
Accent this elegant entrée with crisp lettuce salads, slices of Braided Bread (see recipe, page 207), and glasses of dry white wine.

PER SERVING
Calories _____ 751
Protein _____ 50 g
Carbohydrate _____ 47 g
Fat (total) _____ 39 g
  Saturated _____ 15 g
Cholesterol __ 139 mg
Sodium_____ 914 mg
Potassium _____ 538 mg

CHICKEN GINGER

2 medium boneless, skinless chicken breast halves (6 ounces total)

■ Rinse the chicken and pat dry. Cut chicken into 1-inch pieces. Set aside.

TIME ESTIMATE

Start to finish — 35 min.

¼ cup water
1 tablespoon dry sherry
1 tablespoon soy sauce
1 teaspoon cornstarch
½ teaspoon sugar
¼ teaspoon pepper

■ For sauce, in a small bowl stir together the water, dry sherry, soy sauce, cornstarch, sugar, and pepper. Set aside.

MENU IDEA

Finish off this one-dish meal with warm pieces of Almond-Praline Chocolate Upside-Down Cake (see recipe, page 200) and cold glasses of milk.

1 tablespoon cooking oil
1 tablespoon gingerroot cut into thin slivers
3 cloves garlic, minced
1 small green pepper, cut into ¾-inch pieces (½ cup)
3 green onions, bias-sliced into ½-inch pieces (about ½ cup)
1 cup sliced fresh mushrooms

■ Pour the cooking oil into a wok or large skillet. (Add more oil as necessary during cooking.) Preheat over medium-high heat. Stir-fry gingerroot and garlic in the hot oil for 15 seconds. Add the green pepper and green onions. Stir-fry for 30 seconds more. Add the mushrooms and stir-fry about 1 minute more or till vegetables are crisp-tender. Remove vegetables from the wok or skillet.

PER SERVING

Calories _____ 431
Protein _____ 26 g
Carbohydrate _____ 55 g
Fat (total) _____ 11 g
    Saturated _____ 2 g
Cholesterol _____ 54 mg
Sodium_____ 576 mg
Potassium _____ 563 mg

1½ cups hot cooked rice

■ Add the chicken to the hot wok or skillet. Stir-fry about 3 minutes or till chicken is tender and no pink remains. Push the chicken from the center of the wok.

Stir the sauce. Add the sauce to the center of the wok or skillet. Cook and stir till thickened and bubbly. Return the vegetable mixture to the wok or skillet. Stir all ingredients together to coat with sauce. Cook and stir about 1 minute more or till heated through. Serve immediately over hot cooked rice. Makes 2 servings.

MAPLE-GLAZED STUFFED CORNISH HENS

A choice selection for the holidays! These Cornish hens display a bit of homeyness, as well as a touch of elegance, and make a generous, holiday-size serving.

2 slices bacon
1 small leek *or* 2 green
    onions, thinly sliced
    (¼ cup)
2 tablespoons chopped
    pecans *or* walnuts
⅛ teaspoon dried thyme *or*
    marjoram, crushed
    Dash pepper
¾ cup dry bread cubes
    (1 slice)
1 to 2 tablespoons water

■ In a medium skillet cook the bacon till crisp. Remove bacon and drain on paper towels. Crumble bacon and set aside. Reserve *1 tablespoon* of bacon drippings in skillet.

Cook the leek or green onions and pecans or walnuts in reserved bacon drippings over medium heat till leek is tender and nuts are toasted; remove from heat. Stir in the bacon, thyme or marjoram, and pepper. Stir in bread cubes. Drizzle enough water over bread mixture to moisten, tossing lightly till mixed.

2 1- to 1½-pound Cornish
    game hens
1 teaspoon margarine *or*
    butter, melted

■ Rinse hens and pat dry. Lightly season the cavities with salt and pepper. Lightly stuff the hens with the bread mixture. Skewer neck skin, if present, to back of each hen. Twist wing tips under back, holding skin in place. Tie legs to tail. Place hens, breast side up, on a rack in a shallow roasting pan. Brush with margarine or butter; cover loosely with foil. Roast in a 375° oven for 1 hour.

2 tablespoons maple-
    flavored syrup, maple
    syrup, *or* apricot syrup
1 tablespoon margarine *or*
    butter, melted
2 teaspoons Dijon-style
    mustard *or* 1 teaspoon
    brown mustard

■ Meanwhile, in a small bowl stir together the maple-flavored syrup, margarine or butter, and Dijon-style or brown mustard. Brush *some* of the mixture on the hens. Roast hens, uncovered, about 30 minutes more or till tender and no pink remains, brushing with syrup mixture twice. Makes 2 servings.

TIME ESTIMATE

Preparation ⸺ 20 min.
Roasting ⸺ 1½ hrs.

MENU IDEA

For a complete holiday meal, serve buttered broccoli, Dinner Rolls (see recipe, page 207), and your favorite beverage. Then, if you wish, top off dinner with Country-Style Pear Dumplings (see recipe, page 191) and coffee.

PER SERVING

Calories ⸺ 762
Protein ⸺ 78 g
Carbohydrate ⸺ 28 g
Fat (total) ⸺ 39 g
  Saturated ⸺ 3 g
Cholesterol ⸺ 162 mg
Sodium ⸺ 429 mg
Potassium ⸺ 108 mg

TANGY BARBECUED CHICKEN BREASTS

Bring out the grill and showcase this lip-lickin' good chicken for dinner any day of the week.

¼ cup catsup
1 tablespoon finely
    chopped onion
1 tablespoon vinegar
1 tablespoon light corn
    syrup *or* honey
½ teaspoon lemon juice
    Few dashes bottled hot
    pepper sauce

■ For sauce, in a small saucepan stir together the catsup, onion, vinegar, corn syrup or honey, lemon juice, and hot pepper sauce. Bring to boiling; reduce heat. Simmer mixture, uncovered, for 5 to 10 minutes or to desired consistency. Set aside.

1 whole medium chicken
    breast, halved
    lengthwise, *or* 4
    chicken drumsticks *or*
    thighs, *or* 2 chicken
    legs (about 12 ounces
    total)

■ Rinse the chicken and pat dry. Sprinkle lightly with salt and pepper.

To grill, place the chicken pieces, skin side down, on the rack of an uncovered grill. (See tip, page 27.) Grill directly over *medium* coals for 20 minutes. Turn chicken and grill for 15 to 25 minutes more or till the chicken is tender and no pink remains, brushing often with the sauce during the last 10 minutes of cooking.

Or, to broil, place the chicken pieces, skin side down, on the unheated rack of a broiler pan. Broil 4 to 5 inches from the heat for 20 minutes. Turn chicken and broil for 5 to 15 minutes more or till the chicken is tender and no pink remains, brushing often with the sauce the last 5 minutes of cooking. Pass any remaining sauce. Makes 2 servings.

TIME ESTIMATE

Start to finish _*40 min.
Allow extra time to heat coals.

MENU IDEA

Try this summertime favorite with Cottage-Cheese-Dressed Potato Salad (see recipe, page 140), green beans, and garlic toast.

PER SERVING

Calories	231
Protein	26 g
Carbohydrate	17 g
Fat (total)	7 g
Saturated	2 g
Cholesterol	72 mg
Sodium	429 mg
Potassium	374 mg

ROAST CHICKEN WITH LEMON STUFFING

Transform the leftover chicken from this oven-roasted bird into another marvelous meal. Use it in any recipe calling for cooked chicken.

¼ **cup finely chopped onion**
1 **clove garlic, minced**
2 **tablespoons margarine**
   ***or* butter**
3 **cups dry bread cubes**
   (4 slices)
½ **teaspoon finely shredded**
   lemon peel
¼ **teaspoon dried thyme,**
   crushed
⅛ **teaspoon salt**
⅛ **teaspoon pepper**
1 **slightly beaten egg white**
1 **tablespoon lemon juice**
1 **2½- to 3-pound broiler-**
   fryer chicken

1 **tablespoon cooking oil,**
   margarine, *or* butter,
   melted

■ For stuffing, in a medium saucepan cook the onion and garlic in hot margarine or butter till onion is tender. Remove from heat. Stir in the bread cubes, lemon peel, thyme, salt, and pepper.

In a small mixing bowl combine the egg white, lemon juice, and 1 tablespoon *water*. Drizzle over bread cube mixture, tossing lightly to moisten.

Rinse chicken; pat dry. Lightly season cavity with salt. Pull the neck skin to the back and fasten with a small skewer. Lightly spoon stuffing into body cavity.* Tie drumsticks securely to tail. Twist wing tips under back.

■ Place chicken, breast side up, on a rack in a shallow roasting pan. Insert a meat thermometer into the center of an inside thigh muscle. Brush chicken with cooking oil. Roast, uncovered, in a 375° oven for 1 to 1¼ hours or till chicken is tender and no pink remains and meat thermometer registers 180° to 185°.

Remove chicken from oven. Cover; let stand for 15 to 20 minutes before carving. Divide stuffing between 2 individual plates. Place *4 ounces* of cooked chicken on *each* plate. Refrigerate remaining chicken 1 to 2 days or freeze 2 to 4 months. Makes 2 servings.

Or, spoon stuffing into a 1-quart casserole; drizzle with 1 tablespoon *water*. Cover and chill. Place in oven with chicken the last 20 to 30 minutes of roasting.

TIME ESTIMATE
Preparation ____ 20 min.
Roasting _____ 1 hr.

MENU IDEA
Serve buttered peas, hard rolls, and beverages of your choice.

PER SERVING *
Calories _____ 605
Protein _____ 38 g
Carbohydrate _____ 31 g
Fat (total) _____ 36 g
  Saturated _____ 8 g
Cholesterol ____ 100 mg
Sodium_____ 677 mg
Potassium _____ 396 mg
*Each serving includes 4 ounces of the cooked chicken and half of the stuffing.

SPINACH-CHICKEN À LA KING

Not your traditional chicken à la king—this more sophisticated version is delicately flavored with white wine Worcestershire sauce and fresh spinach, then ladled into rich and flaky pastry shells.

2 frozen patty shells *or* 2 Basic Buttery Biscuits (see recipe, page 215)

■ Bake patty shells according to package directions; remove tops. Or, prepare Basic Buttery Biscuits; split biscuits.

TIME ESTIMATE
Start to finish — 30 min.

½ cup water
2 teaspoons white wine Worcestershire sauce, dry white wine, *or* Worcestershire sauce
1½ teaspoons instant chicken bouillon granules
⅛ teaspoon ground nutmeg Dash pepper
2 cups finely torn fresh spinach

■ In a large saucepan stir together the water, Worcestershire sauce or wine, chicken bouillon granules, nutmeg, and pepper. Bring mixture to boiling; reduce heat. Stir in the spinach.

MENU IDEA
All you'll need with this rich and creamy entrée are crisp lettuce salads with Lemon-Nut Vinaigrette (see recipe, page 136) and your choice of beverages.

1 cup milk
¼ cup all-purpose flour
1 cup chopped cooked chicken *or* turkey (about 5 ounces)
Lemon twists (optional)

■ Meanwhile, stir together the milk and flour. Stir into the spinach mixture. Cook and stir over medium-high heat till thickened and bubbly. Cook and stir for 1 minute more. Stir in the chicken or turkey and heat through.

To serve, ladle the chicken mixture into the baked patty shells or over the biscuits. If desired, garnish with lemon twists. Makes 2 servings.

PER SERVING

Calories	472
Protein	31 g
Carbohydrate	39 g
Fat (total)	21 g
Saturated	2 g
Cholesterol	70 mg
Sodium	1,069 mg
Potassium	699 mg

SPINACH-CHICKEN À LA KING

PECAN-COATED CHICKEN KIEV

Cut into this version of Chicken Kiev and you'll find melted cheese, pecans, and onions oozing out instead of the typical melted butter, onions, and parsley.

2 large boneless, skinless chicken breast halves (8 ounces total)

■ Rinse the chicken and pat dry. Place each breast half between 2 pieces of plastic wrap. Working from the center to the edges, pound chicken lightly with the flat side of a meat mallet to ⅛-inch thickness. Remove plastic wrap. Season lightly with salt and pepper.

2 2x½x½-inch sticks of Havarti *or* provolone cheese (¾ ounce)
1 green onion, thinly sliced (2 tablespoons)
1 tablespoon finely chopped pecans, walnuts, *or* almonds

■ To assemble, place *one* piece of the cheese in the center of *each* chicken piece. Sprinkle *each* piece with *half* of the green onion and nuts. Fold in the sides and roll up jelly-roll style, pressing the edges to seal.

1 beaten egg
1 tablespoon water
2 tablespoons all-purpose flour
3 tablespoons ground pecans, walnuts, *or* almonds

■ In a bowl stir together the egg and water. Then, coat each chicken roll with flour, dip in egg mixture, and roll in pecans, walnuts, or almonds. Cover and chill for 30 minutes to 24 hours.

1 tablespoon cooking oil

■ In a medium skillet cook the chicken rolls in hot cooking oil over medium-high heat about 5 minutes or till golden brown, turning to brown all sides Transfer the chicken rolls to an 8x8x2-inch or 10x6x2-inch baking dish. Bake in a 400° oven for 15 to 18 minutes or till the chicken is tender and no pink remains. Makes 2 servings.

TIME ESTIMATE
Preparation —— 20 min.
Chilling ———— 30 min.
Cooking ———— 20 min.

MENU IDEA
For a palate-pleasing meal, serve Poppy Seed and Orange Pasta (see recipe, page 184), buttered pea pods, orange slices, and glasses of dry white wine.

PER SERVING
Calories ——————412
Protein ———————34 g
Carbohydrate ——— 10 g
Fat (total) ————— 26 g
  Saturated ————— 5 g
Cholesterol —— 186 mg
Sodium————— 190 mg
Potassium ——— 338 mg

MICROWAVE MAGIC

Need to melt margarine or butter for a sauce or soften tortillas for fajitas? Look no further than this handy reference for all sorts of easy microwave hints. We tested these tips in 600- to 700-watt ovens, so if your oven has fewer watts, you may need to add to the cooking time (start with a few more seconds and keep increasing the time as needed). Be sure to use only microwave-safe dishes when cooking in your microwave.

Cooking frozen vegetables: In a 1-quart casserole place 1½ cups loose-pack frozen vegetables. Add 1 tablespoon water. Cook, covered, on 100% power (high) till tender, stirring once. Drain.
   For broccoli cuts, whole kernel corn, and peas allow 2½ to 3 minutes. For cut green beans, crinkle-cut carrots, cauliflower flowerets, and mixed vegetables allow 4 to 5 minutes.

Baking potatoes: Prick medium potatoes (5 to 6 ounces each) with a fork. Cook, uncovered, on 100% power (high) till almost tender, rearranging once. Allow 5 to 7 minutes for 1 potato and 8 to 10 minutes for 2 potatoes. Let stand for 5 minutes.

Softening tortillas: Place four 6- to 8-inch flour tortillas between paper towels. Cook on 100% power (high) for 45 to 60 seconds or till softened.

Melting chocolate: Cook chocolate, uncovered, on 100% power (high) till soft enough to stir smooth, stirring every minute during cooking. (It won't seem melted till stirred.)
   For squares, in a 1-cup measure, allow 1 to 2 minutes for 1 square (1 ounce) and 1½ to 2½ minutes for 2 squares (2 ounces).
   For chocolate pieces, in a 1-cup measure, allow 1 to 2 minutes for ½ cup and, in a 2-cup measure, allow 1½ to 2½ minutes for one 6-ounce package (1 cup).

Melting margarine or butter: Place margarine or butter in a custard cup. Cook, uncovered, on 100% power (high) till melted. Allow 40 to 50 seconds for 2 tablespoons, 45 to 60 seconds for ¼ cup, and 1 to 2 minutes for ½ cup.

Softening margarine or butter: Place margarine or butter in a custard cup. Cook, uncovered, on 10% power (low) till softened. Allow 45 seconds for 2 tablespoons and 1 to 1½ minutes for ¼ to ½ cup.

Softening cream cheese: Place cream cheese in a custard cup. Cook, uncovered, on 100% power (high) till softened. Allow 15 to 30 seconds for 3 ounces cream cheese and 45 to 60 seconds for 8 ounces.

Reheating muffins and rolls: Place 1 or 2 muffins or rolls on a plate. Heat, uncovered, on 100% power (high) for 15 to 20 seconds or till warm.

Reheating soups: Heat chilled soups, uncovered, on 100% power (high) stirring every 30 seconds. In a 2-cup measure, allow 3 to 4 minutes for 1 cup, and in a 4-cup measure, allow 5½ to 7½ minutes for 2 cups.

CHICKEN QUESADILLAS WITH PAPAYA SALSA

½ **of a small papaya, peeled, seeded, and chopped (for identification, see photo, right)**

1 **small nectarine, pitted and chopped**

1 **hot red *or* jalapeño pepper, seeded and finely chopped (see tip, page 12)**

1 **tablespoon snipped cilantro *or* parsley**

½ **teaspoon finely shredded lime peel (set aside)**

1 **tablespoon lime juice**

1 **teaspoon honey**

■ For salsa, in a bowl stir together the papaya, nectarine, hot red or jalapeño pepper, cilantro or parsley, lime juice, and honey. Cover and chill thoroughly.

TIME ESTIMATE

Preparation ———— 20 min.
Marinating ———— 30 min.
Cooking ————— 3 min.
Assembling ——— 15 min.

MENU IDEA

Feature this fresh-tasting Mexican meal with nectarine slices and frozen margaritas.

PER SERVING

Calories ————————420
Protein ————————27 g
Carbohydrate ———— 43 g
Fat (total) ————— 17 g
  Saturated ———— 5 g
Cholesterol ———— 66 mg
Sodium———————326 mg
Potassium ———— 598 mg

2 **medium boneless, skinless chicken breast halves (6 ounces total)**

2 **green onions, thinly sliced (¼ cup)**

3 **tablespoons lime *or* lemon juice**

1 **tablespoon snipped cilantro *or* parsley**

1 **teaspoon honey**

■ Meanwhile, rinse the chicken and pat dry. Cut into 1-inch pieces. Place chicken and green onions in a plastic bag set in a deep mixing bowl. For marinade, in a bowl stir together the lime peel, lime juice, cilantro or parsley, and honey. Pour over chicken and onions in the bag. Close bag and turn to coat well. Marinate at room temperature for 30 minutes or in the refrigerator for 2 hours, turning bag occasionally. Drain chicken and discard marinade. Remove salsa from the refrigerator; set aside.

1 **tablespoon cooking oil**

2 **8-inch flour tortillas**

¼ **cup shredded Monterey Jack *or* cheddar cheese (1 ounce)**

■ In a medium skillet cook chicken in hot oil over medium-high heat for 3 to 4 minutes or till no pink remains, stirring constantly.

On a baking sheet, layer *half* of *each* tortilla with *one-fourth* of salsa and *half* of chicken and cheese. Fold plain halves over filled halves. Bake in a 350° oven 8 to 10 minutes or till golden. Top with remaining salsa. Serves 2.

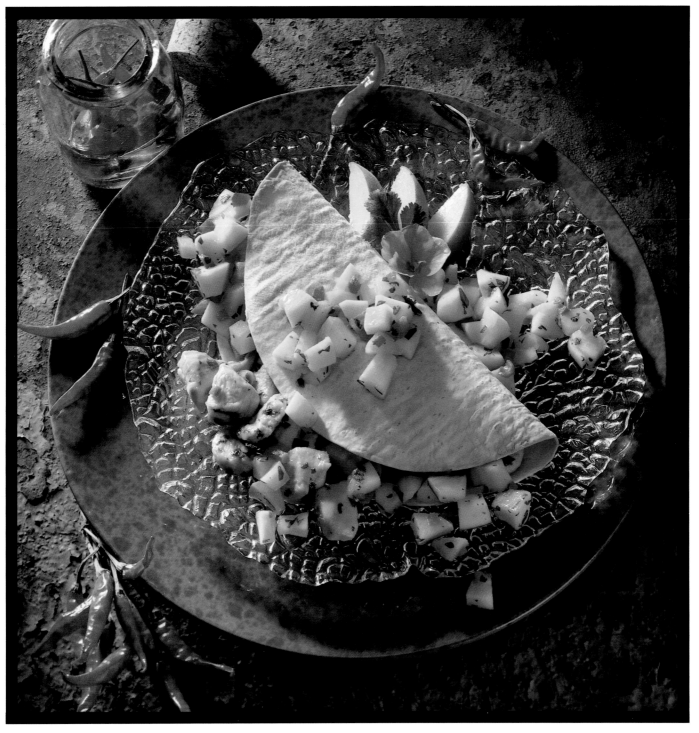

CHICKEN QUESADILLAS WITH PAPAYA SALSA

HEARTY TURKEY SAUSAGE AND VEGETABLE SKILLET

Country-style cooking at its finest—plump and juicy turkey sausage, garden fresh vegetables, and a zippy mustard dressing.

2 **small potatoes** *or* **6 to 8 whole tiny new potatoes**

■ Cut potatoes into ¼-inch-thick slices. Cook the potato slices in a small amount of boiling lightly salted water for 10 to 12 minutes or till tender. Drain.

3 **tablespoons wine vinegar** *or* **vinegar**
2 **tablespoons water**
1 **tablespoon sugar**
1 **tablespoon snipped fresh basil** *or* **1 teaspoon dried basil, crushed**
2 **teaspoons Dijon-style mustard**

■ Meanwhile, for dressing, in a small mixing bowl stir together the wine vinegar or vinegar, water, sugar, basil, and Dijon-style mustard. Set aside.

8 **ounces fully cooked turkey sausage, halved lengthwise and cut into ¼-inch slices**
1 **small zucchini** *or* **yellow summer squash, thinly sliced (about 1 cup)**
1 **small sweet red, green,** *or* **yellow pepper, cut into bite-size strips (½ cup)**
1 **small onion, chopped (⅓ cup)**

■ In a large skillet cook the turkey sausage; zucchini or yellow squash; red, green, or yellow pepper; and onion over medium heat about 7 minutes or till the sausage is heated through and the vegetables are tender, stirring occasionally. Add the potatoes and dressing. Toss to coat all ingredients with dressing. Heat through. Makes 2 servings.

TIME ESTIMATE
Start to finish _ 30 min.

MENU IDEA
All you need to serve with this easy one-dish meal is bread and beverages of your choice. Then, for dessert, try Brickle-Crunch Apple Tarts (see recipe, page 192) and cups of coffee or tea.

PER SERVING
Calories _____ 495
Protein _____ 25 g
Carbohydrate _____ 65 g
Fat (total) _____ 17 g
  Saturated _____ 5 g
Cholesterol _____ 76 mg
Sodium _____ 1,056 mg
Potassium _____ 1,426 mg

TURKEY AND ASPARAGUS STIR-FRY

2 **turkey tenderloin steaks**
   ***or* 2 large boneless,**
   skinless chicken breast
   halves (8 ounces total)
⅓ **cup water**
2 **tablespoons dry white**
   wine *or* water
1 **tablespoon honey**
1 **tablespoon soy sauce**
2 **teaspoons cornstarch**
½ **teaspoon instant chicken**
   bouillon granules

■ Rinse turkey or chicken and pat dry. Cut into thin bite-size strips. Set aside.

For sauce, in a small bowl stir together the water, white wine, honey, soy sauce, cornstarch, and chicken bouillon granules. Set aside.

Start to finish — 40 min.

MENU IDEA
Serve this springtime specialty with mixed fresh fruit, whole wheat rolls, and cold beverages.

PER SERVING
Calories	437
Protein	35 g
Carbohydrate	46 g
Fat (total)	13 g
Saturated	2 g
Cholesterol	71 mg
Sodium	801 mg
Potassium	732 mg

1 **tablespoon cooking oil**
1 **teaspoon grated**
   gingerroot
8 **ounces fresh asparagus,**
   cut into 1-inch pieces
   (1½ cups), *or* ½ of a
   10-ounce package
   frozen cut asparagus,
   thawed
1 **medium carrot, thinly**
   bias-sliced (½ cup)
2 **green onions, sliced**
   (¼ cup)

■ Pour cooking oil into a wok or large skillet. (Add more oil as necessary during cooking.) Preheat over medium-high heat. Stir-fry the gingerroot in the hot oil for 15 seconds. Add asparagus and carrot; stir-fry for 3 minutes. Add the green onions; stir-fry about 1½ minutes more or till crisp-tender. Remove vegetables from the wok. Add the turkey or chicken to the hot wok or skillet. Stir-fry for 2 to 3 minutes or till no pink remains. Push turkey or chicken from center of the wok.

1½ **cups hot cooked couscous,**
   orzo, *or* rice
2 **tablespoons coarsely**
   chopped walnuts *or*
   pecans

■ Stir the sauce. Add the sauce to the center of the wok. Cook and stir till thickened and bubbly. Return the vegetables to the wok. Stir all ingredients together to coat with sauce. Cover and cook about 1 minute or till heated through. Serve immediately over hot cooked couscous, orzo, or rice. Sprinkle with walnuts or pecans. Makes 2 servings.

TURKEY WITH CRANBERRY AND FIG CHUTNEY

Cranberries, an apple, and figs sparkle like jewels in this glossy gingered sauce.

½ **cup cranberries**
½ **cup chopped, peeled apple**
¼ **cup orange juice, apple juice, *or* water**
2 **tablespoons snipped dried figs *or* raisins, *or* 1 tablespoon dried currants**
1 **tablespoon brown sugar *or* sugar**
1 **teaspoon snipped crystallized ginger *or* ⅛ teaspoon ground ginger**

■ For chutney, in a heavy small saucepan stir together the cranberries; apple; orange juice, apple juice, or water; figs, raisins, or currants; brown sugar or sugar; and ginger. Bring to boiling; reduce heat. Simmer, uncovered, for 5 to 7 minutes or to desired consistency, stirring occasionally.

4 **turkey breast slices (8 ounces total)**
1 **tablespoon margarine *or* butter**

■ Meanwhile, rinse the turkey and pat dry. In a medium skillet cook the turkey in hot margarine or butter for 4 to 5 minutes or till the turkey is tender and no pink remains, turning once.

To serve, transfer the turkey to individual plates. Spoon *some* of the warm chutney over the turkey. Pass the remaining chutney. Makes 2 servings.

TIME ESTIMATE
Start to finish — 20 min.

MENU IDEA
For a festive fall meal, try this cranberry-topped turkey with crisp spinach salads, Creamy Mashed Sweet Potatoes (see recipe, page 179), your choice of bread, and cups of hot apple cider or tea.

PER SERVING
Calories —— 279
Protein —— 26 g
Carbohydrate —— 24 g
Fat (total) —— 9 g
  Saturated —— 2 g
Cholesterol —— 59 mg
Sodium —— 125 mg
Potassium —— 459 mg

CHICKEN WITH CRANBERRY AND FIG CHUTNEY

2 **large boneless, skinless chicken breast halves (8 ounces total)**

■ Prepare Turkey with Cranberry and Fig Chutney as directed above, *except* substitute the chicken breast halves for the turkey slices. Cook the chicken for 8 to 10 minutes or till the chicken is tender and no pink remains, turning once.

PER SERVING
Same as *Turkey with Cranberry and Fig Chutney,* except:
Calories —— 293
Cholesterol —— 72 mg

BROILING AND GRILLING POULTRY

If desired, remove the skin from the poultry; rinse and pat dry with paper towels. If desired, sprinkle with salt and pepper.

To broil: Preheat the broiler for 5 to 10 minutes. Arrange the poultry on the unheated rack of the broiler pan with the bone side up. If desired, brush with cooking oil. Place the pan under the broiler so the surface of the poultry is 4 to 5 inches from the heat. (Chicken halves should be 5 to 6 inches from the heat.) Turn the pieces over when browned on one side, usually after half of the broiling time. Chicken halves and meaty pieces should be turned after 20 minutes.

Brush again with oil. The poultry is done when the meat is tender and no pink remains. If desired, brush with a sauce the last 5 minutes of cooking.

To grill: Test for desired temperature of the coals (see tip, page 27). Place poultry on the grill rack, bone side up, directly over the preheated coals. (For ground turkey or chicken patties, use a grill basket.) Grill, uncovered, for the specified time or till poultry is tender and no pink remains. Turn the poultry over after half of the grilling time. If desired, brush often with sauce during the last 10 minutes of cooking.

TYPE OF BIRD	WEIGHT	BROILING TIME	COAL TEMPERATURE	GRILLING TIME
Chicken, broiler-fryer, half*	1¼ to 1½ pounds	28 to 32 minutes	Medium	40 to 50 minutes
Chicken breast halves (boneless)	6 to 8 ounces total	12 to 15 minutes	Medium-hot	15 to 18 minutes
Chicken breast halves, thighs, and drumsticks (with bone)	12 ounces total	25 to 35 minutes	Medium	35 to 45 minutes
Chicken kabobs (boneless breast, cut into 2x½-inch strips and threaded loosely onto skewers)	8 ounces total	8 to 10 minutes	Medium-hot	8 to 10 minutes
Turkey breast steaks or slices	8 ounces total	6 to 8 minutes		Not recommended
Turkey tenderloin steaks	8 ounces total	8 to 10 minutes	Medium	12 to 15 minutes
Turkey or chicken patties (ground raw turkey or chicken)	¾ inch thick	10 to 12 minutes	Medium-hot	15 to 18 minutes

TURKEY STEAKS WITH APPLE AND MAPLE SAUCE

For a more intense maple flavor, use maple-flavored syrup.

**2 turkey tenderloin steaks
   or 2 large boneless,
   skinless chicken breast
   halves (8 ounces total)**
**1 tablespoon margarine *or*
   butter**

■ Rinse the turkey or chicken and pat dry. In a medium skillet cook the turkey or chicken in hot margarine or butter over medium heat for 8 to 10 minutes or till the turkey or chicken is tender and no pink remains, turning once. Transfer the turkey or chicken to individual plates, reserving the drippings in the skillet. Cover the turkey or chicken to keep warm.

**2 tablespoons maple *or*
   maple-flavored syrup**
**1 tablespoon cider vinegar
   or wine vinegar**
**1 teaspoon Dijon-style
   mustard**
**½ teaspoon instant chicken
   bouillon granules**
**1 medium tart red apple,
   cored and thinly sliced
   Fresh sage (optional)**

■ Stir the maple syrup, cider vinegar or wine vinegar, Dijon-style mustard, and chicken bouillon granules into the drippings in the skillet. Add the apple slices. Cook and stir over medium heat for 2 to 3 minutes or till the apple is tender. To serve, spoon the apple mixture over the turkey or chicken. If desired, garnish with sage. Makes 2 servings.

TIME ESTIMATE
Start to finish — 20 min.

MENU IDEA
Baked sweet potato wedges and glasses of sparkling water are great teamed with this apple glazed turkey.

PER SERVING

Calories	262
Protein	26 g
Carbohydrate	25 g
Fat (total)	7 g
Saturated	1 g
Cholesterol	71 mg
Sodium	416 mg
Potassium	373 mg

TURKEY STEAKS WITH APPLE AND MAPLE SAUCE

EAT TWO/FREEZE TWO

CHUTNEY-FILLED CHICKEN AND PASTRY BUNDLES

½ of a 17½-ounce package (1 sheet) frozen puff pastry
4 medium boneless, skinless chicken breast halves (12 ounces total)
2 tablespoons chutney
¼ cup toasted coconut
3 tablespoons soft-style cream cheese
⅛ teaspoon curry powder

---

1 slightly beaten egg white
1 tablespoon water

■ To thaw pastry, let stand at room temperature for 20 minutes. Rinse chicken; pat dry. Place each breast half between 2 pieces of plastic wrap. Working from center to edges, pound lightly with the flat side of a meat mallet to ⅛-inch thickness. Remove wrap.

For filling, snip the chutney. Combine chutney, coconut, cream cheese, and curry powder. Spoon about *1 tablespoon* filling in the center of *each* chicken piece. Fold in sides; roll up jelly-roll style.

■ Unfold pastry. Cut off a ½-inch-wide strip; set aside. Cut remaining pastry into 4 portions. On a floured surface roll each portion into a 7x6-inch rectangle. Center chicken bundles atop pastry rectangles. Wrap pastry over chicken, overlapping long sides. Brush edges with a mixture of egg white and water; seal. Fold over ends (see photo, right). Brush ends with egg mixture; seal. Turn seam side down; brush with egg mixture. Cut shapes from reserved pastry; decorate tops. Brush with egg mixture. Bake 2 bundles immediately; freeze others as directed. Serves 4.

TIME ESTIMATE
Preparation ____ 35 min.
Baking _____ 25 min.

PER SERVING
Calories _____ 460
Protein _____ 26 g
Carbohydrate _____ 31 g
Fat (total) _____ 25 g
    Saturated _____ 4 g
Cholesterol _____ 65 mg
Sodium _____ 474 mg
Potassium _____ 201 mg

TO EAT TWO: Line a baking pan with foil; grease foil. Place 2 bundles in the pan. Grease another sheet of foil. Cover bundles loosely with foil, greased side down. Bake in a 400° oven for 15 minutes. Uncover; bake about 10 minutes more or till pastry is golden and chicken is tender and no pink remains.

TO FREEZE TWO: Seal, label, and freeze 2 bundles for up to 3 months. *To serve,* line a baking pan with foil; grease foil. Unwrap and place 1 or 2 of the frozen bundles in the pan. Grease another sheet of foil. Cover bundles loosely with foil, greased side down. Bake in a 400° oven for 35 minutes. Uncover; bake about 5 minutes more or till pastry is golden and chicken is tender and no pink remains.

PICADILLO CHICKEN LOAVES

Sweet and spicy! Two great tastes you wouldn't expect to find in a meat loaf.

1 beaten egg
¼ cup fine dry bread
    crumbs
¼ cup raisins
2 tablespoons thinly sliced
    pimiento-stuffed olives
2 tablespoons apple juice
    or milk
½ teaspoon onion salt
½ teaspoon ground
    cinnamon
½ teaspoon ground cumin
1 pound ground raw
    chicken *or* turkey
¼ cup toasted chopped
    almonds *or* pecans

■ In a large mixing bowl stir together the egg, bread crumbs, raisins, olives, apple juice or milk, onion salt, cinnamon, and cumin. Add the ground chicken or turkey and the almonds or pecans; mix well.

■ Shape the chicken or turkey mixture into four 4x2½x1-inch loaves. Place each loaf in an individual casserole. Bake 2 casseroles immediately and freeze the remaining casseroles as directed. Makes 4 servings.

TO EAT TWO: Bake 2 of the casseroles, uncovered, in a 350° oven about 25 minutes or till no pink remains. Sprinkle *each* loaf with 1 tablespoon shredded **cheddar *or* Monterey Jack cheese.** Bake about 3 minutes more or till the cheese melts.

TO FREEZE TWO: Seal, label, and freeze 2 of the casseroles for up to 3 months. *To serve,* bake 1 or 2 of the frozen casseroles, uncovered, in a 350° oven for 35 to 40 minutes or till no pink remains. Sprinkle *each* loaf with 1 tablespoon shredded **cheddar *or* Monterey Jack cheese.** Bake about 3 minutes more or till cheese melts.

TIME ESTIMATE
Preparation ____ 15 min.
Baking _____ 30 min.

MENU IDEA
Serve tomato slices on lettuce leaves and a side dish of orzo or couscous with these individual loaves.

PER SERVING
Calories _____ 342
Protein _____ 24 g
Carbohydrate _____ 16 g
Fat (total) _____ 20 g
  Saturated _____ 6 g
Cholesterol ____ 141 mg
Sodium _____ 508 mg
Potassium _____ 381 mg

EAT TWO/FREEZE TWO

EASY CHEESY CHICKEN RAVIOLI

For an even simpler version, use purchased spaghetti sauce instead of the homemade Tomatoey Sauce.

6 ounces ground raw chicken *or* turkey
1 8-ounce container soft-style cream cheese with chive and onion
¼ cup shredded carrot

■ For filling, in a medium mixing bowl stir together the chicken or turkey, cream cheese, and carrot. Set aside.

TIME ESTIMATE	
Start to finish _ 50 min.	

PER SERVING	
Calories	298
Protein	13 g
Carbohydrate	20 g
Fat (total)	19 g
Saturated	8 g
Cholesterol	30 mg
Sodium	586 mg
Potassium	427 mg

20 3½-inch wonton wrappers

■ Place about *1 tablespoon* of the filling in the center of *each* wrapper. Brush edges with water. Fold 1 corner over to the opposite corner, forming a triangle. To seal, press edges together or use a pastry wheel. Cook 2 servings of the ravioli immediately and freeze the remaining ravioli as directed. Serves 4.

TO EAT TWO: Prepare **Tomatoey Sauce** (see recipe, page 110) as directed. Meanwhile, in a Dutch oven bring a large amount of water and 1 tablespoon **cooking oil** to boiling. Drop 2 servings of the ravioli into the boiling water. Reduce heat. Simmer, uncovered, for 3 to 4 minutes or till no pink remains in chicken or turkey; remove with a slotted spoon. Drain on paper towels. Spoon the sauce in the center of 2 individual plates. Arrange the cooked ravioli on top of the sauce. If desired, garnish with fresh **basil.**

TO FREEZE TWO: Place 2 servings of the ravioli in a freezer container. Seal, label, and freeze container for up to 3 months. *To serve,* prepare **Tomatoey Sauce** (see recipe, page 110) as directed. Meanwhile, in a Dutch oven bring a large amount of water and 1 tablespoon **cooking oil** to boiling. Drop the frozen ravioli into the boiling water. Reduce heat. Simmer, uncovered, for 5 to 6 minutes or till no pink remains in chicken or turkey; remove with a slotted spoon. Drain on paper towels. Spoon the sauce in the center of 2 individual plates. Arrange the cooked ravioli on top of the sauce. If desired, garnish with fresh **basil.**

EASY CHEESY CHICKEN RAVIOLI

EAT TWO/FREEZE TWO

TURKEY AND VEGETABLE TORTILLA ROLL-UPS

1 8-ounce container soft-style cream cheese with chive and onion
1 cup milk
2 teaspoons cornstarch
½ cup shredded Monterey Jack, mozzarella, *or* cheddar cheese (2 ounces)

8 8-inch flour tortillas
2 cups chopped cooked turkey *or* chicken
1½ cups loose-pack frozen broccoli, corn, and peppers, thawed and drained
¼ teaspoon pepper

■ For sauce, in a heavy medium saucepan cook and stir cream cheese over medium-low heat till melted. Stir milk into cornstarch. Slowly add milk mixture to cream cheese. Cook and stir till thickened and bubbly. Cook and stir 2 minutes more. Remove from heat. Stir in the shredded cheese. Set aside.

■ Wrap tortillas tightly in foil. Bake in a 350° oven for 10 minutes to soften.

Meanwhile, for filling, in a mixing bowl combine ½ *cup* of the sauce, the turkey or chicken, vegetables, and pepper.

For each roll-up, spoon about ⅓ *cup* of the filling onto *each* tortilla just below the center. Fold bottom edge over filling, just till mixture is covered. Fold opposite sides of tortilla in, just till they meet. Roll up tortilla from the bottom. Place 2 roll-ups, seam side down, in *each* of 4 greased individual casseroles or au gratin dishes. Top with remaining sauce. Bake 2 of the casseroles immediately and freeze the remaining casseroles as directed. Makes 4 servings.

TO EAT TWO: Bake 2 of the casseroles, covered, in a 350° oven for 20 to 25 minutes or till heated through. Sprinkle *each* casserole with ¼ cup shredded **Monterey Jack, mozzarella, *or* cheddar cheese** (1 ounce). Bake, uncovered, about 4 minutes more or till the cheese melts.

TO FREEZE TWO: Seal, label, and freeze 2 of the casseroles for up to 3 months. *To serve,* bake 1 or 2 of the frozen casseroles, covered, in a 350° oven about 1 hour or till heated through. Sprinkle *each* casserole with ¼ cup shredded **Monterey Jack, mozzarella, *or* cheddar cheese** (1 ounce). Bake, uncovered, about 4 minutes or till cheese melts.

TIME ESTIMATE
Preparation ____ 30 min.
Baking _____ 25 min.

MENU IDEA
Offer salads of spinach and fresh fruit topped with Lemon-Nut Vinaigrette (see recipe, page 136).

PER SERVING
Calories _____ 662
Protein _____ 42 g
Carbohydrate _____ 54 g
Fat (total) _____ 32 g
 Saturated _____ 17 g
Cholesterol _____ 97 mg
Sodium_____ 748 mg
Potassium _____ 549 mg

TURKEY TETRAZZINI-STYLE CASSEROLES

6 ounces packaged spaghetti
  or linguine
1 cup loose-pack frozen
  peas
1 cup sliced fresh
  mushrooms *or* one
  4-ounce can sliced
  mushrooms, drained
½ cup chopped onion
3 tablespoons margarine
  or butter

■ Break the pasta into 3- to 4-inch pieces. Cook pasta (see chart, page 185), adding the peas the last 5 minutes of cooking. Drain immediately.

Meanwhile, in a large saucepan cook the fresh mushrooms (if using) and the onion in hot margarine or butter till the onion is tender but not brown, stirring occasionally.

TIME ESTIMATE
Preparation ⎯ 35 min.
Baking ⎯⎯⎯ 15 min.

MENU IDEA
Accent the casseroles with breadsticks, and cucumber slices and tomato wedges drizzled with Garlic Vinaigrette (see recipe, page 137).

3 tablespoons all-purpose
  flour
¼ teaspoon dried tarragon
  or rosemary, crushed
1¼ cups half-and-half, light
  cream, *or* milk
1 teaspoon instant chicken
  bouillon granules
1 cup cut-up process Swiss
  or Gruyère cheese
  (4 ounces)
2 cups cubed cooked
  turkey *or* chicken
2 tablespoons dry white
  wine *or* dry sherry

■ Stir in the flour, tarragon or rosemary, and ⅛ teaspoon *pepper.* Add the half-and-half, light cream, or milk; bouillon granules; and 1 cup *water.* Cook and stir over medium heat till thickened and bubbly. Reduce heat; add the process Swiss or Gruyère cheese. Cook and stir till cheese is melted.

Stir in the turkey or chicken, white wine or dry sherry, and, if using, the canned mushrooms. Add the pasta mixture. Toss to coat. Divide mixture among 4 lightly greased individual casseroles. Bake 2 casseroles immediately; freeze others as directed. Serves 4.

PER SERVING
Calories ⎯⎯⎯⎯⎯ 654
Protein ⎯⎯⎯⎯ 40 g
Carbohydrate ⎯⎯ 51 g
Fat (total) ⎯⎯⎯ 32 g
  Saturated ⎯⎯⎯ 13 g
Cholesterol ⎯⎯ 106 mg
Sodium ⎯⎯⎯⎯ 833 mg
Potassium ⎯⎯⎯ 673 mg

TO EAT TWO: Bake 2 of the casseroles, covered, in a 350° oven for 10 minutes. Sprinkle *each* casserole with 1 tablespoon **sliced almonds or chopped pecans.** Bake, uncovered, for 5 to 10 minutes more or till heated through.

TO FREEZE TWO: Seal, label, and freeze 2 of the casseroles for up to 3 months. *To serve,* bake 1 or 2 of the frozen casseroles, covered, in a 375° oven for 1¼ hours. Stir. Sprinkle *each* casserole with 1 tablespoon **sliced almonds or chopped pecans.** Bake, uncovered, about 15 minutes more or till heated through.

FISH AND SHELLFISH

HOT-AND-SOUR SHRIMP

HOT-AND-SOUR SHRIMP

8 ounces fresh *or* frozen peeled and deveined medium shrimp
⅓ cup water
2 tablespoons white wine vinegar
1 tablespoon soy sauce
1 tablespoon catsup
2 teaspoons cornstarch
1 teaspoon sugar
1 teaspoon instant chicken bouillon granules
⅛ to **¼** teaspoon ground red pepper
2 ounces rice sticks *or* 1½ cups hot cooked rice

■ Thaw shrimp, if frozen. Rinse shrimp and pat dry. Cut shrimp in half lengthwise. Set aside.

For sauce, in a small mixing bowl stir together the water, wine vinegar, soy sauce, catsup, cornstarch, sugar, chicken bouillon granules, and ground red pepper. Set aside.

If using rice sticks, in a medium saucepan cook the rice sticks in boiling water for 1 to 2 minutes or just till tender. Drain and keep warm.

1 tablespoon cooking oil
1 clove garlic, minced
1 teaspoon grated gingerroot
1½ cups thinly sliced bok choy *or* torn fresh spinach
6 green onions, bias-sliced into 1-inch pieces (1 cup)
1 small yellow *or* sweet red pepper, cut into ¾-inch pieces (½ cup)

■ Pour cooking oil into a wok or large skillet. (Add more oil as necessary during cooking.) Preheat over medium-high heat. Stir-fry the garlic and gingerroot in hot oil for 15 seconds. Add bok choy, if using. Stir-fry for 1½ minutes. Add the green onions and yellow or red pepper; stir-fry about 1½ minutes more or till the vegetables are crisp-tender. Remove the vegetables from the wok.

Add the shrimp to the hot wok or skillet. Stir-fry for 2 to 3 minutes or till shrimp turn pink. Push shrimp from the center of wok.

■ Stir the sauce. Add the sauce to center of the wok. Cook and stir till thickened and bubbly. Return vegetables to the wok. Add spinach, if using. Stir all ingredients together to coat with sauce. Cook and stir about 1 minute more or till heated through. Serve over hot cooked rice sticks or rice. Serves 2.

TIME ESTIMATE
Start to finish _ 30 min.

MENU IDEA
Top off this one-dish meal with rice crackers. Then for dessert, serve dishes of frozen yogurt or ice cream with fresh fruit and cups of hot tea or coffee.

PER SERVING
Calories _____ 317
Protein _____ 24 g
Carbohydrate ____ 38 g
Fat (total) _____ 8 g
 Saturated _____ 1 g
Cholesterol ___ 166 mg
Sodium _____ 1,262 mg
Potassium ____ 592 mg

GARLIC AND HERB SHRIMP SAUTÉ

A tasty main dish that's simple and oh so satisfying.

12 ounces fresh *or* frozen large shrimp in shells

■ Thaw shrimp, if frozen. Peel shrimp, leaving tails intact. To devein shrimp, use a sharp knife to make a shallow slit along the back of each shrimp. Remove the sandy black vein, if present. Rinse shrimp and pat dry. Set aside.

2 tablespoons olive oil, margarine, *or* butter
3 cloves garlic, minced
1 small leek, thinly sliced (⅔ cup), *or* 2 green onions, thinly sliced (¼ cup)
¼ teaspoon dried basil, oregano, *or* tarragon, crushed
1 tablespoon snipped parsley
1 tablespoon dry sherry *or* dry white wine
1 tablespoon lemon juice

■ In a medium skillet heat the olive oil, margarine, or butter over medium heat. Add the shrimp, garlic, leek or green onions, and the basil, oregano, or tarragon. Cook for 2 to 4 minutes or till shrimp turn pink, stirring frequently. Remove from heat. Stir in the parsley, dry sherry or white wine, and lemon juice. Makes 2 servings.

TIME ESTIMATE
Start to finish — 25 min.

MENU IDEA
Add a side dish of spinach or tomato fettuccine and slices of yellow summer squash.

PER SERVING
Calories _____ 243
Protein _____ 20 g
Carbohydrate _____ 7 g
Fat (total) _____ 15 g
  Saturated _____ 2 g
Cholesterol ____ 166 mg
Sodium _____ 199 mg
Potassium _____ 266 mg

RUMAKI-STYLE SCALLOP KABOBS

For a special grilled flavor, toss sprigs of fresh basil onto the hot coals.

8 ounces fresh *or* frozen sea
  scallops
¼ cup dry white wine
2 tablespoons olive oil *or*
  cooking oil
2 tablespoons lemon juice
2 teaspoons Dijon-style
  mustard
¼ teaspoon pepper

■ Thaw scallops, if frozen. Halve any large ones. Place scallops in a plastic bag set in a deep mixing bowl. For marinade, in a bowl stir together the white wine, olive oil or cooking oil, lemon juice, Dijon-style mustard, and pepper. Pour over scallops in bag. Close bag and turn to coat scallops well. Marinate at room temperature for 30 minutes or in the refrigerator for 2 hours, turning bag occasionally. Drain scallops, reserving marinade.

1 medium yellow summer
  squash *or* zucchini, cut
  into ½-inch-thick slices

■ Meanwhile, cook the yellow squash or zucchini in a small amount of boiling water for 2 minutes. Drain and set aside.

2 ounces prosciutto *or* fully
  cooked ham, thinly
  sliced
16 large fresh basil leaves
2 or 3 sprigs fresh basil
  (optional)
8 cherry tomatoes

■ Cut prosciutto or ham into 1-inch-wide strips. Wrap each scallop with a basil leaf and then with a strip of meat (see photo, right). On four 9- or 10-inch skewers alternately thread the wrapped scallops and squash.

To grill, if desired, place basil sprigs directly on *medium-hot* coals. (See tip, page 27.) Place skewers on greased rack of an uncovered grill. Grill directly over coals 10 to 12 minutes or till scallops are opaque, brushing scallops and squash with marinade and turning occasionally. Add 2 cherry tomatoes to each skewer the last 1 to 2 minutes of cooking.

Or, to broil, place skewers on the greased unheated rack of a broiler pan. Do not use basil sprigs. Broil 4 to 5 inches from heat 8 to 10 minutes or till scallops are opaque, brushing kabobs with marinade and turning occasionally. Add 2 tomatoes to each skewer for the last 1 minute of cooking. Serves 2.

TIME ESTIMATE

Preparation —— 45 min.
Grilling ——— *10 min.
Allow extra time to heat coals.

MENU IDEA

Accent these elegant scallop kabobs with a side dish of orzo or rice and wedges of radicchio drizzled with Garlic Vinaigrette (see recipe, page 137).

PER SERVING

Calories ————— 323
Protein ————— 29 g
Carbohydrate —— 13 g
Fat (total) ———— 17 g
  Saturated ——— 3 g
Cholesterol —— 53 mg
Sodium———— 718 mg
Potassium —— 851 mg

CAJUN COATED SOFT-SHELL CRABS

At some fish markets you may find these crabs already cleaned. Even if they aren't, they are well worth the extra effort.

2 large *or* 4 small soft-shell blue crabs (10 to 12 ounces total)

■ To clean crabs, carefully grasp each crab between the back legs. Using kitchen shears, cut across the body about ½ inch behind the eyes, removing the face.

Lift the pointed soft top shell on one side. Using your fingers, push up the "devil's fingers" (the spongy projectiles on the exposed side), and pull off. Replace the soft top shell over the body. Repeat on the other side.

Turn the crab over. Pull up the apron-shaped piece; discard. Thoroughly rinse crabs under cold running water to remove the mustard-colored substance. Pat dry.

1 beaten egg
1 tablespoon milk *or* water
¼ cup finely crushed rich round cheese crackers
¼ cup ground pecans, walnuts, *or* almonds
¼ teaspoon dried thyme, crushed
⅛ teaspoon ground red pepper
⅛ teaspoon pepper

■ In a shallow dish stir together the egg and milk or water. On a sheet of waxed paper combine crushed crackers; pecans, walnuts, or almonds; thyme; red pepper; and pepper. Dip crabs in the egg mixture, then roll them in the cracker mixture.

2 tablespoons cooking oil
Lime *or* lemon wedges

■ In a large skillet heat cooking oil. Add the crabs, back side down. Cook crabs over medium heat for 6 to 10 minutes or till golden and crisp, carefully turning once. Drain on paper towels. Serve with lime or lemon wedges. Makes 2 servings.

TIME ESTIMATE

Start to finish _ 20 min.

MENU IDEA

Add a salad of your choice, Cream Cheesy Corn (see recipe, page 176), and slices of sourdough bread.

PER SERVING

Calories	442
Protein	34 g
Carbohydrate	8 g
Fat (total)	31 g
Saturated	4 g
Cholesterol	249 mg
Sodium	487 mg
Potassium	572 mg

POACHED FILLETS WITH ORANGE SAUCE

2 4-ounce fresh *or* frozen
   skinless orange roughy
   or cod fillets (about ½
   inch thick)
½ cup orange juice
½ teaspoon grated
   gingerroot *or* ⅛
   teaspoon ground ginger

1 tablespoon water
1 teaspoon cornstarch
1 tablespoon thinly sliced
   green onion *or* snipped
   chives

■ Thaw fish, if frozen. In a medium skillet stir together the orange juice and gingerroot or ground ginger. Bring the mixture just to boiling. Carefully add the fish. Return just to boiling; reduce heat. Cover and simmer for 4 to 6 minutes or just till fish begins to flake easily. Transfer the fish to individual plates. Cover the fish to keep warm.

■ For sauce, if desired, pour the cooking liquid in the skillet through a strainer. Return the strained liquid to the skillet.

Stir together water and cornstarch. Stir into liquid in skillet. Cook and stir till thickened and bubbly. Cook and stir for 1 minute more.

To serve, spoon the sauce over fish. Sprinkle with green onion or chives. Serves 2.

TIME ESTIMATE

Start to finish _ 20 min.

MENU IDEA

Complement this light and refreshing entrée with a side dish of orzo or rice and fresh spinach salads.

PER SERVING

Calories _____ 177
Protein _____ 18 g
Carbohydrate _____ 8 g
Fat (total) _____ 8 g
  Saturated _____ 0 g
Cholesterol _____ 23 mg
Sodium _____ 73 mg
Potassium _____ 143 mg

BROILING AND GRILLING FISH

Follow the directions and times below to broil or grill fish, cooking the fish just till it begins to flake easily. Season the cooked fish to taste with salt and pepper. If desired, serve lemon wedges with the fish.

COOKING METHOD	FRESH FILLETS OR STEAKS	FROZEN FILLETS OR STEAKS	DRESSED FISH
Broil: Preheat broiler. Place fish on the greased unheated rack of a broiler pan. For fillets, tuck under any thin edges. Brush with melted margarine or butter.	Broil 4 inches from the heat for 4 to 6 minutes per ½-inch thickness. If fish is 1 inch or more thick, turn it over halfway through broiling.	Broil 4 inches from heat 6 to 9 minutes per ½-inch thickness. If fish is 1 inch or more thick, turn it over halfway through broiling.	Not recommended.
Grill: Place fillets in a well-greased grill basket. Place steaks on a greased grill rack.	Grill on an uncovered grill directly over *medium-hot* coals for 4 to 6 minutes per ½-inch thickness, turning once. Brush with melted margarine or butter, if desired.	Not recommended.	Grill on an uncovered grill directly over *medium-hot* coals for 7 to 9 minutes for a ½- to 1½-pound fish. Brush with melted margarine or butter, if desired.

FISH

FLOUNDER AND VEGETABLES EN PAPILLOTE

Baked in a paper package, the fish and vegetables are nestled together. Then, when the package is opened, poof—a tantalizing aroma is revealed.

2 4-ounce fresh *or* frozen skinless flounder *or* sole fillets (about ¼ inch thick)
2 15x12-inch pieces parchment paper

■ Thaw fish, if frozen. Fold each sheet of parchment paper in half lengthwise. Then cut each sheet in a half-heart shape 6 inches longer and 2 inches wider than the fish. (The fold will be the center of the heart.)

2 tablespoons soft-style cream cheese
¼ cup chopped green *or* sweet red pepper
1 thin onion slice, separated into rings

■ Open each paper heart; arrange one fish fillet on the right half of each heart. Tuck under any thin edges of fish. Sprinkle fish with salt and pepper. Spoon cream cheese over the top of the fish. Top with green or red pepper and onion.

To seal, fold the left half of the paper heart over the fish, matching edges. Starting at the top of the heart, seal the package by folding the edges together in a double fold (see photo, right). Fold only a small section at a time to ensure a tight seal. Then twist the tip of the heart to close the package.

1 tablespoon snipped cilantro *or* parsley
2 lime *or* lemon wedges

■ Place bundles on an ungreased baking sheet. Bake in a 450° oven about 10 minutes or till paper puffs up and fish just begins to flake easily (carefully open the paper to check doneness). Transfer the bundles to individual plates.

To serve, cut a large X on the top of each bundle, then pull back the paper. Sprinkle fish with cilantro or parsley. Serve with lime or lemon wedges. Makes 2 servings.

TIME ESTIMATE
Preparation ___ 15 min.
Baking ___ 10 min.

MENU IDEA
Serve this Mexican-seasoned fish with breadsticks and mixed greens with avocado.

PER SERVING
Calories ___ 139
Protein ___ 18 g
Carbohydrate ___ 3 g
Fat (total) ___ 6 g
  Saturated ___ 3 g
Cholesterol ___ 59 mg
Sodium ___ 127 mg
Potassium ___ 316 mg

TROUT IN WHITE WINE SAUCE

Nothing beats the flavor of fresh trout poached in white wine then topped with a delicate mushroom sauce.

2 8-ounce fresh *or* frozen pan-dressed trout *or* other pan-dressed fish
½ cup dry white wine
½ cup water
1 teaspoon lemon juice
¼ teaspoon instant chicken bouillon granules

¾ cup sliced fresh mushrooms *or* one 2-ounce jar sliced mushrooms, drained
2 tablespoons finely chopped onion
1 tablespoon margarine *or* butter
1 tablespoon all-purpose flour
⅛ teaspoon salt
⅛ teaspoon pepper
½ cup milk
2 tablespoons dry white wine

Watercress sprigs (optional)

■ Thaw fish, if frozen. If desired, cut off the heads and tails.

In a large skillet combine the white wine, water, lemon juice, and chicken bouillon granules. Bring the mixture just to boiling. Carefully add the fish. Return just to boiling; reduce heat. Cover and simmer for 10 to 15 minutes or just till fish begins to flake easily.

■ Meanwhile, for sauce, in a small saucepan cook the fresh mushrooms (if using) and onion in hot margarine or butter till tender but not brown. Stir in the flour, salt, and pepper. Add the milk all at once. Cook and stir over medium heat till thickened and bubbly. Cook and stir for 1 minute more. Stir in the white wine and, if using, the sliced mushrooms from the jar.

■ To serve, transfer the fish to individual plates. Discard the poaching liquid. Spoon the sauce over the fish. If desired, garnish with watercress. Makes 2 servings.

TIME ESTIMATE

Start to finish _ 20 min.

MENU IDEA

Add a colorful accompaniment like Carrot and Squash Stir-Fry (see recipe, page 173) and slices of sourdough bread.

PER SERVING

Calories _____ 322
Protein _____ 33 g
Carbohydrate _____ 9 g
Fat (total) _____ 12 g
    Saturated _____ 3 g
Cholesterol ____ 88 mg
Sodium_____ 386 mg
Potassium _____ 984 mg

HEALTHY CHOICES

When it comes to healthy eating, cutting calories and lowering your intake of fat, cholesterol, and sodium are usually the main concerns. With the helpful tips below, you can take steps in the right direction without sacrificing quality or flavor.

■ When selecting chicken, choose chicken breasts over legs or thighs because white meat contains less fat than dark meat. Then, to cut fat even further, remove the skin before cooking.

■ Look for lean cuts of beef, pork, or other meats and trim off and discard any visible fat. Also, select the leanest ground beef, pork, raw turkey, or raw chicken available and drain it after cooking. Be sure to read the label and make sure no skin has been added to the ground turkey or chicken.

■ If you're concerned about reducing fat, serve fish that is reasonably low in fat, such as orange roughy, red snapper, or cod. However, if you're more concerned about reducing cholesterol, serve fish like salmon, tuna, and rainbow or lake trout that are a bit higher in fat, but contain omega-3 fatty acids, substances that may lower blood cholesterol levels. Remember, shrimp, crab, and oysters are relatively high in cholesterol, so choose these infrequently. Other shellfish, such as lobster, clams, and mussels, have lower cholesterol levels and can be eaten more often.

■ Drink and use 1 percent or skim milk in your recipes. Both types of milk contain the same nutrients as 2 percent and whole milk, but contain much less fat and cholesterol and fewer calories.

■ Lighten salads by using reduced-calorie, low-calorie, or nonfat salad dressings.

■ For potato toppings, use low-fat yogurt or sour cream instead of butter.

■ If you're concerned about your sodium intake, use sodium-reduced versions of products such as soy sauce, broth, tomato juice, and canned tomatoes.

SWORDFISH AND MIXED VEGETABLE STIR-FRY

8 ounces fresh *or* frozen swordfish, shark, *or* tuna steaks, cut 1 inch thick

■ Thaw fish, if frozen. Cut fish into 1-inch cubes. Set aside.

TIME ESTIMATE
Start to finish — 20 min.

½ cup water
2 tablespoons white wine Worcestershire sauce *or* Worcestershire sauce
1 teaspoon cornstarch
½ to 1 teaspoon grated gingerroot *or* ⅛ teaspoon ground ginger
½ teaspoon instant chicken bouillon granules
⅛ teaspoon onion powder

■ For sauce, in a small bowl stir together the water, white wine Worcestershire sauce or Worcestershire sauce, cornstarch, gingerroot or ground ginger, chicken bouillon granules, and onion powder. Set aside.

MENU IDEA

Complete your meal by serving Chocolate Chip Oat Cookies (see recipe, page 202) and scoops of ice cream.

PER SERVING

Calories	529
Protein	29 g
Carbohydrate	50 g
Fat (total)	24 g
Saturated	4 g
Cholesterol	43 mg
Sodium	674 mg
Potassium	403 mg

1 tablespoon cooking oil
3 cups loose-pack frozen broccoli, carrots, water chestnuts, and red peppers, thawed and drained

■ Pour cooking oil into a wok or large skillet. (Add more oil as necessary during cooking.) Preheat over medium-high heat. Stir-fry the thawed vegetables for 2 to 3 minutes or till crisp-tender. Remove the vegetables from the wok or skillet.

Add the fish to the hot wok or skillet. Stir-fry for 3 to 5 minutes or just till the fish begins to flake easily. Push fish from the center of the wok or skillet.

1 3-ounce can chow mein noodles *or* 1½ cups hot cooked rice

■ Stir sauce. Add sauce to the center of wok or skillet. Cook and stir till thickened and bubbly. Return vegetables to the wok or skillet. Stir all ingredients together to coat with sauce. Cook and stir about 1 minute more or till heated through. Serve over chow mein noodles or hot rice. Makes 2 servings.

SALMON AND GREEN PEPPERCORN STRUDEL

To yield the correct amount of cooked fish, broil 8 ounces of salmon or tuna steaks (see chart, page 87).

2 teaspoons whole green peppercorns
1 tablespoon margarine *or* butter
4 teaspoons all-purpose flour
¾ cup half-and-half, light cream, *or* milk
1¼ cups flaked cooked salmon *or* tuna

■ In a small saucepan cook green peppercorns in hot margarine or butter for 1 minute. Stir in the flour and dash *salt.* Stir in the half-and-half, light cream, or milk all at once. Cook and stir over medium heat till thickened and bubbly. Remove *half* of the peppercorn mixture from the pan. Cover with plastic wrap and set aside. Stir salmon or tuna into remaining mixture in saucepan. Set aside.

4 sheets frozen phyllo dough (17x12-inch rectangles), thawed
3 tablespoons margarine *or* butter, melted

■ Unfold phyllo dough. Brush 1 sheet of phyllo dough with some of the melted margarine or butter. Top with a second sheet of phyllo, then brush with more margarine. Repeat layering with remaining phyllo sheets and margarine (reserve some of the margarine). Cut the phyllo stack lengthwise in half.

To assemble, spread *half* of the salmon mixture along one short side of *each* phyllo strip to within 1 inch of the long sides. Fold the short end of phyllo over the salmon mixture and roll up, folding in the sides as you roll (see photo, right). Brush the seam with margarine; press to seal. Place rolls, seam side down, in a shallow baking dish. Cut diagonal slits about 1 inch apart in the top layers of each roll. Brush with margarine. Bake in a 400° oven 20 minutes or till phyllo is golden.

1 tablespoon brandy *or* dry white wine
1 tablespoon half-and-half, light cream, *or* milk

■ In a small saucepan heat brandy over medium heat. Add reserved peppercorn mixture, stirring with a wire wisk. Stir in half-and-half. Heat through. Spoon sauce onto individual plates. Place a strudel roll in center. Serves 2.

TIME ESTIMATE
Preparation —— 35 min.
Baking————— 20 min.

MENU IDEA
Accent this elegant entrée with mixed green salads drizzled with your favorite dressing, a side dish of baby zucchini and red onion, and glasses of dry white wine.

PER SERVING
Calories ——————— 710
Protein————————34 g
Carbohydrate ——— 40 g
Fat (total) ————— 45 g
  Saturated ————13 g
Cholesterol —— 119 mg
Sodium———— 551 mg
Potassium —— 516 mg

SALMON AND GREEN PEPPERCORN STRUDEL

PASTA WITH SALMON CREAM SAUCE

Simple, yet sophisticated. Try this creamy, rich cheese sauce studded with fresh salmon pieces and served over hot cooked pasta.

6 ounces fresh *or* frozen skinless, boneless salmon fillets *or* other fish fillets

6 ounces fresh refrigerated *or* 4 ounces packaged spinach *or* plain linguine, fettuccine, *or* spaghetti

■ Thaw fish, if frozen. Cut fish into 1-inch pieces. Set aside.

Cook pasta (see chart, page 185). Drain immediately.

1 cup half-and-half *or* light cream

1 tablespoon cornstarch
Dash ground nutmeg
Dash pepper

■ Meanwhile, for the sauce, in a medium saucepan stir together the half-and-half or light cream, cornstarch, nutmeg, and pepper. Cook and stir over medium heat till thickened and bubbly.

½ cup shredded process Gruyère *or* Swiss cheese (2 ounces)

■ Add the Gruyère or Swiss cheese to the sauce. Cook and stir till melted. Carefully stir in the fish. Return just to boiling; reduce heat. Cover and simmer gently for 3 to 5 minutes or just till fish begins to flake easily. Serve immediately over the hot cooked pasta. Makes 2 servings.

TIME ESTIMATE
Start to finish — 20 min.

MENU IDEA
Serve Lemon-Almond Green Beans (see recipe, page 175) and wheat rolls with this rich and creamy pasta dish.

PER SERVING
Calories	479
Protein	32 g
Carbohydrate	23 g
Fat (total)	29 g
Saturated	15 g
Cholesterol	122 mg
Sodium	189 mg
Potassium	631 mg

GRILLED TUNA STEAKS WITH PINEAPPLE SALSA

A taste of the tropics—pineapple, strawberries, coconut, and macadamia nuts spiked with lemon juice and ginger, then spooned over grilled fresh tuna steaks.

2 **4-ounce fresh *or* frozen tuna, swordfish, *or* halibut steaks, cut 1 inch thick**

1 **8¼-ounce can crushed pineapple**

■ Thaw fish, if frozen. Drain the pineapple, reserving juice.

---

2 **tablespoons chopped macadamia nuts, almonds, *or* pecans**

2 **tablespoons flaked coconut**

1 **tablespoon lemon *or* lime juice**

⅛ **teaspoon ground ginger, nutmeg, *or* cinnamon**

■ Spread the macadamia nuts, almonds, or pecans and the coconut into a thin layer in a pie plate. Bake in a 350° oven for 5 to 10 minutes or till light golden brown, stirring once or twice. Cool.

In a small mixing bowl stir together *2 table-spoons* of the reserved pineapple juice, the drained pineapple, lemon or lime juice, and ginger, nutmeg, or cinnamon. Set aside.

⅓ **cup coarsely chopped strawberries**

■ *To grill,* place the fish steaks on the greased rack of an uncovered grill. (See tip, page 27.) Grill directly over *medium-hot* coals for 5 minutes. Turn fish; brush with some of the remaining pineapple juice. Grill 3 to 7 minutes more or just till fish begins to flake easily.

Or, to broil, place fish steaks on the greased unheated rack of a broiler pan. Broil 4 inches from the heat for 5 minutes. Turn fish; brush with some of the remaining pineapple juice. Broil for 3 to 7 minutes more or just till fish begins to flake easily.

For salsa, stir the nuts, coconut, and strawberries into the pineapple mixture. To serve, transfer fish steaks to individual plates. Spoon some of the salsa over the fish. Pass the remaining salsa. Makes 2 servings.

TIME ESTIMATE

Start to finish _*25 min.
Allow extra time to heat the coals.

MENU IDEA

While you're grilling, add a side dish of sweet peppers and leeks to the grill (see chart, page 181).

PER SERVING

Calories	317
Protein	27 g
Carbohydrate	24 g
Fat (total)	14 g
Saturated	4 g
Cholesterol	42 mg
Sodium	68 mg
Potassium	513 mg

SWORDFISH MARGARITA

2 4-ounce fresh *or* frozen swordfish *or* tuna steaks, cut ½ to 1 inch thick
¾ cup water
1 teaspoon instant chicken bouillon granules
¼ teaspoon ground coriander

■ Thaw fish, if frozen. In a medium skillet combine the water, bouillon granules, and coriander. Bring mixture just to boiling. Measure thickness of fish. Carefully add the fish steaks to the skillet. Spoon liquid over fish; reduce heat. Cover and simmer just till fish begins to flake easily (allow 4 to 6 minutes per ½-inch thickness). Using a slotted spatula, transfer the fish to individual plates. Cover fish to keep warm. Reserve *½ cup* of liquid in skillet. Discard remaining liquid.

1 teaspoon finely shredded lime peel
1 tablespoon lime juice
1½ teaspoons cornstarch
1 teaspoon sugar
Dash pepper
1 tablespoon tequila *or* dry white wine

■ For sauce, in a small bowl stir together the lime peel, lime juice, cornstarch, sugar, and pepper. Add to the reserved liquid in the skillet. Cook and stir till thickened and bubbly. Cook and stir for 2 minutes more. Stir in the tequila or white wine. Drizzle the sauce over the fish. Makes 2 servings.

TIME ESTIMATE
Start to finish _ 20 min.

MENU IDEA
Enhance this dish by serving it with rye rolls and salads made of torn fresh spinach, orange sections, and Sugar Coated Nuts (see recipe, page 138).

PER SERVING
Calories _____ 155
Protein _____ 22 g
Carbohydrate _____ 4 g
Fat (total) _____ 5 g
　Saturated _____ 1 g
Cholesterol _____ 43 mg
Sodium_____ 549 mg
Potassium _____ 328 mg

SMART SHOPPING STRATEGIES

When you're cooking for two, it's often difficult to purchase just the right amount of the fresh ingredient you need. To avoid ending up with leftover ingredients that must be used immediately, look for convenience products, like these, that have a longer storage life:
■ Frozen chopped onion
■ Frozen chopped green pepper
■ Frozen chopped onion, green pepper, and celery
■ Frozen hash brown potatoes
■ Loose-pack frozen vegetables
■ Bottled minced garlic
■ Bottled frozen lemon juice

MUSTARD-TOPPED HALIBUT WITH APPLES

One great recipe—two great tastes! The apple lends the sweetness and the mustard gives the sharpness.

8 ounces fresh *or* frozen halibut steaks, cut ¾ inch thick, *or* haddock *or* orange roughy fillets (½ inch thick)

1 medium cooking apple, cored and sliced into ¼-inch-thick rings

1 tablespoon margarine *or* butter

■ Thaw fish, if frozen. In a large skillet cook the apple slices, covered, in margarine or butter about 2 minutes or till tender. Remove skillet from heat.

Nonstick spray coating

1 teaspoon Dijon-style mustard

¼ cup water

2 tablespoons dry white wine

½ teaspoon instant chicken bouillon granules

⅛ teaspoon onion powder

■ Spray an 8x8x2-inch baking dish with nonstick spray coating. Arrange fish steaks or fillets in dish. If using fillets, turn under any thin edges.

Spread tops of fish with mustard. In a small bowl combine the water, white wine, chicken bouillon granules, and onion powder. Pour mixture around fish. Arrange the apple slices atop and around the fish. Bake, covered, in a 450° oven for 6 to 10 minutes or just till fish begins to flake easily. Transfer the fish and apples to individual plates. Cover food to keep warm.

1 teaspoon margarine *or* butter

■ For sauce, if desired, strain the cooking liquid in the baking dish. Pour the liquid into the same skillet used for cooking the apple. If necessary, boil gently over medium-high heat till *¼ cup* liquid remains. Use a small whisk or fork to blend the margarine or butter into the sauce. Heat through. Pour the sauce over fish and apples. Serve immediately. Serves 2.

TIME ESTIMATE

Start to finish — 25 min.

MENU IDEA

Go ahead and pair this flavorful dish with Crispy Baked Potatoes (see recipe, page 178). The oven temperature needed for baking both dishes is the same.

PER SERVING

Calories	233
Protein	21 g
Carbohydrate	12 g
Fat (total)	12 g
Saturated	2 g
Cholesterol	35 mg
Sodium	452 mg
Potassium	584 mg

SEAFOOD LASAGNA ROLL-UPS

8 packaged lasagna noodles
1 10-ounce package frozen chopped spinach

■ Cook the lasagna noodles (see chart, page 185). Drain immediately. Rinse with *cold* water and drain again.

Cook spinach according to package directions. Drain well, pressing out excess liquid.

1 cup shredded mozzarella cheese (4 ounces)
1 cup ricotta cheese
1 6½-ounce can crabmeat, drained, flaked, and cartilage removed, *or* half of a 6-ounce package frozen, peeled, cooked shrimp, thawed (about ⅔ cup)
1 small sweet red *or* green pepper, finely chopped (½ cup)
½ teaspoon salt

■ For filling, in a medium mixing bowl stir together the spinach, mozzarella cheese, ricotta cheese, crabmeat or shrimp, sweet red or green pepper, salt, and ¼ teaspoon *pepper.*

To assemble the roll-ups, spread about ½ *cup* filling on *each* noodle. Roll up jelly-roll style, beginning from one of the short sides. Place 2 rolls, seam side down, in *each* of 4 lightly greased individual casseroles. Set the casseroles aside.

2 cloves garlic, minced
2 tablespoons margarine *or* butter
1 tablespoon cornstarch
¼ teaspoon pepper
1½ cups milk
2 tablespoons dry white wine
2 tablespoons grated Parmesan cheese

■ For sauce, in a medium saucepan cook garlic in hot margarine or butter for 30 seconds. Stir in the cornstarch, pepper, and dash *salt.* Add milk all at once. Cook and stir till thickened and bubbly. Add wine. Cook and stir for 2 minutes more. Spoon sauce over casseroles. Sprinkle with Parmesan cheese. Bake 2 of the casseroles immediately and freeze remaining casseroles as directed. Serves 4.

TO EAT TWO: Bake 2 of the casseroles, covered, in a 375° oven about 25 minutes or till filling is heated through.

TO FREEZE TWO: Seal, label, and freeze 2 of the casseroles for up to 3 months. *To serve,* bake 1 or 2 of the frozen casseroles, covered, in a 375° oven about 1 hour or till heated through.

TIME ESTIMATE
Preparation —— 30 min.
Baking———— 25 min.

MENU IDEA
Round out this meal with buttered broccoli and salads of radicchio and other greens drizzled with Garlic Vinaigrette (see recipe, page 137).

PER SERVING
Calories —————— 525
Protein ————————33 g
Carbohydrate ———— 47 g
Fat (total) —————— 22 g
  Saturated ————— 11 g
Cholesterol ———— 89 mg
Sodium————— 791 mg
Potassium ——— 702 mg

MEDITERRANEAN-STYLE FISH ROLLS

**4 4-ounce fresh *or* frozen
    flounder, sole, *or* other
    fish fillets**
**12 ounces asparagus spears
    or one 10-ounce
    package frozen
    asparagus spears**

■ Thaw fish, if frozen. Cut the fresh asparagus, if using, into 6-inch spears; discard woody stems. Cook the fresh asparagus, covered, in a small amount of boiling water for 8 to 10 minutes or till crisp-tender. Or, if using frozen asparagus, cook according to package directions. Drain well.

Place 4 or 5 asparagus spears crosswise on each fillet. Roll up jelly-roll style, starting from a narrow end. Place rolls, seam side down, in 4 greased individual casseroles.

¼ cup finely chopped onion
**2 teaspoons olive oil *or*
    cooking oil**
2 teaspoons cornstarch
**½ teaspoon dried basil,
    crushed**
**¼ teaspoon dried oregano,
    crushed**
1 8-ounce can tomato sauce
**1 4-ounce can diced green
    chili peppers, drained**
1 tablespoon lemon juice

■ For sauce, in a small saucepan cook the onion in olive oil or cooking oil till tender. Stir in the cornstarch, basil, and oregano. Add the tomato sauce, chili peppers, and lemon juice. Cook and stir till thickened and bubbly. Cook and stir for 2 minutes more. Spoon the sauce over fish rolls. Bake 2 of the casseroles immediately and freeze remaining casseroles as directed. Makes 4 servings.

TIME ESTIMATE
Preparation ___ 25 min.
Baking _____ 25 min.

MENU IDEA
Try a side dish of whole tiny new potatoes and crisp lettuce wedges drizzled with Tomato-Basil Vinaigrette (see recipe, page 139).

PER SERVING
Calories	224
Protein	29 g
Carbohydrate	11 g
Fat (total)	8 g
Saturated	3 g
Cholesterol	81 mg
Sodium	817 mg
Potassium	903 mg

TO EAT TWO: Bake 2 of the casseroles, uncovered, in a 350° oven about 20 minutes or till fish is nearly done. Sprinkle *each* fish roll with 2 tablespoons shredded **Monterey Jack cheese.** Bake, uncovered, 3 minutes more or just till fish begins to flake easily and cheese is melted. If desired, garnish with **lemon slices** and sliced pitted **ripe olives.**

TO FREEZE TWO: Seal, label, and freeze 2 of the casseroles for up to 3 months. *To serve,* bake 1 or 2 of the frozen casseroles, covered, in a 350° oven for 60 to 70 minutes or till fish is nearly done. Sprinkle *each* fish roll with 2 tablespoons shredded **Monterey Jack cheese.** Bake, uncovered, for 3 to 5 minutes more or just till fish begins to flake easily and cheese is melted. If desired, garnish with **lemon slices** and sliced pitted **ripe olives.**

Meatless Main Dishes

BUTTERMILK AND SWISS FONDUE

BUTTERMILK AND SWISS FONDUE

Buttermilk lends a pleasing tanginess to the cheese flavor. Non-alcoholic wine and sparkling white grape juice are other tasty options.

6 ounces process Swiss *or* Gruyère cheese, torn *or* shredded

1 tablespoon all-purpose flour

1 cup buttermilk, dry white wine, *or* apple cider
Dash ground nutmeg *or* mace, *or* ½ teaspoon caraway seed

2 tablespoons chopped walnuts *or* pecans

3 cups cubed French, sourdough, *or* whole wheat bread

2 cups assorted vegetable dippers (such as radicchio leaves; baby yellow summer squash halves; sweet orange, red, *or* green pepper strips; Belgian endive leaves; bias-sliced carrots; broccoli flowerets; cauliflower flowerets)

■ In a small bowl toss together Swiss or Gruyère cheese and flour. In a medium saucepan heat buttermilk, wine, or apple cider over medium heat till small bubbles rise to the surface. Stir in cheese mixture, little by little, making sure cheese has melted before adding more. (Stir constantly and continue to add cheese till all is mixed in.) Stir till cheese mixture bubbles gently. Stir in nutmeg, mace, or caraway seed.

■ Pour cheese mixture into a small fondue pot. Keep cheese mixture warm over fondue burner. Sprinkle with walnuts or pecans. Serve with bread cubes and vegetable dippers. Makes 2 servings.

TIME ESTIMATE
Start to finish _ 30 min.

MENU IDEA
Serve glasses of wine with the meal. Then splurge with chocolate brownies for dessert.

PER SERVING
Calories _____ 544
Protein _____ 32 g
Carbohydrate _____ 39 g
Fat (total) _____ 29 g
  Saturated _____ 15 g
Cholesterol _____ 76 mg
Sodium _____ 1,544 mg
Potassium _____ 720 mg

LENTIL AND CHEESE TOSTADAS

1½ **cups water**
¾ **cup dry lentils**
¼ **cup chopped onion**
1 **tablespoon snipped cilantro**
½ **teaspoon salt**
½ **teaspoon ground cumin**
1 **clove garlic, minced**

■ In a medium saucepan stir together water, lentils, onion, cilantro, salt, cumin, and garlic. Bring to boiling; reduce heat. Cover and simmer about 30 minutes or till lentils are tender and liquid is absorbed. (For identification of uncooked and cooked lentils, see photo, right.) Use a fork to mash the cooked lentils.

TIME ESTIMATE
Start to finish _ 40 min.

½ **of a medium avocado, seeded and peeled**
1 **teaspoon lemon juice**
2 **tostada shells**
¼ **cup salsa**
1 **cup shredded lettuce**
¾ **cup shredded Monterey Jack *or* cheddar cheese**
1 **small tomato, chopped**
2 **tablespoons sliced pitted ripe olives**

■ Chop avocado and toss with lemon juice. To serve, place tostada shells on 2 individual plates. Spread with lentil mixture. Top with the salsa and avocado. Then add lettuce, cheese, tomato, and olives. Makes 2 servings.

PER SERVING
Calories _____ 587
Protein _____ 34 g
Carbohydrate ____ 63 g
Fat (total) _____ 26 g
  Saturated _____ 10 g
Cholesterol _____ 37 mg
Sodium _____ 1,101 mg
Potassium ____ 1,281 mg

LENTIL AND CHEESE BURRITOS

4 **10-inch flour tortillas**

■ Prepare Lentils and Cheese Tostadas as above, *except* omit tostada shells. Wrap flour tortillas in foil. Heat in a 350° oven 10 minutes to soften. Spoon *one-fourth* of the lentil mixture onto *each* tortilla just below center. Top with salsa and cheese. Fold bottom edge of tortilla up and over filling, just till mixture is covered. Fold in opposite sides of tortilla, just till they meet. Roll up tortilla from the bottom. Secure with wooden toothpicks. Arrange burritos on a baking sheet. Bake in a 350° oven for 10 to 12 minutes or till heated through. Remove toothpicks. Serve on lettuce with avocado, tomato, and olives.

PER SERVING
Calories _____ 864
Protein _____ 41 g
Carbohydrate ____ 116 g
Fat (total) _____ 32 g
  Saturated _____ 11 g
Cholesterol _____ 37 mg
Sodium _____ 1,469 mg
Potassium ____ 1,368 mg

CARAMELIZED ONION AND BLUE CHEESE PIZZA

3 medium onions, thinly
  sliced (about 2 cups)
2 tablespoons margarine
  or butter

■ In a large saucepan cook onions, uncovered, in hot margarine or butter over low heat about 30 minutes or till onions are very soft and golden, stirring occasionally.

2 large pita bread rounds,
  split horizontally, *or*
  four 7-inch flour
  tortillas

■ Meanwhile, place pita bread halves or tortillas on a baking sheet. Bake in a 350° oven about 15 minutes or till pita halves or tortillas are crisp and lightly browned.

1½ cups cream-style cottage
  cheese
¼ cup crumbled blue *or*
  feta cheese
⅓ cup toasted chopped
  walnuts *or* pecans

■ In a blender container or food processor bowl combine the cottage cheese and blue or feta cheese. Cover and blend or process till smooth. Spread cottage cheese mixture over pita bread halves or tortillas. Top with onions and walnuts or pecans. Increase oven temperature to 450°. Bake pizzas in the 450° oven for 8 to 10 minutes or till heated through. Makes 2 servings.

TIME ESTIMATE
Start to finish — 50 min.

MENU IDEA
Toss crisp greens and assorted fresh vegetables with your favorite dressing. Top off your salads with Dilled Bagel Crisps (see recipe, page 138).

PER SERVING

Calories	649
Protein	33 g
Carbohydrate	51 g
Fat (total)	35 g
Saturated	11 g
Cholesterol	34 mg
Sodium	1,313 mg
Potassium	527 mg

STEPS TO SPEEDIER COOKING

In a hurry? Organization is the key to getting meals ready on the double. Make your time in the kitchen more efficient by dovetailing or overlapping steps so you accomplish two things at once. Here are some suggestions:

■ First, turn on the oven or broiler so the appliance will be preheated when you need it. (This takes about 10 minutes.) Then, read the recipe and get out the utensils you'll need.

■ While waiting for water to boil or meat to brown, measure ingredients, chop vegetables, open cans, or make a sauce.

■ While the main dish is cooking, put together a side dish and set the table.

■ Put away containers and wash utensils used in preparation as you finish using them to cut cleanup time at the end.

PILAF PRIMAVERA

Savor the rich, nutty flavor that comes forth when you toast the rice.

¾ **cup brown rice**
2 **teaspoons olive oil *or*
   cooking oil**

■ To toast the rice, in a medium saucepan cook rice in hot olive oil or cooking oil over medium heat till the rice is golden, stirring occasionally.

1¾ **cups water**
1 **medium onion, chopped
   (½ cup)**
2 **teaspoons snipped fresh
   dillweed *or* ¼ teaspoon
   dried dillweed**
1 **teaspoon snipped fresh
   thyme *or* ⅛ teaspoon
   dried thyme, crushed**
1 **teaspoon instant chicken
   bouillon granules**
⅛ **teaspoon pepper**
1 **medium zucchini *or*
   yellow summer squash,
   halved lengthwise and
   sliced (1¼ cups)**
1 **medium sweet red *or*
   green pepper, cut into
   ¾-inch squares (1 cup)**
1 **stalk celery, sliced
   (½ cup)**

■ *Carefully* add the water. Stir in the onion, dillweed, thyme, bouillon granules, and pepper. Bring to boiling; reduce heat. Cover and simmer for 35 minutes. Stir in the zucchini or yellow summer squash, sweet red or green pepper, and celery. Cover and simmer about 10 minutes more or till rice and vegetables are tender and liquid is absorbed.

½ **cup shredded Swiss
   cheese (2 ounces)**
¼ **cup cashews *or* toasted
   slivered almonds**

■ Stir the Swiss cheese and cashews or almonds into the rice mixture. Serve immediately. Makes 2 servings.

TIME ESTIMATE

Start to finish — 55 min.

MENU IDEA

Spread your favorite bagels or English muffins with a little margarine or butter, then sprinkle them with garlic powder. Toast them under the broiler till the margarine is bubbly.

PER SERVING

Calories	548
Protein	19 g
Carbohydrate	70 g
Fat (total)	23 g
Saturated	8 g
Cholesterol	26 mg
Sodium	661 mg
Potassium	718 mg

RICE PATTIES FLORENTINE WITH YOGURT SAUCE

1 cup water
⅔ cup brown rice

■ In a medium saucepan bring water to boiling. Slowly add rice to water and return to boiling. Cover and simmer about 35 minutes or till rice is tender. Cool rice for 5 minutes.

½ of a 10-ounce package frozen chopped spinach, thawed and well drained
½ cup shredded carrot
¼ cup fine dry bread crumbs
¼ cup grated Parmesan cheese
¼ cup toasted pumpkin seed *or* chopped almonds
1 beaten egg
1 teaspoon white wine Worcestershire sauce *or* Worcestershire sauce

■ Stir the spinach, carrot, bread crumbs, Parmesan cheese, pumpkin seed or almonds, egg, and white wine Worcestershire sauce or Worcestershire sauce into the rice. Mix well.

1 beaten egg
1 tablespoon milk
½ cup fine dry bread crumbs
2 tablespoons margarine, butter, olive oil, *or* cooking oil

■ Shape rice mixture into four ¾-inch-thick patties. Stir together the egg and milk. Carefully dip patties in egg mixture, then coat them with bread crumbs. Cook rice patties in hot margarine, butter, olive oil, or cooking oil over medium heat about 4 minutes on each side or till golden. (If patties brown too quickly, reduce heat to medium-low.)

½ cup plain yogurt
¼ teaspoon dried dillweed
Spinach leaves *or* shredded zucchini (optional)

■ Meanwhile, for sauce, in a small bowl stir together the yogurt and dillweed.
　To serve, if desired, arrange spinach leaves or shredded zucchini on individual plates. Top with rice patties and sauce. Serves 2.

TIME ESTIMATE
Start to finish ——— 1 hr.

MENU IDEA
Brush fresh ears of sweet corn with a flavored butter (see recipes, page 177).

PER SERVING
Calories ——————— 821
Protein ——————— 36 g
Carbohydrate ——— 92 g
Fat (total) ——————— 36 g
　Saturated ——————— 10 g
Cholesterol ——— 227 mg
Sodium——————— 968 mg
Potassium ——— 955 mg

PEPPERS STUFFED WITH CINNAMON BULGUR

Take in the pleasurable aroma of cinnamon as it weaves its flavor through the whole grain.

1¾ cups water
1 medium carrot, shredded (½ cup)
¼ cup chopped onion
1 teaspoon instant chicken bouillon granules
3 inches stick cinnamon

■ In a medium skillet combine water, carrot, onion, bouillon granules, and stick cinnamon. Bring to boiling; reduce heat. Cover and simmer for 5 minutes.

¾ cup bulgur
½ cup raisins

■ Stir in the bulgur and raisins. Remove from heat. Cover and let stand for 5 minutes. Remove the stick cinnamon from the bulgur mixture. Drain off excess liquid.

1 large sweet red, yellow, *or* green pepper

■ Meanwhile, halve pepper lengthwise, removing stem end, seeds, and membranes.

½ cup shredded Muenster, brick, *or* mozzarella cheese (2 ounces)
2 tablespoons chopped pecans *or* sliced almonds

■ Stir Muenster, brick, or mozzarella cheese and pecans or almonds into the bulgur mixture. Spoon mixture into pepper halves.

½ cup water

■ Place pepper halves in skillet. Add water; bring to boiling. Cover and simmer for 5 to 10 minutes or till filling is heated through and pepper is crisp-tender. Makes 2 servings.

TIME ESTIMATE
Start to finish — 30 min.

MENU IDEA
Bake a batch of your favorite muffins to pass during the meal.

PER SERVING
Calories ——————— 493
Protein ——————— 16 g
Carbohydrate ——— 82 g
Fat (total) ——————— 15 g
　Saturated ——————— 6 g
Cholesterol ——— 27 mg
Sodium——————— 653 mg
Potassium ——— 792 mg

POLENTA WITH TOMATO-BEAN SAUCE

Win the diner's dash by fixing the polenta and sauce the day before serving. Then just heat and eat. Or, for a super-quick sauce, substitute 1¼ cups purchased meatless spaghetti sauce for the Tomatoey Sauce.

1½ **cups water**
½ **cup yellow cornmeal**
½ **cup cold water**
½ **teaspoon salt**

■ For polenta, in a medium saucepan bring the 1½ cups water to boiling. In a mixing bowl stir together the cornmeal, ½ cup cold water, and salt. Slowly add cornmeal mixture to boiling water, stirring constantly. Cook and stir till mixture returns to boiling. Reduce heat to very low. Cover and simmer for 15 minutes, stirring occasionally.

■ Spread hot cornmeal mixture in an 8x8x2-inch baking dish. Cover and chill about 4 hours or till firm. (Polenta may be chilled for up to 24 hours.)

½ **cup shredded mozzarella,**
Monterey Jack, *or*
cheddar cheese
(2 ounces)

■ Sprinkle the mozzarella, Monterey Jack, or cheddar cheese over the chilled polenta. Bake, covered, in a 350° oven about 25 minutes or till heated through. Cut into 4 squares.

Tomatoey Sauce (see
recipe, page 110)
1 **15- to 16-ounce can red**
kidney, butter, *or* lima
beans, drained
1 **8½-ounce can lima**
beans, drained

■ Meanwhile, prepare Tomatoey Sauce. Stir in beans. Heat through.

■ To serve, transfer the polenta to individual plates. Spoon the sauce over the polenta. Makes 2 servings.

TIME ESTIMATE

Preparation	25 min.
Chilling	4 hrs.
Baking	25 min.

MENU IDEA

Accent the polenta dish with Carrot and Squash Stir-Fry (see recipe, page 173) and glasses of milk.

PER SERVING

Calories	588
Protein	30 g
Carbohydrate	92 g
Fat (total)	13 g
Saturated	4 g
Cholesterol	16 mg
Sodium	1,466 mg
Potassium	1,529 mg

MIXED VEGETABLE AND TOFU CHOW MEIN

1 cup fresh pea pods *or* ½ of
    a 6-ounce package
    frozen pea pods,
    thawed
½ cup water
2 tablespoons dry sherry
    or dry white wine
1 tablespoon soy sauce
2 teaspoons cornstarch
½ teaspoon instant chicken
    bouillon granules

■ Slice the pea pods in half crosswise at a diagonal; set aside. For sauce, in a small bowl stir together the water, dry sherry or dry white wine, soy sauce, cornstarch, and chicken bouillon granules. Set aside.

1 tablespoon cooking oil
2 cloves garlic, minced
½ cup thinly sliced carrot
1 cup shredded Chinese
    cabbage *or* cabbage
1 small yellow summer
    squash *or* zucchini,
    thinly sliced (about
    1 cup)
2 green onions, bias-sliced
    into 1-inch lengths

■ Pour cooking oil into a wok or large skillet. (Add more oil as necessary during cooking.) Preheat over medium-high heat. Stir-fry the garlic in hot oil 15 seconds. Add carrot; stir-fry for 1 minute. Add the fresh pea pods (if using), regular cabbage (if using), summer squash or zucchini, and green onions; stir-fry 3 to 4 minutes more or till vegetables are crisp-tender. Remove the vegetables from the wok.

4 ounces firm tofu (fresh
    bean curd), cut into ½-
    inch cubes
1 7-ounce jar whole straw
    mushrooms *or* one 4½-
    ounce jar sliced
    mushrooms, drained
½ cup cashews *or* peanuts
    Chow mein noodles
    (optional)

■ Add the tofu to the hot wok or skillet. Carefully stir-fry for 2 to 3 minutes or till lightly browned. Remove tofu from wok.

Stir the sauce. Add the sauce to the wok or skillet. Cook and stir till thickened and bubbly. Return cooked vegetables and tofu to the wok. Add the thawed pea pods (if using), Chinese cabbage (if using), and mushrooms. Stir all ingredients together to coat with sauce. Cook and stir about 1 minute more or till heated through. Stir in cashews or peanuts. If desired, spoon over chow mein noodles. Serve immediately. Makes 2 servings.

TIME ESTIMATE
Start to finish — 35 min.

MENU IDEA
Enjoy the chow mein with hot tea and rice crackers or breadsticks.

PER SERVING
Calories _____ 402
Protein _____ 15 g
Carbohydrate _____ 30 g
Fat (total) _____ 26 g
  Saturated _____ 4 g
Cholesterol _____ 0 mg
Sodium _____ 1,150 mg
Potassium _____ 810 mg

MOO SHU VEGETABLE AND EGG CREPES

12 asparagus spears, cut into 3-inch lengths

2 carrots, cut into 3-inch-long sticks

2 green onions, cut into 2-inch lengths

■ In a large saucepan cook the asparagus, carrots, and green onions in a small amount of boiling lightly salted water for 7 to 9 minutes or till vegetables are crisp-tender. Drain.

2 tablespoons bottled sweet-and-sour sauce

1 tablespoon orange *or* pineapple juice

½ teaspoon grated gingerroot *or* ⅛ teaspoon ground ginger

■ Meanwhile, for sauce, in a small bowl stir together the sweet-and-sour sauce, orange or pineapple juice, and gingerroot or ground ginger. Set aside.

4 eggs

2 tablespoons water

2 teaspoons cooking oil

■ For crepes, in a small mixing bowl combine the eggs and water. Using a fork, beat till combined but not frothy. In an 8- or 10-inch skillet with flared sides, heat *1 teaspoon* of the cooking oil till a drop of water sizzles. Lift and tilt the pan to coat the sides of the skillet with oil. Add *half* of the egg mixture (about ½ cup) to the skillet; cook over medium heat. As the eggs set, run a spatula around the edge of the skillet, lifting eggs and letting the uncooked portion flow underneath. When the eggs are set but still shiny, transfer the crepe to a warm plate; cover with plastic wrap. Repeat with the remaining egg mixture and oil.

2 tablespoons toasted chopped walnuts *or* almonds

■ To assemble, spread some of the sauce onto each crepe. Arrange steamed vegetables on *one-quarter* of each crepe, fanning vegetables at the edge of crepe. Fold each crepe in half over the vegetables; fold again into quarters (see photo, right). Top with remaining sauce; sprinkle with the walnuts or almonds. Makes 2 servings.

TIME ESTIMATE

Start to finish — 25 min.

MENU IDEA

Delight in buttery croissants with this brunch or dinner entrée.

PER SERVING

Calories _____ 320
Protein _____ 17 g
Carbohydrate ____ 20 g
Fat (total) _____ 20 g
　Saturated _____ 4 g
Cholesterol ___ 426 mg
Sodium_____ 199 mg
Potassium ____ 699 mg

SPINACH-STUFFED PASTA SHELLS

16 packaged jumbo shells *or* 8 packaged manicotti shells
1 10-ounce package frozen chopped spinach, thawed
2 beaten eggs
1 cup ricotta cheese
1 cup shredded mozzarella cheese (4 ounces)
1 cup shredded cheddar cheese (4 ounces)
½ cup freshly shredded *or* grated Parmesan cheese
   Tomatoey Sauce

■ Cook pasta (see chart, page 185). Drain immediately. Rinse with cold water; drain well.

Meanwhile, drain thawed spinach well, pressing out excess liquid.

For filling, combine eggs; ricotta, mozzarella, and cheddar cheeses; *half* of the Parmesan cheese; and the spinach. Spoon about *3 tablespoons* filling into *each* jumbo shell or about ⅓ *cup* filling into *each* manicotti shell.

Place 4 jumbo shells or 2 manicotti shells into each of 4 individual casseroles. Top with sauce; sprinkle with remaining Parmesan cheese. Bake 2 casseroles immediately; freeze remaining casseroles as directed. Serves 4.

TO EAT TWO: Bake 2 of the casseroles, covered, in a 350° oven about 25 minutes or till heated through.

TO FREEZE TWO: Seal, label, and freeze 2 of the casseroles for up to 3 months. *To serve,* bake 1 or 2 of the frozen casseroles, covered, in a 375° oven about 1 hour or till heated through.

TIME ESTIMATE
Start to finish — 40 min.

MENU IDEA
Warm, crusty sourdough rolls are the perfect accompaniment.

PER SERVING
Calories	561
Protein	36 g
Carbohydrate	37 g
Fat (total)	31 g
Saturated	17 g
Cholesterol	191 mg
Sodium	939 mg
Potassium	755 mg

TOMATOEY SAUCE

⅓ cup chopped onion
1 clove garlic, minced
1 tablespoon margarine *or* butter
1 14½-ounce can whole Italian-style tomatoes, cut up
2 tablespoons tomato paste
½ teaspoon dried Italian seasoning, crushed
¼ teaspoon sugar

■ In a saucepan cook onion and garlic in hot margarine or butter till onion is tender but not brown. Carefully stir in *undrained* tomatoes, tomato paste, Italian seasoning, sugar, dash *salt,* and dash *pepper.* Simmer, uncovered, about 10 minutes or till sauce is of desired consistency, stirring occasionally.

SPINACH-STUFFED PASTA SHELLS

WHITE-CHILI-STYLE PASTA SAUCE

1 medium onion, chopped
   (½ cup)
2 cloves garlic, minced
1 tablespoon margarine *or*
   butter

■ In a medium saucepan cook the onion and garlic in hot margarine or butter till onion is tender but not brown.

TIME ESTIMATE
Start to finish — 20 min.

MENU IDEA
Arrange herb-buttered zucchini or yellow summer squash slices next to the sauce-covered pasta.

2 tablespoons all-purpose
   flour
⅛ teaspoon pepper
1⅓ cups milk

■ Stir in the all-purpose flour and pepper. Add the milk all at once. Cook and stir over medium heat till thickened and bubbly. Cook and stir for 1 minute more.

PER SERVING

Calories	524
Protein	27 g
Carbohydrate	67 g
Fat (total)	16 g
Saturated	9 g
Cholesterol	43 mg
Sodium	951 mg
Potassium	645 mg

1½ cups shredded process
   Swiss, Gruyère, *or*
   American cheese
   (6 ounces)
1 15-ounce can great
   northern *or* red kidney
   beans, drained
1 4-ounce can diced green
   chili peppers, drained

■ Add the Swiss, Gruyère, or American cheese and stir till cheese is melted. Stir in the great northern or red kidney beans and the green chili peppers.

■ Pour *half* of the sauce mixture into 1 or 2 individual freezer containers and freeze as directed. Leave remaining mixture in saucepan and cook immediately. Makes 4 servings.

TO EAT TWO: Cook and stir the remaining sauce mixture in the saucepan till heated through. Serve sauce over 2 cups hot cooked **linguine, spaghetti,** *or* **other pasta.**

TO FREEZE TWO: Seal, label, and freeze the freezer containers for up to 3 months. *To serve,* place 1 or 2 of the frozen portions in a saucepan. Cover and cook over medium-low heat about 30 minutes or till heated through, stirring occasionally. Serve *each* portion over 1 cup hot cooked **linguine, spaghetti,** *or* **other pasta.**

HEARTY SPINACH AND TOFU RISOTTO

2 cups water
1 cup brown rice
1 8-ounce package tofu
   (fresh bean curd),
   drained

½ cup chopped onion
1 clove garlic, minced
2 tablespoons cooking oil
1 14½-ounce can whole
   Italian-style tomatoes,
   cut up
1 teaspoon dried oregano
   or basil, crushed
1 10-ounce package frozen
   chopped spinach,
   thawed and well
   drained
¼ cup shredded Swiss *or*
   cheddar cheese
   (1 ounce)
½ teaspoon salt
¼ teaspoon pepper

■ In a medium saucepan bring water to boiling. Slowly add rice to water and return to boiling; reduce heat. Cover and simmer about 35 minutes or till rice is tender.

Meanwhile, place the tofu in a blender container or food processor bowl. Cover and blend or process till smooth. Set aside.

■ In a large saucepan cook the onion and garlic in hot oil till onion is tender but not brown. Carefully stir in the *undrained* tomatoes and oregano or basil. Bring to boiling; reduce heat. Simmer, uncovered, for 3 minutes. Stir in the tofu, cooked rice, drained spinach, shredded Swiss or cheddar cheese, salt, and pepper.

Spoon rice mixture into 4 greased individual casseroles. Bake 2 of the casseroles immediately and freeze the remaining casseroles as directed. Makes 4 servings.

TIME ESTIMATE

Preparation ___ 45 min.
Baking_____ 25 min.

MENU IDEA

Dress up cantaloupe wedges with a few brightly colored berries. Top them with a dollop of plain or vanilla yogurt.

PER SERVING

Calories _____ 387
Protein_____ 16 g
Carbohydrate _____ 48 g
Fat (total) _____ 16 g
   Saturated _____ 4 g
Cholesterol _____ 13 mg
Sodium_____ 540 mg
Potassium _____ 671 mg

TO EAT TWO: Bake 2 of the casseroles, uncovered, in a 350° oven about 25 minutes or till hot. Sprinkle *each* casserole with 1 tablespoon shredded **Swiss *or* cheddar cheese** and ½ teaspoon toasted **sesame seed.**

TO FREEZE TWO: Seal, label, and freeze 2 of the casseroles for up to 3 months. *To serve,* bake 1 or 2 of the frozen casseroles, covered, in a 350° oven about 1 hour or till heated through. Sprinkle *each* casserole with 1 tablespoon shredded **Swiss *or* cheddar cheese** and ½ teaspoon toasted **sesame seed.**

SALADS

LEMON CHICKEN SALAD

LEMON CHICKEN SALAD

Select only edible flowers to garnish salads or other foods. To be edible, flowers must be nontoxic varieties and free of chemicals. Some edible varieties include nasturtiums, pansies, marigolds, roses, violas, and chamomiles.

2 medium boneless, skinless chicken breast halves (6 ounces total)
¼ cup lemon juice
1 teaspoon lemon-pepper seasoning
1 tablespoon olive oil *or* cooking oil

■ Rinse chicken and pat dry. Place chicken in a plastic bag set in a deep mixing bowl. Pour lemon juice over chicken in bag. Close bag and turn chicken to coat well. Marinate at room temperature for 30 minutes or in the refrigerator for 1 hour, turning bag occasionally. Drain chicken, discarding lemon juice.

Sprinkle both sides of chicken breast halves with lemon-pepper seasoning, pressing into surface.

In a medium skillet cook chicken in hot olive oil or cooking oil over medium heat for 8 to 10 minutes or till chicken is tender and no pink remains, turning often to brown evenly. Remove from skillet. Cut chicken across the grain into ½-inch-wide strips.

2 tablespoons honey
2 tablespoons coarse-grain brown mustard *or* Dijon-style mustard
2 teaspoons lemon juice

■ Meanwhile, for dressing, in a small bowl stir together the honey, brown or Dijon-style mustard, and lemon juice. Set aside.

3 cups torn mixed greens
1 cup chopped, seeded cucumber
1 medium tomato, seeded and chopped
¼ cup alfalfa sprouts
   Fresh nasturtiums *or* other edible flowers (optional)

■ Divide mixed greens, cucumber, tomato, and alfalfa sprouts between 2 individual salad bowls or plates. Arrange the hot chicken strips atop the greens and vegetables. If desired, garnish with the nasturtiums or other edible flowers. Serve with the dressing. Makes 2 servings.

TIME ESTIMATE
Preparation —— 15 min.
Marinating —— 30 min.
Cooking —— 10 min.

MENU IDEA
For a light and refreshing meal, serve soft breadsticks and icy glasses of lemonade with this salad.

PER SERVING
Calories —— 294
Protein —— 23 g
Carbohydrate —— 28 g
Fat (total) —— 11 g
   Saturated —— 2 g
Cholesterol —— 54 mg
Sodium —— 663 mg
Potassium —— 658 mg

WALDORF CHICKEN SALAD

For tasty sandwiches, spoon this fruity chicken salad into split pita bread halves or onto split croissants.

½ **cup vanilla yogurt**
⅛ **teaspoon apple pie spice**
   or **pumpkin pie spice,**
   or **ground allspice,**
   ginger, *or* **cinnamon**

■ For dressing, in a small bowl stir together the yogurt and spice. Set aside.

¾ **cup chopped apple**
1 **teaspoon lemon juice**
1 **cup chopped cooked**
   chicken *or* **turkey**
¼ **cup sliced celery**
¼ **cup raisins, snipped**
   dried cherries *or*
   cranberries, *or* **snipped**
   pitted dates
¼ **cup seedless red** *or* **green**
   grapes, halved

■ In a medium mixing bowl toss the apple with the lemon juice. Stir in the chicken or turkey; celery; raisins, cherries, cranberries, or dates; and grapes. Add the dressing. Stir till thoroughly combined. Cover and chill for 30 minutes to 1 hour to blend flavors.

Lettuce leaves
2 **tablespoons sliced**
   almonds *or* **chopped**
   peanuts, walnuts, *or*
   pecans

■ To serve, line 2 individual salad bowls or plates with lettuce leaves. Stir the chicken mixture. Spoon chicken mixture atop lettuce. Sprinkle with almonds, peanuts, walnuts, or pecans. Makes 2 servings.

TIME ESTIMATE
Preparation —— 20 min.
Chilling ——— 30 min.

MENU IDEA
Blueberry-Oatmeal Muffins (see recipe, page 212) or buttery croissants are great accompaniments for this flavorful salad.

PER SERVING
Calories ————— 306
Protein ————— 26 g
Carbohydrate ——— 36 g
Fat (total) ———— 7 g
   Saturated ——— 2 g
Cholesterol —— 62 mg
Sodium———— 103 mg
Potassium —— 608 mg

HOT CURRIED CHICKEN SALAD WITH CRISPY PITA CHIPS

On a chilly day, warm up with a serving of this hearty, hot chicken salad accompanied by homemade pita chips.

1 tablespoon margarine *or* butter, melted

¼ teaspoon dried basil, crushed

Dash ground red pepper (optional)

1 large pita bread round

■ In a small bowl stir together the melted margarine or butter, basil, and, if desired, ground red pepper.

For pita chips, split the pita bread horizontally in half. Lightly brush each cut half with the margarine mixture. Cut each half into 6 wedges. Spread wedges in a single layer on a baking sheet. Bake in a 350° oven about 10 minutes or till crisp.

TIME ESTIMATE
Start to finish _ 25 min.

MENU IDEA
Top off this meal with Fudge Brownies with Cocoa Glaze (see recipe, page 201) and scoops of vanilla ice cream.

¼ cup mayonnaise *or* salad dressing

1 tablespoon chutney, snipped

¼ teaspoon curry powder

1 cup chopped cooked chicken *or* turkey

¼ cup sliced celery

¼ cup shredded carrot

1 tablespoon thinly sliced green onion

■ Meanwhile, in a small mixing bowl stir together the mayonnaise or salad dressing, chutney, and curry powder.

In a small saucepan combine the chicken or turkey, celery, carrot, and green onion. Stir in the mayonnaise mixture. Heat and stir over low heat till chicken mixture is heated through.

PER SERVING

Calories	581
Protein	28 g
Carbohydrate	38 g
Fat (total)	36 g
Saturated	6 g
Cholesterol	75 mg
Sodium	589 mg
Potassium	496 mg

Lettuce leaves

½ of an 8-ounce can pineapple tidbits, drained

2 tablespoons chopped peanuts

■ To serve, line 2 individual plates with lettuce leaves. Stir the pineapple into the chicken mixture. Spoon chicken mixture atop lettuce. Sprinkle with peanuts. Serve with warm pita chips. Makes 2 servings.

FRESH FRUIT AND CHICKEN PLATES

A pomegranate is a seasonal fruit available only September through December. If you'd like to use pomegranate seeds year-round, buy pomegranates in season and freeze the seeds in freezer containers up to 1 year.

2 medium boneless,
 skinless chicken breast
 halves (6 ounces total)
¼ cup Lemon-Nut
 Vinaigrette (see recipe,
 page 136)

■ Rinse the chicken and pat dry. Place chicken in a plastic bag set in a deep mixing bowl. Pour the vinaigrette over the chicken in the bag. Close bag and turn chicken to coat well. Marinate at room temperature for 30 minutes or in the refrigerator for 2 hours, turning the bag occasionally. Drain the chicken, reserving vinaigrette.

Place the chicken on the unheated rack of a broiler pan. Broil 4 inches from the heat for 3 minutes. Turn chicken and brush with reserved vinaigrette. Broil for 3 to 5 minutes more or till the chicken is tender and no pink remains, brushing frequently with the vinaigrette. Cut the chicken across the grain into 1-inch-wide strips.

Lettuce leaves
1 small papaya, halved,
 seeded, peeled, and
 sliced; 1 peach, peeled,
 pitted, and sliced; *or* 1
 nectarine, pitted and
 sliced
1 small avocado, halved,
 pitted, peeled, and
 sliced
1 tablespoon lemon juice
1 pomegranate *or* ¼ cup
 fresh raspberries
¼ cup Lemon-Nut
 Vinaigrette (see recipe,
 page 136)

■ To assemble, line 2 individual plates with lettuce leaves. Alternately arrange the papaya, peach, or nectarine slices and the avocado slices around the outer edge of each lettuce-lined plate. Sprinkle lemon juice over the fruit. Overlap the chicken slices in a circle in the center of the fruit.

Cut the pomegranate open, if using. With a fork, remove the seeds. Discard the membrane. Sprinkle the pomegranate seeds or raspberries over the chicken and fruit. Drizzle with the Lemon-Nut Vinaigrette. Makes 2 servings.

TIME ESTIMATE

Preparation ____ 10 min.
Marinating ____ 30 min.
Cooking _____ 10 min.

MENU IDEA

Team these colorful salads with Sweet Cheese Rolls (see recipe, page 209) or the muffins of your choice.

PER SERVING

Calories _____ 548
Protein _____ 23 g
Carbohydrate _____ 30 g
Fat (total) _____ 40 g
 Saturated _____ 5 g
Cholesterol _____ 54 mg
Sodium _____ 64 mg
Potassium _____ 1,077 mg

WILTED SPINACH AND CHICKEN SALAD

Try turkey in this spectacular salad. Just substitute 6 ounces of turkey tenderloin steaks for the chicken.

2 medium boneless, skinless chicken breast halves (6 ounces total)
1 tablespoon olive oil *or* cooking oil

■ Rinse the chicken and pat dry. Cut into thin bite-size strips. In a large skillet cook the chicken in hot olive oil or cooking oil over medium heat for 2 to 3 minutes or till tender and no pink remains, stirring frequently. Remove the chicken from the skillet.

2 slices bacon

■ Wipe out the skillet. In the same skillet cook the bacon till crisp. Remove bacon, reserving *1 tablespoon* drippings in skillet. Drain bacon on paper towels. Crumble bacon.

4 cups torn fresh spinach
½ cup enoki mushrooms *or* other sliced fresh mushrooms
¼ cup shredded carrot

■ In a large salad bowl combine the chicken, bacon, spinach, mushrooms, and carrot. Toss to mix. Set aside.

1 tablespoon olive oil *or* cooking oil
1 shallot, finely chopped, *or* 1 green onion, thinly sliced
¼ cup half-and-half, light cream, *or* whipping cream
2 tablespoons wine vinegar
Dash pepper
⅓ cup Parmesan-Herb Croutons (see recipe, page 138) *or* purchased croutons

■ Add the olive oil or cooking oil to the reserved drippings in skillet. Add shallot or green onion. Cook and stir till tender but not brown. Stir in the half-and-half, light cream, or whipping cream, scraping up any browned bits. Add the wine vinegar and pepper, stirring vigorously. Heat through but *do not* boil. Pour hot mixture over spinach mixture in bowl. Toss till coated.

To serve, divide salad mixture between 2 individual plates. Sprinkle with croutons. Serve immediately. Makes 2 servings.

TIME ESTIMATE
Start to finish _ 30 min.

MENU IDEA
Complement this country-style salad with piping hot Dinner Rolls (see recipe, page 207).

PER SERVING
Calories _____ 403
Protein _____ 28 g
Carbohydrate _____ 14 g
Fat (total) _____ 27 g
  Saturated _____ 7 g
Cholesterol _____ 71 mg
Sodium _____ 366 mg
Potassium _____ 968 mg

FRUITED TURKEY SALAD WITH CREAMY ORANGE DRESSING

A choice salad to make in the spring when asparagus is small and tender and strawberries are sweet and juicy.

8 ounces fresh asparagus, cut into 1-inch pieces (1½ cups), *or* ½ of a 10-ounce package frozen cut asparagus

■ If using fresh asparagus, cook in boiling lightly salted water for 7 to 9 minutes or till nearly tender. Or, if using frozen asparagus, cook according to package directions. Drain asparagus. Let stand in cold water to cool; drain.

½ of a 3-ounce package cream cheese, softened
1 teaspoon sugar
½ teaspoon finely shredded orange peel
1 to 2 tablespoons orange juice
¼ teaspoon poppy seed

■ Meanwhile, for dressing, in a small mixing bowl beat together the cream cheese, sugar, and orange peel till smooth. Gradually beat in enough orange juice to make dressing of drizzling consistency. Stir in the poppy seed. Set aside.

4 cups torn mixed greens
8 ounces fully cooked smoked turkey breast portion, cut into ½-inch cubes, *or* 2 cups cubed cooked chicken
1 cup sliced fresh strawberries, sliced peaches, raspberries, *and/or* blueberries
¼ cup cashews, unblanched whole almonds, *or* pecan halves

■ In a mixing bowl combine the asparagus, mixed greens, turkey or chicken, and strawberries, peaches, raspberries, and/or blueberries. Gently toss to mix.

To serve, divide the salad mixture between 2 individual plates or salad bowls. Sprinkle with cashews, almonds, or pecans. Drizzle with the dressing. Makes 2 servings.

TIME ESTIMATE

Start to finish — 25 min.

MENU IDEA

Accent this fresh salad with Sweet Yogurt Scones (see recipe, page 217) or whole wheat rolls and the beverages of your choice.

PER SERVING

Calories	388
Protein	33 g
Carbohydrate	23 g
Fat (total)	21 g
Saturated	7 g
Cholesterol	75 mg
Sodium	1,011 mg
Potassium	1,092 mg

FRUITED TURKEY SALAD WITH CREAMY ORANGE DRESSING

PIZZA-STYLE TACO SALAD

6 **ounces ground raw chicken** *or* **turkey** *or* **lean ground beef** *or* **pork**
1 **clove garlic, minced**
½ **cup taco sauce**
½ **of an 8-ounce can (⅓ cup) red kidney beans, drained**
2 **tablespoons water**
1 **teaspoon chili powder**
Dash ground cumin

■ For meat mixture, in a medium skillet cook meat and garlic over medium heat till no pink remains. Drain off any fat. Stir in the taco sauce, kidney beans, water, chili powder, and cumin. Bring to boiling; reduce heat. Cover and simmer for 10 minutes.

2 **8-inch flour tortillas**
1 **tablespoon margarine** *or* **butter, melted**

■ Lightly brush both sides of each tortilla with margarine or butter. Place tortillas on an ungreased baking sheet. Bake in a 400° oven for 7 to 10 minutes or till lightly browned.

2 **cups torn lettuce**
1 **medium tomato, chopped (½ cup)**
½ **of a small avocado, seeded, peeled, and chopped**
½ **cup shredded cheddar** *or* **Monterey Jack cheese (2 ounces)**
½ **of a 2¼-ounce can (⅓ cup) sliced pitted ripe olives, drained**

■ Meanwhile, in a medium mixing bowl combine the lettuce, tomato, avocado, cheddar or Monterey Jack cheese, and olives. Add the hot meat mixture. Toss to mix.

¼ **cup shredded cheddar** *or* **Monterey Jack cheese (1 ounce)**
Dairy sour cream (optional)
Taco sauce (optional)

■ To serve, transfer the tortillas to 2 individual plates. Spoon the salad mixture atop each tortilla. Sprinkle with cheese. If desired, serve with sour cream and taco sauce. Makes 2 servings.

TIME ESTIMATE
Start to finish — 30 min.

MENU IDEA
Finish off your meal with slices of a mouth-watering dessert— Strawberry-Cream-Cheese Torte (see recipe, page 197).

PER SERVING
Calories _____ 659
Protein _____ 33 g
Carbohydrate _____ 43 g
Fat (total) _____ 42 g
  Saturated _____ 15 g
Cholesterol ____ 105 mg
Sodium_____ 931 mg
Potassium ____ 1,027 mg

SUMMER FRUIT AND BARLEY SALAD

When nectarines and peaches are out of season, try the Winter Fruit and Barley Salad, featuring an orange, apple, or pear.

1¼ cups water
¾ cup quick-cooking barley
¾ cup Gouda, gjetost, Colby, *or* Cojack cheese cut into ¼-inch cubes (3 ounces)
⅓ cup Lemon-Nut Vinaigrette (see recipe, page 136)

Bibb *or* other lettuce leaves
1 medium nectarine, pitted and sliced, *or* 1 medium peach, peeled, pitted, and sliced
2 medium plums, pitted and sliced, *or* 2 kiwi fruit, peeled and sliced

■ In a medium saucepan bring water to boiling. Add barley; return to boiling. Reduce heat. Cover and simmer for 10 minutes. Pour barley into a colander. Run cold water through colander to cool barley.

In a medium mixing bowl stir together the barley, cheese, and Lemon-Nut Vinaigrette. Cover and chill in the refrigerator for 1 to 24 hours or in the freezer for 20 minutes.

■ To serve, line 2 individual plates with Bibb or other lettuce leaves. Arrange nectarine or peach slices and plum or kiwi slices in a fan shape near one edge of each plate. Spoon barley mixture onto the plates next to the sliced fruit. Makes 2 servings.

TIME ESTIMATE
Preparation —— 25 min.
Chilling —————— 1 hr.

MENU IDEA
Serve slices of Banana-Brickle Bread (see recipe, page 210) or croissants with this meatless main-dish salad.

PER SERVING
Calories —————— 556
Protein —————— 18 g
Carbohydrate —— 66 g
Fat (total) ———— 29 g
  Saturated ———— 9 g
Cholesterol —— 48 mg
Sodium———— 349 mg
Potassium —— 500 mg

WINTER FRUIT AND BARLEY SALAD

1 orange, peeled and sectioned, *or* 1 apple *or* pear, cored and sliced

■ Prepare the Summer Fruit and Barley Salad as directed above, *except* substitute the orange, apple, or pear for the nectarine or peach.

PER SERVING
Same as *Summer Fruit and Barley Salad,* except:
Calories —————— 553
Potassium —— 474 mg

MARINATED BEEF AND GARDEN VEGETABLE SALAD

2 **medium tomatoes, cut
into thin wedges**
4 **ounces sliced cooked
beef** *or* **pork, cut into
thin strips (1 cup)**
½ **cup Edam** *or* **Gouda
cheese cut into ½-inch
cubes (2 ounces)**
½ **of a small onion, thinly
sliced and separated
into rings**
½ **of a small green** *or*
**yellow pepper, cut into
thin strips (⅓ cup)**

■ In a medium mixing bowl combine the to-matoes, beef or pork, Edam or Gouda cheese, onion, and green or yellow pepper. Set aside.

TIME ESTIMATE

Preparation ____ 10 min.
Marinating _____ 1 hr.

MENU IDEA

Complement this
Italian-style salad with
slices of Italian bread
or crackerlike
breadsticks.

PER SERVING

Calories _____ 418
Protein _____ 27 g
Carbohydrate ____ 11 g
Fat (total) _____ 31 g
  Saturated _____ 9 g
Cholesterol ____ 70 mg
Sodium _____ 413 mg
Potassium ____ 712 mg

3 **tablespoons olive oil** *or*
salad oil
3 **tablespoons wine vinegar**
1 **tablespoon mayonnaise**
or **salad dressing**
1 **tablespoon snipped fresh
basil** *or* **1 teaspoon
dried basil, crushed**
1 **clove garlic, minced**
Lettuce leaves
2 **tablespoons pine nuts** *or*
chopped walnuts

■ For dressing, in a screw-top jar combine the olive oil, wine vinegar, mayonnaise, basil, garlic, ⅛ teaspoon *salt,* and ⅛ teaspoon *pepper.* Cover and shake well. Pour over vegetable mixture. Toss lightly to coat. Cover and let stand at room temperature 1 hour, stirring occasionally. (*Or,* cover and chill for 4 to 24 hours, stirring occasionally. Before serving, let stand at room temperature 30 minutes.)

To serve, line 2 individual plates with let-tuce. Using a slotted spoon, spoon vegetable mixture atop. Sprinkle with nuts. Serves 2.

MARINATED BEEF, PASTA, AND GARDEN VEGETABLE SALAD

½ **cup corkscrew, medium
shell,** *or* **rope macaroni**

■ Prepare Marinated Beef and Garden Veg-etable Salad as directed above, *except* cook pasta (see chart, page 185). Drain. Rinse with cold water; drain well. Add pasta to vegetable mixture before adding dressing. Omit chill-ing option. Serve as above.

PER SERVING

Same as *Marinated Beef
and Garden Vegetable
Salad,* except:
Calories _____ 523
Protein _____ 31 g
Carbohydrate ____ 33 g
Potassium ____ 767 mg

SPINACH AND BASIL SALAD WITH BEEF

A light and luscious pear dressing delicately coats the greens. For an even simpler version of the dressing, substitute a small jar of pear baby food for the fresh pear.

½ of a small very ripe pear, cored and peeled

1 tablespoon white wine vinegar *or* cider vinegar

¼ teaspoon white wine Worcestershire sauce *or* Worcestershire sauce

Dash pepper

2 cups lightly packed torn fresh spinach

1 cup sliced fresh mushrooms

½ cup lightly packed fresh basil leaves

6 ounces sliced cooked beef, cut into thin strips (about 1 cup)

2 small oranges, peeled and sectioned, *or* one 11-ounce can mandarin orange sections, drained

■ For dressing, in a blender container or food processor bowl combine the pear, white wine vinegar or cider vinegar, white wine Worcestershire sauce or Worcestershire sauce, and pepper. Cover and blend or process till smooth.

■ In a bowl toss together the spinach, mushrooms, and basil leaves. Add the beef strips and orange or mandarin orange sections. Toss lightly to mix. Add the dressing; toss to mix. Divide salad mixture between 2 individual salad bowls or plates. Makes 2 servings.

TIME ESTIMATE
Start to finish _ 25 min.

MENU IDEA
Choose sweet muffins, such as Blueberry-Oatmeal Muffins (see recipe, page 212), to serve with this salad.

PER SERVING
Calories _____ 274
Protein _____ 28 g
Carbohydrate _____ 24 g
Fat (total) _____ 8 g
　Saturated _____ 3 g
Cholesterol _____ 65 mg
Sodium _____ 118 mg
Potassium ____ 1,121 mg

BEEF SALAD WITH POTATO CRISPS

Give the potato crisps some pizzazz by lightly sprinkling them with garlic salt, onion salt, or salt before baking.

1 medium potato
Nonstick spray coating

■ For potato crisps, cut potato into ⅛-inch-thick slices. Spray a baking sheet with non-stick coating. Arrange potato slices in a single layer on baking sheet. Bake in a 450° oven 20 minutes or till crisp and golden brown. Remove from baking sheet. Cool 10 minutes.

3 tablespoons chutney, snipped; apricot preserves; *or* orange marmalade
2 tablespoons olive oil *or* salad oil
2 tablespoons red wine vinegar, balsamic vinegar, *or* cider vinegar
1 tablespoon water
⅛ teaspoon pepper

■ Meanwhile, for dressing, in a small mixing bowl stir together the chutney, apricot preserves, or orange marmalade; olive oil or salad oil; red wine vinegar, balsamic vinegar, or cider vinegar; water; and pepper. Let stand at room temperature at least 20 minutes.

3 cups torn mixed greens
6 ounces sliced cooked beef *or* pork, cut into ½-inch-wide strips (about 1 cup)
2 medium carrots, cut into julienne strips (1 cup), *or* 1 cup jicama cut into julienne strips
2 green onions, sliced (¼ cup), *or* 2 tablespoons chopped onion
¼ cup shredded cheddar, Colby, *or* Cojack cheese (1 ounce)

■ Divide mixed greens evenly among 2 individual plates. Arrange the potato crisps, beef or pork strips, carrot or jicama strips, onion, and cheese atop. Stir dressing; drizzle over salads. Makes 2 servings.

TIME ESTIMATE

Start to finish — 45 min.

MENU IDEA

For dessert, offer Cinnamon and Sugar Slices (see recipe, page 203) and scoops of orange sherbet.

PER SERVING

Calories	587
Protein	32g
Carbohydrate	55 g
Fat (total)	27 g
Saturated	8 g
Cholesterol	80 mg
Sodium	440 mg
Potassium	1,269 mg

BEEF SALAD WITH POTATO CRISPS

ITALIAN-STYLE CHEF SALAD WITH CREAMY PESTO DRESSING

3 cups torn mixed greens
½ cup mozzarella *or*
    provolone cheese cut
    into julienne strips
    (2 ounces)
2 ounces thinly sliced fully
    cooked ham *or* turkey,
    cut into thin strips
1 ounce thinly sliced
    salami *or* prosciutto,
    cut into thin strips
1 small tomato, cut into
    thin wedges
½ of a small yellow *or*
    green pepper, sliced
    into rings
½ of a small onion, thinly
    sliced and separated
    into rings
½ of a 6-ounce jar
    marinated artichoke
    hearts, drained and
    halved
    Creamy Pesto Dressing

■ Divide the greens between 2 individual salad bowls or plates. Arrange the mozzarella or provolone cheese, ham or turkey, salami or prosciutto, tomato, yellow or green pepper, onion, and artichoke hearts over the greens. Drizzle with the Creamy Pesto Dressing. Makes 2 servings.

TIME ESTIMATE
Start to finish — 25 min.

MENU IDEA
Try slices of Pepperoni-Parmesan Bread (see recipe, page 211) or crusty hard rolls with this luscious salad.

PER SERVING
Calories _____ 456
Protein _____ 22 g
Carbohydrate _____ 14 g
Fat (total) _____ 36 g
  Saturated _____ 10 g
Cholesterol _____ 63 mg
Sodium _____ 1,074 mg
Potassium _____ 698 mg

CREAMY PESTO DRESSING

3 tablespoons mayonnaise
    or salad dressing
2 tablespoons dairy sour
    cream *or* plain yogurt
1 tablespoon grated
    Parmesan cheese
1 tablespoon pesto*
1 clove garlic, minced
1 to 2 tablespoons milk

■ In a small mixing bowl stir together the mayonnaise or salad dressing, sour cream or yogurt, Parmesan cheese, pesto, and garlic. If necessary, stir in milk, 1 teaspoon at a time, to make the dressing of desired consistency. Makes ½ cup.

  *If desired, prepare Pesto (see recipe, page 156) or use purchased pesto.

PORK AND PEAR SPINACH SALAD

Brie is a rich cheese with a mild flavor that is usually purchased in small rounds. Since this recipe uses only part of a small round, serve the remaining Brie with fresh fruit and slices of French bread as a snack or appetizer.

4 cups torn fresh spinach

1 medium pear *or* apple, cored and sliced, *or* 1½ cups red *or* green seedless grapes

1 cup cooked pork *or* beef cut into julienne strips

½ of a small red or white onion, thinly sliced and separated into rings

1 ounce Brie cheese, cut into thin wedges *or* cubes, *or* ¼ cup crumbled blue *or* feta cheese (1 ounce)

2 tablespoons toasted broken walnuts *or* pecans *or* slivered almonds

■ Divide the torn spinach between 2 individual salad bowls or plates. Arrange the pear, apple, or grapes; pork or beef; and onion atop the spinach. Sprinkle with the Brie, blue, or feta cheese and the walnuts, pecans, or almonds.

2 tablespoons olive oil *or* salad oil

2 tablespoons vinegar *or* white wine vinegar

1½ teaspoons sugar

¼ teaspoon celery seed

⅛ teaspoon dry mustard *or* ½ teaspoon Dijon-style mustard

■ For dressing, in a screw-top jar combine the olive oil or salad oil, vinegar or white wine vinegar, sugar, celery seed, and dry mustard or Dijon-style mustard. Cover and shake well. Drizzle the dressing over the salads. Makes 2 servings.

TIME ESTIMATE

Start to finish __ 25 min.

MENU IDEA

Serve a variety of crackers with the salad. Then, for dessert, dish up servings of your favorite frozen yogurt.

PER SERVING

Calories	453
Protein	31 g
Carbohydrate	24 g
Fat (total)	29 g
Saturated	7 g
Cholesterol	72 mg
Sodium	231 mg
Potassium	1,113 mg

HOT SAUSAGE AND LENTIL SLAW

For a wonderful eating adventure, indulge in this exceptional version of cabbage slaw. Tender lentils, smoked sausage, various vegetables, and a zippy vinaigrette cook together to create a fantastic blend of flavors.

1½ **cups water**
¾ **cup dry lentils, rinsed and drained**

■ In a medium saucepan stir together the water and lentils. Bring to boiling; reduce heat. Cover and simmer about 30 minutes or till lentils are tender. If liquid is not absorbed, drain the lentils.

6 **ounces fully cooked smoked Polish sausage, bratwurst,** *or* **kielbasa**
1 **cup loose-pack frozen whole kernel corn**
¼ **cup chopped sweet red** *or* **green pepper**
2 **tablespoons water**

■ Meanwhile, cut sausage in half lengthwise. Slice into ¼-inch-thick pieces. In a large skillet combine the sausage, corn, sweet red or green pepper, and water. Cook, covered, over medium heat about 4 minutes or till the sausage and corn are heated through and pepper is tender.

3 **cups shredded cabbage** *or* **shredded cabbage with carrot**
¼ **cup Pepper** *or* **Garlic Vinaigrette (see recipes, page 137)**
Purple kale, cabbage, *or* **lettuce leaves**
Pepper *or* **Garlic Vinaigrette (optional)**

■ Stir the cooked lentils, shredded cabbage, and ¼ cup Pepper or Garlic Vinaigrette into the skillet. Cover and cook for 2 to 3 minutes more or till the cabbage is wilted and the mixture is heated through, stirring once.

To serve, line 2 individual plates with purple kale, cabbage, or lettuce leaves. Spoon slaw mixture atop. If desired, pass additional vinaigrette. Makes 2 servings.

TIME ESTIMATE
Start to finish _ 45 min.

MENU IDEA
Accent this hot and hearty slaw with crusty whole wheat rolls or slices of whole wheat bread.

PER SERVING
Calories _____ 748
Protein _____ 37 g
Carbohydrate _____ 70 g
Fat (total) _____ 39 g
  Saturated _____ 11 g
Cholesterol _____ 60 mg
Sodium_____ 780 mg
Potassium _____ 1,315 mg

HOT SAUSAGE AND LENTIL SLAW

SPRINGTIME PORK SALAD WITH STRAWBERRY VINAIGRETTE

Since the sweetness of fresh strawberries varies from season to season, so will the sweetness of this dressing.

3 cups torn mixed greens
6 ounces sliced cooked
   pork *or* beef, cut into
   ½-inch-wide strips
   (about 1 cup)
⅔ cup sliced strawberries
½ cup jicama *or* carrot cut
   into julienne strips

■ Divide the mixed greens between 2 individual salad bowls or plates. Arrange the pork or beef, strawberries, and jicama or carrot atop the greens. Set aside.

⅓ cup Strawberry
   Vinaigrette
¼ cup Sugar-Coated Nuts
   (see recipe, page 138)

■ Prepare Strawberry Vinaigrette as directed. Drizzle the vinaigrette over the greens. Sprinkle with the Sugar-Coated Nuts. Makes 2 servings.

TIME ESTIMATE
Start to finish _ 25 min.

MENU IDEA
Add a basket of Cinnamon 'n' Spice Oatmeal Muffins (see recipe, page 212).

PER SERVING*
Calories _____ 306
Protein _____ 30 g
Carbohydrate _____ 19 g
Fat (total) _____ 14 g
   Saturated _____ 3 g
Cholesterol _____ 66 mg
Sodium _____ 73 mg
Potassium _____ 739 mg
Includes Strawberry Vinaigrette.

STRAWBERRY VINAIGRETTE

⅓ cup cut-up strawberries
1 tablespoon red wine
   vinegar *or* vinegar
¼ to ½ teaspoon sugar
   Dash pepper

■ In a blender container place the strawberries, red wine vinegar or vinegar, sugar, and pepper. Cover and blend till smooth. Makes five 1-tablespoon servings.

PER TABLESPOON
Calories _____ 4
Protein _____ 0 g
Carbohydrate _____ 1 g
Fat (total) _____ 0 g
   Saturated _____ 0 g
Cholesterol _____ 0 mg
Sodium _____ 1 mg
Potassium _____ 18 mg

FRESH SALMON SALAD NIÇOISE

1 6-ounce fresh *or* frozen salmon *or* tuna steak, cut 1 inch thick

■ Thaw fish, if frozen. Place fish steak on the greased unheated rack of a broiler pan. Broil 4 inches from the heat for 5 minutes. Turn fish and broil for 3 to 7 minutes more or just till fish begins to flake easily. Cool to room temperature. Break or cut salmon into large chunks. (You should have about 1 cup.)

3 whole tiny new potatoes
¾ cup loose-pack frozen cut green beans

■ In a medium covered saucepan cook the potatoes in boiling lightly salted water for 7 minutes. Add green beans. Return to boiling. Cover and boil gently 4 to 6 minutes more or till nearly tender; drain. Rinse with cold water and drain again. Quarter the potatoes.

½ cup cherry *or* yellow baby pear tomatoes, halved
½ of a 3½-ounce (½ cup) can whole pitted ripe olives, drained
½ of a small red *or* white onion, thinly sliced and separated into rings
2 tablespoons Lemon-Nut Vinaigrette (see recipe, page 136) *or* Tomato-Basil Vinaigrette (see recipe, page 139)

■ In a medium bowl combine the potatoes, green beans, cherry or pear tomatoes, olives, and red or white onion. Pour the vinaigrette over the vegetable mixture. Toss to coat.

2 cups torn mixed greens
1 hard-cooked egg, cut into wedges
2 tablespoons Lemon-Nut Vinaigrette (see recipe, page 136) *or* Tomato-Basil Vinaigrette (see recipe, page 139)

■ Divide the mixed greens between 2 individual plates. Spoon the vegetable mixture over the greens. Arrange the salmon or tuna and the hard-cooked egg on top of the vegetables. Drizzle with vinaigrette. Serves 2.

TIME ESTIMATE

Start to finish — 45 min.

MENU IDEA

For a sophisticated meal, complement this elegant French-style salad with an assortment of rolls and glasses of dry white wine.

PER SERVING

Calories —————— 466
Protein —————— 26 g
Carbohydrate ——— 38 g
Fat (total) ———— 24 g
  Saturated ———— 4 g
Cholesterol —— 162 mg
Sodium —————— 281 mg
Potassium —— 1,030 mg

133

TUNA AND WHITE BEAN SALAD

For a flavor twist, substitute ⅓ cup Garlic Vinaigrette or Pepper Vinaigrette (see recipes, page 137) for the dressing.

1 **15-ounce can cannellini *or* great northern beans, rinsed and drained**
1 **3¼-ounce can tuna *or* skinless, boneless salmon, drained and broken into chunks**
1 **medium tomato, seeded and chopped**
¼ **cup chopped green or yellow pepper**
¼ **cup chopped onion**
2 **tablespoons sliced pitted ripe olives (optional)**

■ In a large mixing bowl stir together the cannellini or great northern beans, tuna or salmon, tomato, green or yellow pepper, onion, and, if desired, olives. Set aside.

2 **tablespoons olive oil *or* salad oil**
2 **tablespoons white wine vinegar *or* vinegar**
1 **tablespoon snipped fresh basil *or* 1 teaspoon dried basil, crushed**
1 **clove garlic, minced**
1 **teaspoon Dijon-style mustard *or* ¼ teaspoon dry mustard**
¼ **teaspoon pepper**

■ For dressing, in a screw-top jar combine the olive oil or salad oil, white wine vinegar or vinegar, basil, garlic, Dijon-style mustard or dry mustard, and pepper. Cover and shake well. Pour the dressing over the bean mixture. Toss to coat. Serve immediately or cover and refrigerate for up to 24 hours.

Lettuce leaves
Fresh basil (optional)

■ To serve, line 2 individual salad bowls or plates with lettuce. Spoon bean mixture atop. If desired, garnish with fresh basil. Makes 2 servings.

TIME ESTIMATE
Start to finish — 20 min.

MENU IDEA
As accompaniments, serve orange slices and rye or whole wheat bagels.

PER SERVING
Calories _____ 388
Protein _____ 27 g
Carbohydrate ____ 40 g
Fat (total) _____ 15 g
Saturated ____ 2 g
Cholesterol ____ 24 mg
Sodium_____ 246 mg
Potassium _____ 978 mg

GREEK-STYLE PASTA AND SHRIMP SALAD

A wonderful version of pasta salad—tender shrimp, corkscrew macaroni, fresh spinach, feta cheese, and ripe olives tossed together and marinated in a light, dill vinaigrette.

8 ounces fresh *or* frozen peeled and deveined shrimp

■ Thaw shrimp, if frozen. To cook shrimp, simmer, uncovered in 2 cups *water* and ½ teaspoon *salt* for 1 to 3 minutes or till shrimp turn pink, stirring occasionally. Rinse under cold running water. Drain and set aside.

1⅓ cups packaged corkscrew *or* medium shell macaroni

■ Cook pasta (see chart, page 185). Drain immediately.

¼ cup olive oil *or* salad oil
¼ cup wine vinegar
1 tablespoon snipped fresh dillweed *or* ½ teaspoon dried dillweed
2 cloves garlic, minced
⅛ teaspoon pepper

■ Meanwhile, for dressing, in a screw-top jar combine the olive oil or salad oil, wine vinegar, dillweed, garlic, and pepper. Cover and shake well.

1 cup shredded fresh spinach
½ cup crumbled feta cheese (2 ounces) *or* 2 ounces Gouda cheese, cut into ½-inch cubes
2 tablespoons sliced pitted ripe olives, drained
4 cherry tomatoes, quartered, *or* 1 small tomato, seeded and chopped

■ In a large mixing bowl combine the shrimp, pasta, spinach, feta or Gouda cheese, and olives. Add dressing and toss to mix. Cover and refrigerate for 1 to 24 hours to blend flavors. Stir in cherry tomatoes before serving.

Fresh spinach

■ To serve, line 2 individual salad bowls or plates with spinach. Spoon salad mixture atop spinach. Makes 2 servings.

TIME ESTIMATE
Preparation ____ 25 min.
Chilling _____ 1 hr.

MENU IDEA
Slices of rye or pumpernickel bread make a tasty accompaniment to this salad.

PER SERVING
Calories _____ 710
Protein _____ 35 g
Carbohydrate _____ 64 g
Fat (total) _____ 36 g
  Saturated _____ 8 g
Cholesterol ____ 191 mg
Sodium _____ 622 mg
Potassium _____ 660 mg

SALAD SPECTACULAR

Splash a dash of any of these dressings on a salad or use them to marinate meat, poultry, or fish (see directions, below). Also, for a flavor twist, brush these dressings on meat, poultry, or fish when you're broiling or grilling (see directions, pages 38, 39, 73, and 87).

Lemon-Nut Vinaigrette:
Combine ¼ cup *walnut, salad, or olive oil;* 1 teaspoon finely shredded *lemon or lime peel* (if desired); ¼ cup *lemon or lime juice;* 2 tablespoons ground *walnuts, almonds, or pecans;* and 1 tablespoon *honey.* Mix well. Makes ⅔ cup.

Nutrition information per tablespoon: 62 calories, 0 g protein, 2 g carbohydrate, 6 g total fat (1 g saturated), 0 mg cholesterol, 0 mg sodium, 15 mg potassium

To marinate with one of the dressings, place the meat, poultry, or fish in a plastic bag set in a deep bowl. Pour about *⅓ cup* dressing into the bag. Close bag; turn to coat well. Marinate at room temperature for 30 minutes or in the refrigerator for 3 hours, turning bag occasionally. Drain, reserving dressing. If desired, brush the reserved dressing on the meat, poultry, or fish during cooking.

Pepper Vinaigrette:
Combine ¼ cup *salad or olive oil;* 2 tablespoons *wine vinegar;* 2 tablespoons *lemon juice;* 1 teaspoon *honey;* ¼ teaspoon dried *thyme, oregano, or basil,* crushed; ¼ teaspoon *pepper;* and ¼ teaspoon *crushed red pepper.* Mix well. Makes ½ cup.

Nutrition information per tablespoon: 65 calories, 0 g protein, 1 g carbohydrate, 7 g total fat (1 g saturated), 0 mg cholesterol, 1 mg sodium, 9 mg potassium

Oriental Vinaigrette:
Combine ¼ cup *salad oil,* 3 tablespoons *rice vinegar or white vinegar,* 1 tablespoon *soy sauce,* 1 teaspoon *sugar,* 1 teaspoon grated *gingerroot,* ½ teaspoon *sesame oil or* 1 teaspoon toasted *sesame seed,* and ⅛ teaspoon *pepper.* Mix well. Makes ⅔ cup.

Nutrition information per tablespoon: 52 calories, 0 g protein, 1 g carbohydrate, 6 g total fat (1 g saturated), 0 mg cholesterol, 97 mg sodium, 8 mg potassium

Garlic Vinaigrette:
Combine ⅓ cup *salad or olive oil;* ⅓ cup *white wine vinegar or vinegar;* 1 tablespoon snipped *parsley;* 3 or 4 cloves *garlic,* minced; 1 teaspoon *sugar;* and 1 teaspoon *Dijon-style mustard or* ¼ teaspoon *dry mustard.* Mix well. Makes ⅔ cup.

Nutrition information per tablespoon: 65 calories, 0 g protein, 1 g carbohydrate, 7 g total fat (1 g saturated), 0 mg cholesterol, 17 mg sodium, 10 mg potassium

Honey-Mustard Dressing:
Combine ⅓ cup *salad oil,* 2 tablespoons *lemon juice,* 2 tablespoons *honey,* 2 tablespoons coarse-grain *brown mustard or Dijon-style mustard,* and 1 clove *garlic,* minced. Mix well. Makes ¾ cup.

Nutrition information per tablespoon: 67 calories, 0 g protein, 3 g carbohydrate, 6 g total fat (1 g saturated), 0 mg cholesterol, 33 mg sodium, 10 mg potassium

SALAD SPECTACULAR

Sugar-Coated Nuts

Place ¼ cup *sugar* in a heavy skillet. Cook over medium-high heat, without stirring, till sugar begins to melt, shaking skillet occasionally to heat evenly. Reduce heat to medium-low; cook about 5 minutes more or till sugar is melted and golden, stirring occasionally after sugar begins to melt and bubble. Add ¾ cup broken *walnuts, pecans, or cashews*. Stir till nuts are coated. Spread on buttered foil. Cool; break apart.

To store, place in an airtight container and store at room temperature for up to 1 week. Makes about 1 cup.

Nutrition information per tablespoon: 48 calories, 1 g protein, 4 g carbohydrate, 3 g total fat (0 g saturated), 0 mg cholesterol, 1 mg sodium, 28 mg potassium

Spiced Nuts

Combine ¾ cup broken *walnuts or pecans,* 1 tablespoon softened *margarine or butter,* ¼ teaspoon *salt,* ¼ teaspoon ground *red pepper,* and ¼ teaspoon ground *cumin.* Spread nuts in a single layer in a shallow baking pan. Bake in a 350° oven for 5 to 10 minutes or till light brown, stirring once or twice. Cool.

To store, place in an airtight container and refrigerate for up

to 1 month. Bring to room temperature before serving. Makes ¾ cup.

Nutrition information per tablespoon: 57 calories, 1 g protein, 1 g carbohydrate, 6 g total fat (1 g saturated), 0 mg cholesterol, 56 mg sodium, 40 mg potassium

Parmesan-Herb Croutons

Cut 4 slices *white, whole wheat, or rye bread* into ½-inch cubes. In a large skillet melt 3 tablespoons *margarine or butter.* Add 2 cloves *garlic,* minced; cook 1 minute. Stir in 3 tablespoons grated *Parmesan cheese* and ½ teaspoon dried *Italian seasoning or oregano,* crushed. Add bread cubes and stir till coated.

Spread cubes in a single layer in a baking pan. Bake in a 300° oven 10 minutes. Stir; bake about 10 minutes more or till dry and crisp. Cool.

To store, place in an airtight container and refrigerate for up to 1 month. Bring to room temperature before serving. Makes 2 cups.

Nutrition information per tablespoon: 22 calories, 1 g protein, 2 g carbohydrate, 1 g total fat (0 g saturated), 0 mg cholesterol, 39 mg sodium, 6 mg potassium

Dilled Bagel Crisps

Vertically cut 2 *plain, whole*

wheat, or onion bagels into ¼-inch-thick wedges. In a large skillet melt ¼ cup *margarine or butter.* Stir in ½ teaspoon *dillweed* and ⅛ teaspoon *garlic or onion powder.* Stir in wedges.

Spread wedges in a single layer in a baking pan. Bake in a 300° oven 10 minutes. Stir; bake about 15 minutes more or till dry and crisp. Cool.

To store, place in an airtight container and refrigerate for up to 1 month. Bring to room temperature before serving. Makes 2 cups.

Nutrition information per 2 tablespoons: 48 calories, 1 g protein, 4 g carbohydrate, 3 g total fat (1 g saturated), 0 mg cholesterol, 71 mg sodium, 11 mg potassium

Cheese 'n' Nut Toasts

Spread 1 ounce *soft goat cheese or Brie cheese* over 5 *melba toast rounds.* Sprinkle with 1 tablespoon finely chopped *pecans or almonds.* Place rounds, nut side up, on the unheated rack of a broiler pan. Broil 4 to 5 inches from the heat about 2 minutes or till cheese is heated through. Serve immediately. Makes 5 rounds.

Nutrition information per round: 51 calories, 3 g protein, 4 g carbohydrate, 3 g total fat (0 g saturated), 6 mg cholesterol, 69 mg sodium, 17 mg potassium

GARDEN VEGETABLE AND PASTA SALAD

A spectacular salad to serve in the summer—super easy and super fresh!

½ cup green beans cut into
    1-inch pieces *or* ½ cup
    loose-pack frozen cut
    green beans
⅓ cup packaged medium
    shell *or* corkscrew
    macaroni *or* other
    pasta (1 ounce)

¼ cup sweet red *or* green
    pepper cut into ½-inch
    squares
¼ cup sliced carrot
¼ cup Tomato-Basil
    Vinaigrette
1 tablespoon finely
    shredded *or* grated
    Parmesan cheese

■ If using fresh green beans, cook, covered, in a large amount of boiling lightly salted water for 15 minutes. Add the pasta; return to boiling and cook for 5 to 8 minutes more or till tender. Or, if using frozen beans, cook the pasta in a large amount of boiling lightly salted water for 4 minutes. Add frozen beans; return to boiling and cook for 3 to 5 minutes more or till tender. Drain. Rinse with cold water and drain well.

■ In a medium bowl combine the green beans, pasta, sweet red or green pepper, and carrot. Add Tomato-Basil Vinaigrette. Toss to coat. Cover and chill for 2 to 24 hours, stirring occasionally. (If necessary, add additional dressing before serving.)

To serve, divide vegetable mixture between 2 individual plates. Sprinkle with Parmesan cheese. Makes 2 side-dish servings.

TIME ESTIMATE

Preparation ____ 35 min.
Chilling _____ 2 hrs.

PER SERVING*

Calories _____ 172
Protein _____ 5 g
Carbohydrate _____ 21 g
Fat (total) _____ 8 g
  Saturated _____ 1 g
Cholesterol _____ 2 mg
Sodium _____ 68 mg
Potassium _____ 267 mg
Includes Tomato-Basil Vinaigrette.

TOMATO-BASIL VINAIGRETTE

1 large tomato, peeled,
    seeded, and cut up
3 tablespoons salad oil
3 tablespoons wine vinegar
2 tablespoons snipped
    fresh basil*
1 clove garlic, minced
¼ teaspoon sugar

■ In a blender container or food processor bowl place the tomato, salad oil, wine vinegar, basil, garlic, sugar, and ⅛ teaspoon *pepper*. Cover and blend or process till smooth. To store, cover and chill for up to 3 days. Makes ¾ cup.

*If fresh basil is not available, substitute 1½ teaspoons dried basil, crushed.

PER SERVING

Calories _____ 34
Protein _____ 0 g
Carbohydrate _____ 1 g
Fat (total) _____ 3 g
  Saturated _____ 0 g
Cholesterol _____ 0 mg
Sodium _____ 3 mg
Potassium _____ 34 mg

COTTAGE-CHEESE-DRESSED POTATO SALAD

Trim the calories without sacrificing flavor by using low-fat cottage cheese and reduced-calorie mayonnaise or salad dressing.

1 large potato (about 8 ounces), 8 ounces whole tiny new potatoes, *or* 1½ cups loose-pack frozen hash brown potatoes

■ In a large saucepan cook potatoes, covered, in boiling lightly salted water just till tender. (Allow 20 to 25 minutes for the large potato, 15 to 20 minutes for the new potatoes, or 10 to 12 minutes for the frozen hash brown potatoes.) Drain potatoes well. Peel and cube the large potato or quarter the new potatoes.

¼ cup sliced celery
2 tablespoons chopped green *or* sweet red pepper
1 tablespoon finely chopped onion

■ In a medium mixing bowl combine the celery, green or sweet red pepper, and onion. Add the cooked potatoes. Gently toss to mix.

¼ cup cream-style cottage cheese
2 tablespoons mayonnaise *or* salad dressing
2 teaspoons milk
1 teaspoon coarse-grain brown mustard *or* prepared mustard
¼ teaspoon salt
⅛ teaspoon dried dillweed *or* celery seed

■ For dressing, in a blender container combine the cottage cheese, mayonnaise or salad dressing, milk, brown or prepared mustard, salt, and dillweed or celery seed. Cover and blend till mixture is smooth. Add dressing to the potato mixture. Toss to coat.

1 tablespoon milk (optional)

■ Cover and chill for 3 to 24 hours. If salad seems dry after chilling, stir in milk to moisten. Makes 2 side-dish servings.

TIME ESTIMATE

Preparation —— 35 min.
Chilling ———— 3 hrs.

MENU IDEA

For a summertime meal, offer grilled steaks, tomato slices, and the icy cold beverages of your choice.

PER SERVING

Calories ————— 264
Protein ————— 7 g
Carbohydrate —— 32 g
Fat (total) ——— 12 g
 Saturated ——— 3 g
Cholesterol —— 13 mg
Sodium———— 509 mg
Potassium —— 644 mg

APPLE AND SPINACH SLAW

2 tablespoons mayonnaise *or* salad dressing
2 tablespoons plain yogurt *or* dairy sour cream
1 tablespoon honey
1 teaspoon Dijon-style mustard
½ cup chopped apple
1 cup coarsely shredded cabbage
½ cup coarsely shredded fresh spinach
2 tablespoons chopped onion

■ For dressing, in a small bowl stir together the mayonnaise or salad dressing, yogurt or sour cream, honey, Dijon-style mustard, and dash *salt.* Stir in apple.

In a medium mixing bowl combine the cabbage, spinach, and onion. Toss to mix. Add the dressing and toss to coat. Makes 2 side-dish servings.

TIME ESTIMATE
Start to finish _ 15 min.

PER SERVING
Calories _____ 175
Protein _____ 2 g
Carbohydrate _____ 19 g
Fat (total) _____ 12 g
Saturated _____ 2 g
Cholesterol _____ 9 mg
Sodium _____ 183 mg
Potassium _____ 254 mg

MELON SALAD WITH CREAMY APRICOT DRESSING

½ cup vanilla *or* plain yogurt
2 tablespoons flaked coconut
1 tablespoon apricot preserves

■ For dressing, in a small bowl stir together the yogurt, coconut, and apricot preserves. Cover and chill.

TIME ESTIMATE
Start to finish _ 20 min.

PER SERVING
Calories _____ 212
Protein _____ 5 g
Carbohydrate _____ 35 g
Fat (total) _____ 7 g
Saturated _____ 2 g
Cholesterol _____ 3 mg
Sodium _____ 46 mg
Potassium _____ 647 mg

½ of a medium cantaloupe *or* honeydew melon, seeded
Leaf lettuce (optional)
½ cup halved strawberries, *or* blueberries
2 tablespoons chopped walnuts *or* pecans
Dash ground nutmeg *or* cinnamon (optional)

■ Use a melon baller to scoop out pulp of melon, reserving shell. Cut melon shell into 2 wedges. If desired, line the shell wedges with lettuce leaves. In a medium bowl combine the melon balls and strawberries or blueberries. Spoon the fruit mixture over the melon-shell wedges. Drizzle with dressing. Sprinkle with nuts and, if desired, spice. Makes 2 side-dish servings.

141

SANDWICHES AND SOUPS

MEDITERRANEAN TUNA POCKETS   and   CHEESE SOUP WITH PESTO

MEDITERRANEAN TUNA POCKETS

These capers aren't tricks—they're actually the flower buds of the caper bush. Capers have a pungent, slightly bitter flavor and are usually pickled in vinegar or packed in salt.

1　**3½-ounce can tuna *or* skinless, boneless salmon, drained and broken into chunks**
1　**hard-cooked egg, chopped**
¼　**cup chopped, seeded tomato**
2　**tablespoons sliced pitted ripe olives**
1　**tablespoon chopped red *or* white onion**
1　**tablespoon capers, drained and rinsed (optional)**

■ In a medium mixing bowl stir together the tuna or salmon, egg, tomato, olives, onion, and, if desired, capers. Set aside.

¼　**cup mayonnaise *or* salad dressing**
1　**tablespoon lemon juice**
1　**clove garlic, minced**
⅛　**teaspoon pepper**

■ For dressing, in a small mixing bowl stir together the mayonnaise or salad dressing, lemon juice, garlic, and pepper. Stir dressing into the tuna or salmon mixture.

2　**small pita bread rounds**
　Leaf lettuce

■ To serve, cut the pita bread rounds in half crosswise, forming 4 pockets. Line each pocket with lettuce leaves. Spoon about *⅓ cup* of the tuna or salmon mixture into *each* pita pocket. To serve, if desired, cut the pockets in half, forming 8 triangles. Makes 2 servings.

TIME ESTIMATE
Start to finish — 35 min.

MENU IDEA
Tummy-warming Cheese Soup with Pesto (see recipe, page 156) goes well with these hearty sandwiches.

PER SERVING
Calories _____ 434
Protein _____ 19 g
Carbohydrate _____ 31 g
Fat (total) _____ 26 g
　Saturated _____ 4 g
Cholesterol ____ 142 mg
Sodium_____ 653 mg
Potassium _____ 285 mg

HAM AND CHEESE SANDWICH SPIRALS

Change the filling from easy to super simple. Just use a 4-ounce container of semi-soft cheese spiced with garlic and herbs for the filling.

½ of an 8-ounce container
    soft-style cream cheese
1 tablespoon snipped fresh
    basil *or* ½ teaspoon
    dried basil, crushed
2 teaspoons snipped fresh
    oregano *or* ½ teaspoon
    dried oregano, crushed
¼ teaspoon garlic salt
⅛ teaspoon pepper

■ For filling, in a medium mixing bowl stir together the soft-style cream cheese, basil, oregano, garlic salt, and pepper.

2 8-inch flour tortillas
3 ounces very thinly sliced
    fully cooked ham,
    turkey, *or* chicken
1 ounce very thinly sliced
    Swiss, provolone, *or*
    mozzarella cheese
2 tablespoons alfalfa
    sprouts (optional)

■ To assemble, gently spread each tortilla with the filling. Arrange the ham, turkey, or chicken slices atop the filling. Top the meat slices with the Swiss, provolone, or mozzarella cheese slices. If desired, sprinkle with alfalfa sprouts.

2 lettuce leaves
1 medium tomato, chopped

■ Place lettuce leaves and chopped tomato along one edge of each tortilla. Starting with the edge with the lettuce, roll up each tortilla jelly-roll style. Cover and chill the tortilla rolls for 1 to 24 hours.

    To serve, cut tortilla rolls in half crosswise or cut into 1-inch slices. Makes 2 servings.

TIME ESTIMATE

Preparation —— 15 min.
Chilling ———— 1 hr.

MENU IDEA

Complement these snazzy sandwiches with three-bean salad spooned into small lettuce cups.

PER SERVING

Calories ———— 443
Protein ———— 22 g
Carbohydrate —— 26 g
Fat (total) ———— 29 g
  Saturated ———— 14 g
Cholesterol ——— 97 mg
Sodium———1,156 mg
Potassium ——— 451 mg

VEGETARIAN REUBEN SANDWICH

Crunchy vegetables, zesty sauerkraut, and satisfying cheese join forces to create a mouth-watering combo.

4 slices dark *or* light rye, pumpernickel, *or* marble bread

2 tablespoons Thousand Island *or* Russian salad dressing

■ Spread *one* side of *two* bread slices with the Thousand Island or Russian salad dressing. Place bread slices, dressing side up, on the unheated rack of a broiler pan.

8 thin slices cucumber *or* zucchini

4 thin slices tomato

6 thin slices green *or* sweet red pepper rings

4 thin slices red *or* yellow onion, separated into rings

½ cup sauerkraut, rinsed and well drained

■ Layer the cucumber or zucchini slices, tomato slices, green or sweet red pepper rings, onion rings, and sauerkraut atop the bread.

4 slices Swiss, Monterey Jack, *or* cheddar cheese (4 ounces)

■ Place the cheese slices on the remaining 2 slices of bread. Place bread slices, cheese side up, on the unheated rack of the broiler pan alongside the vegetable-topped bread. Broil 4 inches from the heat about 1 minute or till cheese is melted.

To serve, invert the bread slices with cheese atop the vegetables. Makes 2 servings.

TIME ESTIMATE

Start to finish — 15 min.

MENU IDEA

For a light meal, serve a refreshing fruit salad, such as Melon Salad with Creamy Apricot Dressing (see recipe, page 141).

PER SERVING

Calories ————— 468
Protein ————— 24 g
Carbohydrate ——— 43 g
Fat (total) ———— 24 g
  Saturated ——— 12 g
Cholesterol ——— 56 mg
Sodium ———— 770 mg
Potassium ——— 675 mg

PASTRAMI KABOB SANDWICHES

If your skewers are a little too long, fill the extra space with cherry tomatoes, olives, or pickles.

⅓ cup soft-style cream cheese with chives and onion *or* soft-style cream cheese with toasted onion *or* plain soft-style cream cheese

2 tablespoons shredded carrot

2 tablespoons finely chopped sweet red *or* green pepper

1 teaspoon cream-style prepared horseradish *or* horseradish mustard (optional)

■ In a small bowl stir together the cream cheese, carrot, sweet red or green pepper, and, if desired, horseradish or horseradish mustard.

4 slices rye, whole wheat, *or* marble bread

5 ounces thinly sliced pastrami, corned beef, *or* cooked beef

6 to 8 spinach leaves *or* 2 lettuce leaves

■ If desired, toast the rye, whole wheat, or marble bread. (See tip, page 150.) Spread the cream cheese mixture on 2 of the bread slices. Top with the pastrami, corned beef, or cooked beef; spinach or lettuce leaves; and remaining bread slices.

■ Use a sharp knife to cut each sandwich diagonally into 4 portions. Thread 4 portions each onto two 6- to 8-inch wooden skewers. Makes 2 servings.

TIME ESTIMATE
Start to finish _ 15 min.

MENU IDEA
Try this sandwich with glasses of iced tea and a few crunchy vegetables, such as green onions, radishes, broccoli, jicama, carrot, or pea pods.

PER SERVING
Calories _____ 370
Protein _____ 20 g
Carbohydrate _____ 31 g
Fat (total) _____ 19 g
Saturated _____ 10 g
Cholesterol ____ 41 mg
Sodium_____1,539 mg
Potassium _____ 411 mg

PASTRAMI KABOB SANDWICHES

CHEESY SOUR CREAM AND ONION BURGERS

¾ cup sliced fresh
    mushrooms
1 small onion, thinly sliced
    and separated into
    rings
2 teaspoons margarine *or*
    butter

■ In a small saucepan cook mushrooms and onion in margarine or butter over medium-low heat for 10 to 15 minutes or till onion is very tender, stirring occasionally. Set aside.

¼ cup dairy sour cream
2 tablespoons fine dry
    bread crumbs
1 teaspoon Dijon-style *or*
    prepared mustard
⅛ teaspoon salt
⅛ teaspoon pepper
8 ounces ground beef,
    pork, raw turkey, *or*
    raw chicken

■ Meanwhile, in a mixing bowl stir together the sour cream, bread crumbs, mustard, salt, and pepper. Stir in ground beef, pork, turkey, or chicken. Shape meat mixture into two ¾-inch-thick patties.

2 slices Monterey Jack,
    Swiss, *or* provolone
    cheese (1½ to 2 ounces
    total)
2 kaiser rolls *or*
    hamburger buns, split
    and toasted (see tip,
    page 150)
  Dijon-style *or* prepared
    mustard (optional)

■ *To broil,* place meat patties on the unheated rack of a broiler pan. Broil 3 to 4 inches from the heat for 8 minutes. Turn and broil 8 to 10 minutes more or till no pink remains. Place a slice of cheese atop each burger. Broil about 1 minute more or till cheese begins to melt.

Or, to grill, place meat patties on the rack of an uncovered grill. (See tip, page 27.) Grill directly over *medium-hot* coals for 8 minutes. Turn and grill for 8 to 10 minutes more or till no pink remains. Place a slice of cheese atop each burger. Grill about 1 minute more or till cheese begins to melt.

To serve, place each burger on the bottom half of a toasted bun. Top with mushrooms and onion, then a bun top. If desired, serve with mustard. Makes 2 servings.

TIME ESTIMATE
Start to finish _ 25 min.

MENU IDEA
Go picnic-style with baked beans and glasses of lemonade.

PER SERVING
Calories _____ 551
Protein _____ 34 g
Carbohydrate _____ 32 g
Fat (total) _____ 32 g
   Saturated _____ 14 g
Cholesterol ____ 103 mg
Sodium_____ 768 mg
Potassium _____ 523 mg

TERIYAKI SESAME BURGERS

Here's the best of both worlds—an all-American burger teamed up with tangy Oriental flavors.

2 tablespoons plum preserves
½ teaspoon toasted sesame seed

■ For sauce, in a small saucepan combine preserves and sesame seed. Heat and stir over low heat till preserves are melted. Keep warm.

¼ cup finely chopped water chestnuts
1 tablespoon teriyaki sauce
1 teaspoon toasted sesame seed
¼ teaspoon onion *or* garlic salt
⅛ teaspoon pepper
8 ounces ground beef, pork, raw turkey, *or* raw chicken

■ In a mixing bowl stir together the water chestnuts, teriyaki sauce, sesame seed, onion or garlic salt, and pepper. Stir in ground beef, pork, turkey, or chicken. Shape meat mixture into two ¾-inch-thick patties.

■ *To broil,* place meat patties on the unheated rack of a broiler pan. Broil 3 to 4 inches from the heat for 8 minutes. Turn and broil 8 to 10 minutes more or till no pink remains.

Or, to grill, place meat patties on the rack of an uncovered grill. (See tip, page 27.) Grill directly over *medium-hot* coals for 8 minutes. Turn and grill for 8 to 10 minutes more or till no pink remains.

2 hamburger buns, split and toasted (see tip, page 150) (optional)

■ To serve, if desired, place burgers on toasted buns. Spoon sauce over burgers. Makes 2 servings.

TIME ESTIMATE
Start to finish — 35 min.

MENU IDEA
Stir-fried pea pods and carrots or Lemon and Wild Rice Soup (see recipe, page 160) make a good match with the burgers.

PER SERVING
Calories _____ 418
Protein _____ 27 g
Carbohydrate _____ 41 g
Fat (total) _____ 16 g
  Saturated _____ 6 g
Cholesterol _____ 71 mg
Sodium_____ 886 mg
Potassium _____ 394 mg

GREEK-STYLE POCKET SANDWICHES

A spicy meat filling topped with yogurt lends typically Greek flavors to this quick sandwich.

8 ounces ground beef, lamb, raw turkey, *or* raw chicken

■ For filling, in a medium saucepan cook beef, lamb, turkey, or chicken till no pink remains. Drain off fat.

1 8-ounce can stewed tomatoes
¼ teaspoon ground allspice *or* cinnamon
⅛ teaspoon garlic salt
⅛ teaspoon pepper

■ Stir in *undrained* tomatoes, allspice or cinnamon, garlic salt, and pepper. Bring to boiling; reduce heat. Cover and simmer for 10 minutes, stirring often. Uncover and simmer for 5 to 10 minutes more or till most of the liquid has evaporated, stirring often.

1 pita bread round, halved crosswise, *or* two 6-inch flour tortillas
¼ cup plain yogurt
1 tablespoon thinly sliced green onion

■ To serve, spoon filling into each pita half or onto each tortilla. Top with yogurt and green onion. If using tortillas, fold in the opposite sides of each tortilla, overlapping slightly. Secure with wooden toothpicks. Serves 2.

TIME ESTIMATE
Start to finish — 30 min.

MENU IDEA
Arrange orange slices on lettuce leaves and sprinkle them with Sugar-Coated Nuts (see recipe, page 138).

PER SERVING
Calories	337
Protein	28 g
Carbohydrate	26 g
Fat (total)	13 g
Saturated	5 g
Cholesterol	73 mg
Sodium	649 mg
Potassium	648 mg

TOASTING BUNS, ROLLS, AND BREAD

A little extra touch, like toasting the bun or bread for a sandwich, makes a great sandwich taste even better. Plus, it keeps the bread from getting too wet. For purchased sliced bread, use a countertop toaster. For larger pieces of bread or buns and rolls, follow these directions for the broiler or grill.

■ *To broil,* place bun or roll halves or bread, cut side up, on a baking sheet. Broil 3 to 5 inches from the heat for 1 to 2 minutes or till lightly toasted.

■ *To grill,* place bun or roll halves or bread, cut side down, on a grill rack directly over the coals. Grill about 1 minute or till lightly toasted.

RED HOT BRATS IN BEER

As they simmer, the bratwursts gather a tangy flavor from the beer.

2 fresh (uncooked) bratwursts (about 6 ounces total)
1 12-ounce can (1½ cups) beer
1 teaspoon bottled hot pepper sauce
1 teaspoon Worcestershire sauce
¾ teaspoon ground red pepper
¼ teaspoon chili powder

■ Use a fork to prick several holes in the skin of each bratwurst. In a large saucepan combine the bratwursts, beer, hot pepper sauce, Worcestershire sauce, ground red pepper, and chili powder. Bring to boiling; reduce heat. Cover and simmer about 20 minutes or till no pink remains in the bratwursts. Drain.

■ *To grill,* place bratwursts on the rack of an uncovered grill. (See tip, page 27.) Grill directly over *medium-hot* coals for 7 to 8 minutes or till each bratwurst's skin is golden, turning frequently.

Or, to broil, place bratwursts on the unheated rack of a broiler pan. Broil 4 to 5 inches from the heat for 5 minutes. Turn and broil for 5 to 7 minutes more or till each bratwurst's skin is golden.

2 frankfurter buns, split and toasted (see tip, page 150)
Sauerkraut (optional)
Coarse-grain brown *or* horseradish mustard (optional)

■ To serve, place bratwursts on the toasted buns. If desired, top with sauerkraut and mustard. Makes 2 servings.

TIME ESTIMATE
Start to finish _ 40 min.

MENU IDEA
Pretzels and Cottage-Cheese-Dressed Potato Salad (see recipe, page 140) complete this all-star menu.

PER SERVING
Calories _____ 545
Protein _____ 22 g
Carbohydrate _____ 26 g
Fat (total) _____ 38 g
    Saturated _____13 g
Cholesterol _____ 80 mg
Sodium_____1,673 mg
Potassium _____ 431 mg

GRILLED APPLE-CHEDDARWICHES

4 slices cinnamon-raisin
  bread
2 teaspoons mayonnaise *or*
  salad dressing
4 slices cheddar cheese
  (4 ounces)
1 small apple, cored and
  thinly sliced into 8
  rings
1 tablespoon margarine *or*
  butter, softened

■ Spread 2 slices of the bread with the mayonnaise or salad dressing. Layer each of these bread slices with 1 slice of cheese, half of the apple slices, and another slice of cheese. Top with another slice of bread. Spread the outsides of the bread with margarine or butter.

Place on a preheated griddle or in a large preheated skillet. Cook over medium-low heat for 6 to 8 minutes or till bread is golden and cheese is melted, turning once. Serve immediately. Makes 2 servings.

TIME ESTIMATE
Start to finish — 15 min.

PER SERVING
Calories	479
Protein	18 g
Carbohydrate	36 g
Fat (total)	30 g
Saturated	14 g
Cholesterol	63 mg
Sodium	629 mg
Potassium	242 mg

EASY IDEAS FOR LEFTOVERS

Search your refrigerator for food, such as cooked meat, vegetables, cheese, yogurt, and rice. Then mix them with a dash of seasoning or a pinch of herb and you've changed your average leftovers into a flavorful new dish. Here's some ideas you can try.

■ Quesadillas: For each quesadilla, arrange a combination of *cooked meat, shredded cheese, refried beans, chopped tomato, green pepper, and/or onion* on half of a *flour tortilla*. Fold tortilla in half; press down gently. In a skillet cook quesadillas over medium-high heat about 4 minutes or till hot, turning once.

■ Vegetable Pita Pockets: Cut *pita bread rounds* into quarters. Spread *creamy salad dressing* inside each quarter. Place *cooked vegetable pieces* in each pita quarter. Sprinkle *shredded cheddar or mozzarella cheese* inside each pita quarter. Place on baking sheet. Bake in a 375° oven about 5 minutes or till cheese melts.

■ Fried Rice: Combine a beaten *egg* and dashes of *soy sauce, dry white wine or rice wine,* and *pepper.* Set aside. Pour a little *cooking oil* into a wok or large skillet. Preheat over medium-high heat. Add *loose-pack frozen vegetables,* thawed and well-drained; stir-fry for 3 to 4 minutes or till crisp-tender. Add *chilled cooked rice.* Drizzle egg mixture over rice, stirring rice constantly. Cook and stir for 6 to 8 minutes or till mixture is hot.

SAUCY BARBECUE SANDWICHES

Here's a slick tip—freeze leftover cooked meat in two-serving packages. The small portions will thaw quickly and be ready to use in these simple sandwiches or in main-dish salads.

¼ **cup chopped onion**
1 **clove garlic, minced**
2 **teaspoons olive oil** *or*
   cooking oil
¼ **cup catsup**
1 **tablespoon honey**
1 **tablespoon vinegar**
¼ **teaspoon chili powder**
   Dash ground cumin
   Dash pepper
6 **ounces thinly sliced**
   cooked turkey, chicken,
   beef, *or* **pork**

■ In a small saucepan cook the onion and garlic in the hot oil till onion is tender but not brown. Stir in the catsup, honey, vinegar, chili powder, cumin, and pepper. Bring to boiling. Stir in the turkey, chicken, beef, or pork. Reduce heat; cover and simmer for 10 minutes.

2 **onion hamburger buns** *or*
   kaiser rolls, split
2 **thin slices smoked**
   cheddar, Swiss, *or*
   Monterey Jack cheese
   (optional)

■ Meanwhile, to toast buns or rolls, place the bun or roll halves, cut side up, on a baking sheet. Broil 3 to 5 inches from the heat for 1 minute. If desired, place 1 slice of cheese on the cut side of each bun or roll top. Broil about 30 seconds more or till buns or rolls are toasted and cheese begins to melt.

   Alfalfa sprouts (optional)
   Tomato slices (optional)
   Thinly sliced green
   pepper rings (optional)

■ To serve, spoon the meat mixture onto the bottom halves of buns or rolls. If desired, top with alfalfa sprouts, tomato slices, and green pepper rings. Top with bun or roll tops. Makes 2 servings.

TIME ESTIMATE
Start to finish _ 25 min.

MENU IDEA
Complete this winning menu with tangy coleslaw or pasta salad and sugar cookies.

PER SERVING
Calories _____ 378
Protein _____ 30 g
Carbohydrate _____ 43 g
Fat (total) _____ 10 g
   Saturated _____ 2 g
Cholesterol _____ 59 mg
Sodium_____ 693 mg
Potassium _____ 527 mg

153

COBB-STYLE CHICKEN SANDWICH

Cobb salad, an entrée created at the renowned Brown Derby restaurant in California, inspired this snappy-tasting meal-on-a-bun. Chicken, cheese, bacon, and avocado are all part of the classic salad.

4 slices bacon

■ In a large skillet cook bacon over medium heat till crisp. Drain bacon on paper towels; set aside. Reserve *2 tablespoons* of the drippings in the skillet; discard the remaining drippings.

2 large boneless, skinless chicken breast halves (8 ounces total)
1 tablespoon honey
2 slices Swiss, cheddar, *or* Monterey Jack cheese

■ Place each chicken breast half between 2 pieces of plastic wrap. Working from the center to the edges, pound the chicken lightly with the flat side of a meat mallet to ¼-inch thickness.

Cook chicken in reserved bacon drippings over medium heat for 4 to 6 minutes or till chicken is tender and no pink remains, turning once. Brush chicken with honey; top with cheese.

2 kaiser *or* individual French-style rolls, *or* whole wheat buns, split and toasted (see tip, page 150)
1 tablespoon Dijon-style *or* coarse-grain mustard
1 small tomato, thinly sliced (optional)
½ of a small ripe avocado, sliced (optional)
Alfalfa sprouts *or* leaf lettuce (optional)
Chive flowers (optional)

■ To serve, spread roll or bun halves with the mustard. Add the chicken with cheese, bacon, and, if desired, tomato, avocado, and alfalfa sprouts or lettuce. Top with roll or bun tops. If desired, garnish with chive flowers. Makes 2 servings.

TIME ESTIMATE
Start to finish — 20 min.

MENU IDEA
Simple side dishes, such as potato or corn chips and strawberries or grapes, keep this meal quick to fix.

PER SERVING
Calories ———— 652
Protein ———— 45 g
Carbohydrate ——— 43 g
Fat (total) ———— 35 g
  Saturated ———— 14 g
Cholesterol —— 135 mg
Sodium———— 1,028 mg
Potassium ———— 356 mg

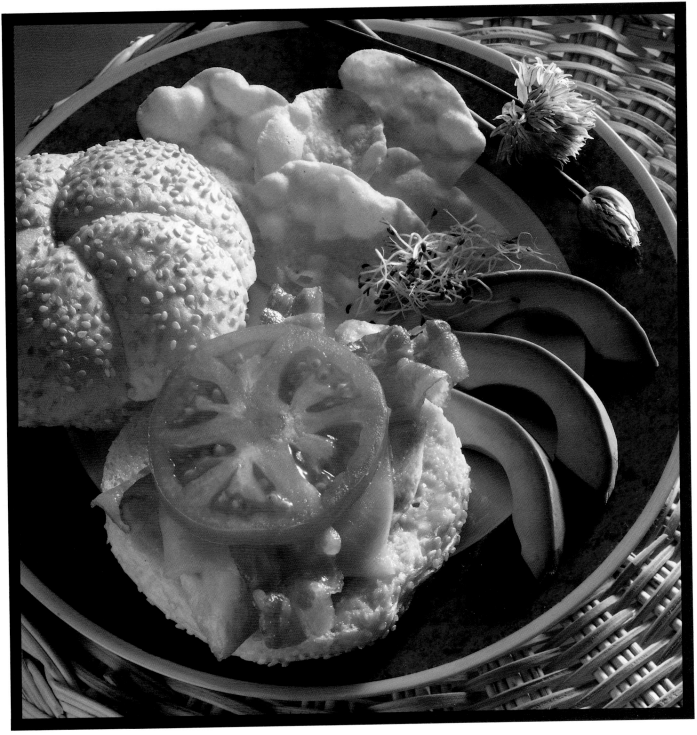

COBB-STYLE CHICKEN SANDWICH

SOUPS • *MAIN DISH*

CHEESE SOUP WITH PESTO

Pesto, a tantalizing mix of fresh basil, garlic, cheese, nuts, and oil, adds a burst of flavor to soup, pasta, or bread. (Pictured on page 142.)

Pesto
1¼ cups water
½ cup shredded carrot
¼ cup chopped onion
 1 tablespoon tomato paste
1½ teaspoons instant
      chicken bouillon
      granules

 1 cup milk
 2 tablespoons all-purpose
      flour
¾ cup shredded American
      cheese (3 ounces)
½ cup shredded Edam,
      cheddar, *or* American
      cheese (2 ounces)
   Chopped tomato
      (optional)
   Fresh parsley (optional)

■ Prepare Pesto as directed below. Set aside *2 tablespoons* of Pesto. Store the remaining Pesto as directed.

In a medium saucepan stir together the water, carrot, onion, tomato paste, and bouillon granules. Bring to boiling; reduce heat. Cover and simmer about 5 minutes or till the onion is tender.

■ Combine the milk and flour. Stir into mixture in saucepan. Cook and stir till thickened and bubbly. Cook and stir for 1 minute more. Toss cheeses together; stir into milk mixture. Cook and stir till cheese is melted. *Do not boil.*

To serve, ladle the soup into individual bowls. Swirl or stir reserved Pesto into soup. If desired, garnish with chopped tomato and parsley. Makes 2 servings.

TIME ESTIMATE
Start to finish — 35 min.

MENU IDEA
Create an upscale soup-and-sandwich meal by arranging Mediterranean Tuna Pockets (see recipe, page 143) around the bowls of soup.

PER SERVING
Calories _____ 641
Protein _____ 27 g
Carbohydrate ____ 24 g
Fat (total) _____ 50 g
  Saturated _____ 19 g
Cholesterol _____ 82 mg
Sodium _____ 1,840 mg
Potassium _____ 668 mg

PESTO

½ cup firmly packed fresh
      basil leaves
¼ cup toasted pecans,
      walnuts, *or* almonds
 3 tablespoons grated
      Parmesan *or* Romano
      cheese
 2 tablespoons olive oil *or*
      cooking oil
 1 clove garlic, minced

■ In a blender container or food processor bowl combine basil, nuts, cheese, oil, and garlic. Cover; blend or process till a paste forms.

To store Pesto, place in an airtight container. Chill for up to 2 days or freeze up to 1 month. Before serving, bring to room temperature. Toss leftover Pesto with hot cooked pasta or use it in Italian-Style Chef Salad with Creamy Pesto Dressing (see recipe, page 128). Makes five 1-tablespoon servings.

PER TABLESPOON
Calories _____ 97
Protein _____ 2 g
Carbohydrate _____ 1 g
Fat (total) _____ 10 g
  Saturated _____ 2 g
Cholesterol _____ 2 mg
Sodium _____ 53 mg
Potassium _____ 45 mg

CHICKEN MEATBALL SOUP

1 **slightly beaten egg white**

2 **tablespoons fine dry bread crumbs**

1 **tablespoon snipped fresh sage, ¼ teaspoon dried sage, crushed, *or* ¼ teaspoon poultry seasoning**

¼ **teaspoon salt**

6 **ounces ground raw chicken *or* turkey**

3 **cups chicken broth**

⅛ **teaspoon pepper**

½ **cup fine noodles**

3 **cups coarsely chopped *or* torn fresh spinach**

■ In a medium mixing bowl stir together the egg white, bread crumbs, sage or poultry seasoning, and salt. Add the ground raw chicken or turkey and mix well. Set aside.

In a medium saucepan stir together the chicken broth and pepper. Bring to boiling; stir in noodles. Reduce heat. Drop meat mixture by small spoonfuls into the simmering broth. Cover and cook for 10 to 12 minutes or till no pink remains in the meat, stirring occasionally.

Gently stir spinach into soup and heat through. To serve, ladle soup into individual bowls. Makes 2 servings.

TIME ESTIMATE

Start to finish _ 25 min.

MENU IDEA

Warm Buttermilk Corn Bread (see recipe, page 216) and fresh fruit round out the meal.

PER SERVING

Calories	275
Protein	27 g
Carbohydrate	15 g
Fat (total)	12 g
Saturated	3 g
Cholesterol	77 mg
Sodium	1,607 mg
Potassium	837 mg

DRIED TOMATOES

Dried tomatoes are great for cooking because they're packed with flavor. They are vine-ripened tomatoes, cut in half and dried. Those dried in the sun are usually labeled "sun-dried" tomatoes and those dried in a dehydrator are called "dried" tomatoes.

Several forms of dried tomatoes are available in supermarkets, gourmet shops, and specialty stores. The tomatoes are sold in halves, slices, and bits, either dry or packed in oil (marinated).

To substitute the dry form for oil-packed, you must rehydrate the dry tomatoes. Just cover dry tomatoes with boiling water, let them stand for 2 minutes, then drain.

To store the dry form, keep the tomatoes in an airtight container out of direct light or in a refrigerator or freezer for up to 1 year. You can store oil-packed tomatoes in the refrigerator for up to 6 months after opening, but make sure the oil covers the tomatoes.

HEARTY BEEF AND SQUASH STEW

Warm yourself on a brisk autumn day with a bowl of fresh, homemade stew and biscuits.

6 ounces beef stew meat, cut
    into ¾-inch pieces
1 tablespoon cooking oil
1 12-ounce jar brown
    gravy
1 medium leek, thinly
    sliced (⅓ cup), *or* 1
    small onion, cut into
    thin wedges
⅓ cup dry red *or* white
    wine*
¼ cup water
¼ teaspoon dried thyme *or*
    basil, crushed
    Dash pepper

■ In a medium saucepan brown the beef in hot oil. Drain off fat. Stir in the gravy, leek or onion, red or white wine, water, thyme or basil, and pepper. Bring to boiling; reduce heat. Cover and simmer for 30 minutes.

2 cups cubed, peeled
    butternut *or* acorn
    squash
2 medium carrots, cut into
    1-inch pieces (1 cup)

■ Stir in butternut or acorn squash and carrots. Cover and simmer about 30 minutes more or till meat and vegetables are tender.

■ To serve, ladle stew into individual bowls. Makes 2 servings.
   *If desired, substitute ⅓ cup *apple juice or water* and 1 tablespoon *vinegar* for the wine.

TIME ESTIMATE

Start to finish —1¼ hrs.

MENU IDEA

Bake Basic Buttery Biscuits (see recipe, page 215) to serve alongside the stew.

PER SERVING

Calories _____ 426
Protein _____ 28 g
Carbohydrate _____ 40 g
Fat (total) _____ 16 g
  Saturated _____ 5 g
Cholesterol _____ 63 mg
Sodium_____ 1,028 mg
Potassium _____ 1,193 mg

CARAWAY POTATO CHOWDER

2 medium potatoes, peeled and chopped (2 cups), *or* 2 cups loose-pack frozen hash brown potatoes
1 cup water
¼ cup chopped onion
1 teaspoon instant chicken bouillon granules

■ In a medium saucepan combine chopped potatoes or frozen hash brown potatoes, water, onion, and bouillon granules. Bring to boiling; reduce heat. Cover and simmer about 10 minutes or till potatoes are tender. *Do not drain.* Slightly mash the potatoes.

1¼ cups milk
2 tablespoons all-purpose flour
1 teaspoon caraway seed
⅛ teaspoon pepper *or* ¼ teaspoon lemon-pepper seasoning

■ In a small mixing bowl stir together the milk and flour. Stir into the potato mixture. Stir in the caraway seed and pepper or lemon-pepper seasoning. Cook and stir till thickened and bubbly.

½ cup chopped fully cooked ham *or* smoked turkey sausage
½ of an 8-ounce can (⅓ cup) sauerkraut, rinsed and well drained

■ Stir in ham or turkey sausage and sauerkraut. Cook and stir till heated through. To serve, ladle chowder into individual bowls. Makes 2 servings.

TIME ESTIMATE
Start to finish _ 30 min.

MENU IDEA
Fill out this menu with sliced apples or pears, crispy breadsticks or crackers, and glasses of milk.

PER SERVING
Calories _____ 295
Protein _____ 18 g
Carbohydrate _____ 44 g
Fat (total) _____ 6 g
  Saturated _____ 3 g
Cholesterol _____ 33 mg
Sodium _____ 1,168 mg
Potassium _____ 895 mg

CARAWAY FISH CHOWDER

6 ounces (½ to ¾ inch thick) skinless, boneless fish fillets cut into 1-inch pieces

■ Prepare Caraway Potato Chowder as directed above, *except* omit the ham or turkey sausage. Stir the fish into potato mixture along with the caraway seed and pepper. Bring almost to boiling; reduce heat. Cover and simmer gently for 2 to 3 minutes or just till fish begins to flake easily.

PER SERVING
Calories _____ 304
Protein _____ 24 g
Carbohydrate _____ 44 g
Fat (total) _____ 4 g
  Saturated _____ 2 g
Cholesterol _____ 50 mg
Sodium _____ 753 mg
Potassium _____ 940 mg

LEMON AND WILD RICE SOUP

Savor this delicate lemony soup that's similar to the Oriental favorite, egg drop soup.

2 cups chicken broth
3 tablespoons wild rice

■ In a medium saucepan bring chicken broth to boiling. Meanwhile, rinse and drain wild rice. Add wild rice to chicken broth; reduce heat. Cover and simmer about 40 minutes or till rice is tender.

2 to 3 teaspoons lemon juice
Dash pepper
1 beaten egg
1 tablespoon sliced green onion

■ Stir in lemon juice and pepper. Pour the egg into the broth mixture in a steady stream while stirring 2 or 3 times to create shreds.

To serve, ladle soup into individual bowls. Garnish with sliced green onion. Makes 2 side-dish servings.

TIME ESTIMATE
Start to finish — 50 min.

MENU IDEA
This zesty side-dish soup pairs well with broiled or grilled chicken.

PER SERVING
Calories _____ 125
Protein _____ 10 g
Carbohydrate _____ 12 g
Fat (total) _____ 4 g
   Saturated _____ 1 g
Cholesterol _____ 108 mg
Sodium _____ 808 mg
Potassium _____ 302 mg

LEMON AND WILD RICE SOUP WITH HAM

1 cup chopped fully cooked ham

■ Prepare Lemon and Wild Rice Soup as directed above, *except* stir ham into soup with the lemon juice. Makes 2 main-dish servings.

PER SERVING
Calories _____ 234
Protein _____ 28 g
Carbohydrate _____ 12 g
Fat (total) _____ 8 g
   Saturated _____ 3 g
Cholesterol _____ 146 mg
Sodium _____ 1,737 mg
Potassium _____ 524 mg

TORTELLINI AND FRESH SPINACH SOUP

½ **cup shredded carrot**
¼ **cup chopped onion**
2 **teaspoons instant chicken bouillon granules**
1 **teaspoon dried Italian seasoning, crushed**
½ **cup packaged cheese tortellini (2 ounces)**
1 **cup fresh spinach, coarsely chopped**
1 **tablespoon grated Parmesan cheese**

■ In a large saucepan stir together the carrot, onion, bouillon granules, Italian seasoning, 3 cups *water,* and dash *pepper.* Bring to boiling; reduce heat. Stir in tortellini. Cover and simmer for 15 minutes.

Stir in spinach and cook about 15 seconds or just till spinach is wilted. To serve, ladle soup into individual bowls. Sprinkle with Parmesan cheese. Makes 2 side-dish servings.

TIME ESTIMATE
Start to finish — 30 min.

PER SERVING
Calories ———————— 132
Protein ———————— 8 g
Carbohydrate ———— 20 g
Fat (total) ————————— 3 g
  Saturated ———————— 1 g
Cholesterol ———— 20 mg
Sodium————— 1,106 mg
Potassium ————— 346 mg

WRAP-IT-UP

Proper packaging will keep the foods you put in your freezer as fresh as when you made them. Here are some suggestions:

■ For liquids, leave enough headspace in the container for the food to expand as it freezes. (In wide-top containers leave ½ inch for pints and 1 inch for quarts; in narrow-top containers leave ¾ inch for pints and 1½ inches for quarts.) For foods packaged in freezer wrap, foil, or bags, press out as much air as possible before sealing the package. Tightly seal bags and containers. Seal freezer wrap and foil with a drugstore fold (fold long edges together in a series of locked folds, then fold short ends under); secure with freezer tape.

■ If a casserole is to be frozen in a baking dish, wrap the dish with heavy foil and seal. When the recipe contains an acidic ingredient, such as tomatoes, cover the food with plastic wrap, then with foil. The plastic wrap will prevent a reaction between the foil and the food during storage. The foil can be used as a cover when heating the food, but the plastic wrap should be removed before cooking.

■ Always label packages with the contents, quantity or number of servings, date frozen, and any special instructions.

TRIPLE-CORN CHOWDER

Cornmeal imparts a new and interesting texture to this pleasantly flavored soup. But, if you're out of cornmeal, use 4 teaspoons all-purpose flour instead.

1 cup loose-pack frozen whole kernel corn
¼ cup chopped green *or* sweet red pepper
¼ cup water
2 tablespoons chopped onion
1 teaspoon instant chicken bouillon granules
Dash pepper

■ In a medium saucepan stir together the frozen corn, green or sweet red pepper, water, onion, bouillon granules, and pepper. Bring to boiling; reduce heat. Cover and simmer about 5 minutes or till the corn is tender. *Do not drain.*

1 cup milk
2 tablespoons yellow cornmeal
¼ cup chopped sliced dried beef *or* fully cooked ham

■ In a small mixing bowl stir together the milk and cornmeal. Stir into saucepan. Cook and stir till thickened and bubbly. Cook and stir for 1 minute more. Stir in the dried beef or ham. Heat through.

2 tablespoons corn nuts *or* coarsely broken corn chips (optional)

■ To serve, ladle chowder into individual bowls. If desired, garnish with corn nuts or chips. Makes 2 side-dish servings.

TIME ESTIMATE
Start to finish _ 20 min.

MENU IDEA
With this full-flavored soup, serve pork or chicken sandwiches, and chocolate chunk cookies.

PER SERVING
Calories _____ 215
Protein _____ 14 g
Carbohydrate _____ 33 g
Fat (total) _____ 4 g
Saturated _____ 2 g
Cholesterol _____ 45 mg
Sodium_____ 1,267 mg
Potassium _____ 453 mg

TRIPLE-CORN CHOWDER

VEGETABLE BEEF SOUP

12 ounces lean ground beef
3 cups water
1 16-ounce can tomatoes,
     cut up
½ of a 9-ounce package
     (1 cup) frozen baby
     lima beans
1 cup loose-pack frozen
     whole kernel corn
1 medium potato, peeled
     and cubed (⅔ cup), *or*
     ⅔ cup loose-pack
     frozen hash brown
     potatoes
1 medium carrot, sliced
     (½ cup)
1 small onion, chopped
     (⅓ cup)
1 tablespoon instant beef
     bouillon granules
2 teaspoons Worcestershire
     sauce
½ teaspoon dried
     marjoram, crushed
½ teaspoon dried oregano,
     crushed
¼ teaspoon pepper

■ Brown ground beef in a large saucepan or Dutch oven. Drain off fat.

Stir in the water, *undrained* tomatoes, lima beans, corn, cubed potato or frozen hash brown potatoes, carrot, onion, bouillon granules, Worcestershire sauce, marjoram, oregano, and pepper.

Pour *half* of the soup into 1 or 2 individual freezer containers and freeze as directed. Leave remaining soup in the saucepan and cook immediately. Makes 4 servings.

TIME ESTIMATE
Start to finish — 40 min.

MENU IDEA
Round up a crispy selection of crackers and spoon fruit over slices of pound cake.

PER SERVING
Calories _____ 275
Protein _____ 25 g
Carbohydrate _____ 33 g
Fat (total) _____ 6 g
  Saturated _____ 2 g
Cholesterol _____ 50 mg
Sodium_____ 980 mg
Potassium _____ 946 mg

TO EAT TWO: Bring remaining 2 servings of soup in the saucepan to boiling; reduce heat. Cover and simmer for 20 to 25 minutes or till vegetables are tender. Ladle soup into individual bowls.

TO FREEZE TWO: Seal, label, and freeze the freezer containers for up to 3 months. *To serve,* transfer 1 or 2 of the frozen portions to a medium saucepan. Cover and cook over medium heat for 25 to 30 minutes or till heated through and vegetables are tender, stirring occasionally. Ladle soup into individual bowls.

RICH ONION AND BEEF SOUP

2 **cups thinly sliced onions**
2 **tablespoons margarine**
   _or_ butter
2 **14½-ounce cans beef**
   broth

½ **cup dry white _or_ red wine,**
   _or_ beer
3 **tablespoons all-purpose**
   flour
½ **teaspoon sugar**
½ **teaspoon dry mustard**
2 **cups cubed cooked beef**
   (about 10 ounces total)

■ In a large saucepan cook onions, covered, in hot margarine or butter over medium-low heat for 8 to 10 minutes or till very tender, stirring occasionally. Carefully stir in beef broth. Bring to boiling; reduce heat. Cover and simmer for 10 minutes.

■ Meanwhile, in a small mixing bowl stir together the wine or beer, flour, sugar, and dry mustard. Stir into broth mixture. Cook and stir till slightly thickened and bubbly. Cook and stir for 1 minute more. Stir in the beef.

Pour _half_ of the soup into 1 or 2 individual freezer containers and freeze as directed. Leave remaining soup in the saucepan and cook immediately. Makes 4 servings.

TO EAT TWO: Cook remaining 2 servings of soup in the saucepan about 2 minutes or till heated through. Meanwhile, place two ¾-inch-thick slices of **French bread** on a baking sheet. Broil 3 to 5 inches from the heat for 1 to 2 minutes or till bread is toasted. Sprinkle toasted bread with ½ cup shredded **Gruyère, Jarlsberg, _or_ Swiss cheese.** Broil about 1 minute more or till cheese is light brown and bubbly. Ladle soup into individual bowls. Top with bread slices.

TO FREEZE TWO: Seal, label, and freeze the freezer containers for up to 2 months. _To serve,_ place 1 or 2 of the frozen portions of soup in a saucepan. Cover and cook over medium heat for 15 to 20 minutes or till heated through, stirring occasionally. Meanwhile, for _each_ serving, place one ¾-inch-thick slice of **French bread** on a baking sheet. Broil 3 to 5 inches from the heat for 1 to 2 minutes or till bread is toasted. Sprinkle each slice of toasted bread with ¼ cup shredded **Gruyère, Jarlsberg, _or_ Swiss cheese.** Broil about 1 minute more or till cheese is light brown and bubbly. Ladle each portion of soup into an individual bowl. Top with a bread slice.

TIME ESTIMATE
Start to finish _ 35 min.

MENU IDEA
Slice fresh fruit to serve with the soup and indulge in a piece of cheesecake for dessert.

PER SERVING
Calories _____ 451
Protein _____ 37 g
Carbohydrate ____ 24 g
Fat (total) _____ 20 g
   Saturated _____ 8 g
Cholesterol ____ 91 mg
Sodium _____ 1,033 mg
Potassium ____ 556 mg

BEEF STEAK CHILI WITH BEANS

1 **pound beef top round steak**
1 **tablespoon cooking oil**
¾ **cup chopped onion**
2 **cloves garlic, minced**

■ Trim fat from meat. Partially freeze meat for 30 minutes. Thinly slice meat across the grain into bite-size strips. In a large saucepan or Dutch oven brown *half* of the meat in hot oil. Remove from pan. Brown remaining meat with the onion and garlic, adding more oil, if necessary. Drain off fat. Return all meat, onion, and garlic to pan.

1 **28-ounce can tomatoes, cut up**
⅔ **cup water**
1 **4-ounce can diced green chili peppers, drained, *or* ¼ cup chopped, canned jalapeño chili peppers**
4 **teaspoons chili powder**
1 **tablespoon brown sugar**
1½ **teaspoons dried oregano, crushed**
1 **teaspoon instant beef bouillon granules**
½ **teaspoon ground cumin**
1 **15-ounce can pinto *or* red kidney beans, drained**

■ Stir in the *undrained* tomatoes, water, green chili peppers or jalapeño peppers, chili powder, brown sugar, oregano, bouillon granules, and cumin. Bring to boiling; reduce heat. Cover and simmer about 1 hour or till meat is tender and chili is of desired consistency. Remove from heat. Stir in the beans.

Pour *half* of the chili into 1 or 2 individual freezer containers and freeze as directed. Leave remaining chili in the saucepan and cook immediately. Makes 4 servings.

TIME ESTIMATE
Preparation ____ 50 min.
Cooking _____ 65 min.

MENU IDEA
Mix orange sections and sliced strawberries to serve on the side and enjoy custard for dessert.

PER SERVING
Calories _____ 365
Protein _____ 36 g
Carbohydrate ____ 37 g
Fat (total) _____ 9 g
  Saturated _____ 2 g
Cholesterol ____ 71 mg
Sodium _____ 932 mg
Potassium ____1,279 mg

TO EAT TWO: Cook the remaining 2 servings of chili in the saucepan, covered, about 5 minutes more or till heated through. Ladle chili into individual bowls. If desired, top with dairy **sour cream *or* shredded cheddar cheese.**

TO FREEZE TWO: Seal, label, and freeze the freezer containers for up to 3 months. *To serve,* place 1 or 2 of the frozen portions in a medium saucepan. Cover and cook over medium heat about 20 minutes or till heated through, stirring occasionally. Ladle into individual bowls. If desired, top with dairy **sour cream *or* shredded cheddar cheese.**

BEEF STEW WITH LENTILS

A half pound of meat is enough to serve four when you mix it with hearty lentils and lots of vegetables.

8 ounces beef *or* pork stew meat, cut into ½-inch pieces	■ In a large saucepan brown the beef or pork on all sides in hot oil; drain off fat.
1 tablespoon cooking oil	

3½ cups beef broth	■ Stir in the beef broth, *undrained* tomatoes, lentils, onion, celery, carrot, and bay leaf. Bring to boiling; reduce heat. Simmer, uncovered, for 35 to 45 minutes or till meat and lentils are tender.
1 8-ounce can stewed tomatoes	
¾ cup dry lentils, rinsed and drained	
1 medium onion, chopped (½ cup)	
1 stalk celery, sliced (½ cup)	
1 medium carrot, sliced (½ cup)	
1 bay leaf	

1 cup loose-pack frozen cut green beans	■ Remove bay leaf. Stir in frozen beans. Spoon *half* of the stew into 1 or 2 individual freezer containers and freeze as directed. Leave remaining stew in the saucepan and cook immediately. Makes 4 servings.

TO EAT TWO: Cook remaining 2 servings of stew in the saucepan, covered, about 10 minutes more or till beans are tender. Ladle stew into individual bowls.

TO FREEZE TWO: Seal, label, and freeze the freezer containers for up to 3 months. *To serve,* place 1 or 2 of the frozen portions in a medium saucepan. Cover and cook over medium heat for 20 to 25 minutes or till heated through and green beans are tender, stirring occasionally. Ladle stew into individual bowls.

■ TIME ESTIMATE ■
Start to finish ——— 1 hr.

■ MENU IDEA ■
While the stew simmers, bake Blueberry and Coconut Crisp (see recipe, page 196) for dessert.

■ PER SERVING ■
Calories ——————— 300
Protein ——————— 28 g
Carbohydrate ——— 31 g
Fat (total) ————— 8 g
    Saturated ——— 2 g
Cholesterol ——— 44 mg
Sodium——————— 891 mg
Potassium ——— 855 mg

BEANY HAM SOUP

½ of a 16-ounce package
   mixed dry soup beans
   or great northern
   beans
3 cups water

3 cups water
2 cups chopped, peeled
   tomatoes *or* one 16-
   ounce can tomatoes,
   cut up
1 1- to 1½-pound meaty
   ham bone, 1 to 1½
   pounds smoked pork
   hocks, *or* 1½ cups
   cubed fully cooked ham
1 cup chopped celery
1 cup chopped onion
1 tablespoon snipped fresh
   thyme *or* 1 teaspoon
   dried thyme, crushed
2 teaspoons instant beef
   bouillon granules
¼ teaspoon pepper
1 bay leaf

■ Rinse beans. In a large saucepan combine beans and water. Bring to boiling; reduce heat. Simmer for 2 minutes. Remove from heat. Cover and let stand for 1 hour. (*Or,* skip boiling the water and soak beans overnight in the covered pan.) Drain and rinse beans.

■ In the same pan stir together beans, the 3 cups *fresh* water, fresh tomatoes or *undrained* canned tomatoes, ham bone or pork hocks (if using), celery, onion, thyme, bouillon granules, pepper, and bay leaf. Bring to boiling; reduce heat. Cover and simmer about 1½ hours or till beans are tender.

Discard bay leaf. Remove ham bone or pork hocks. When cool enough to handle, cut meat off bones. Stir meat or cubed ham (if using) into soup.

Spoon *half* of the soup into 1 or 2 individual freezer containers and freeze as directed. Leave remaining soup in saucepan and cook immediately. Makes 4 servings.

TIME ESTIMATE
Start to finish __2¾ hrs.

MENU IDEA
Match a tossed salad drizzled with Honey-Mustard Dressing (see recipe, page 137) with this wholesome soup.

PER SERVING
Calories_____304
Protein_____27 g
Carbohydrate_____41 g
Fat (total)_____4 g
   Saturated_____1 g
Cholesterol_____29 mg
Sodium_____1,201 mg
Potassium_____1,108 mg

TO EAT TWO: Cook remaining 2 servings of soup in saucepan about 2 minutes or till heated through. If desired, use a fork to mash some of the beans against the side of the saucepan to slightly thicken soup. Ladle soup into individual bowls.

TO FREEZE TWO: Seal, label, and freeze the freezer containers for up to 3 months. *To serve,* place 1 or 2 of the frozen portions in a saucepan. Cover and cook over medium heat about 35 minutes or till heated through, stirring occasionally. If desired, use a fork to mash some of the beans against the side of the saucepan to slightly thicken soup. Ladle soup into individual bowls.

FRESH TOMATO SOUP

3 medium tomatoes, peeled
  and quartered, *or* one
  16-ounce can tomatoes
½ cup chopped onion
½ cup chopped celery
½ of a 6-ounce can (⅓ cup)
  tomato paste
1 tablespoon snipped
  parsley
2 teaspoons instant
  chicken bouillon
  granules
2 teaspoons lime juice *or*
  lemon juice
1 teaspoon sugar
  Few dashes bottled hot
  pepper sauce

■ If desired, seed the *fresh* tomatoes. In a large saucepan combine the fresh tomatoes or *undrained* canned tomatoes, onion, celery, tomato paste, parsley, bouillon granules, lime or lemon juice, sugar, hot pepper sauce, and 1½ cups *water.* Bring to boiling; reduce heat. Cover and simmer about 20 minutes or till celery and onion are very tender.

TIME ESTIMATE
Start to finish _ 40 min.

MENU IDEA
Pair this zesty soup with small chef's salads or bratwursts on buns.

PER SERVING
Calories _____ 57
Protein _____ 2 g
Carbohydrate _____ 13 g
Fat (total) _____ 1 g
  Saturated _____ 0 g
Cholesterol _____ 0 mg
Sodium_____ 644 mg
Potassium _____ 489 mg

■ Place *one-third* of the mixture in a blender container. Cover and blend till smooth. (*Or,* place *half* of the soup in a food processor bowl. Cover and process till smooth.) Repeat with the remaining mixture.

Pour *half* of the soup into 1 or 2 individual freezer containers and freeze as directed. Return remaining soup to saucepan and cook immediately. Makes 4 side-dish servings.

TO EAT TWO: Cook and stir remaining 2 servings of soup in the saucepan about 2 minutes or till heated through. Ladle soup into individual bowls. If desired, garnish with snipped **parsley.**

TO FREEZE TWO: Seal, label, and freeze the freezer containers for up to 3 months. *To serve,* place 1 or 2 of the frozen portions in a medium saucepan. Cover and cook over medium heat for 20 to 25 minutes or till heated through, stirring occasionally. Ladle soup into individual bowls. If desired, garnish with snipped **parsley.**

*E*AT TWO/FREEZE TWO

PUMPKIN AND VEGETABLE SOUP

¼ **cup chopped onion**
1 **tablespoon margarine *or* butter**
1 **14½-ounce can chicken broth**
½ **cup finely chopped peeled potato *or* loose-pack frozen hash brown potatoes**
½ **cup loose-pack frozen corn**
¼ **cup finely chopped sweet red *or* green pepper**

■ In a large saucepan cook onion in hot margarine or butter till tender but not brown. Stir in chicken broth, finely chopped potato or frozen hash brown potatoes, corn, and sweet red or green pepper. Cover and simmer about 15 minutes or till vegetables are tender.

TIME ESTIMATE
Start to finish _ 35 min.

MENU IDEA
Select chicken salad or broiled chicken breasts brushed with apple jelly to serve with this luscious soup.

PER SERVING
Calories _____ 178
Protein _____ 6 g
Carbohydrate ___ 17 g
Fat (total) _____ 11 g
  Saturated _____ 5 g
Cholesterol ___ 23 mg
Sodium _____ 523 mg
Potassium ___ 406 mg

½ **of a 16-ounce can (1 cup) pumpkin**
¼ **teaspoon salt**
⅛ **teaspoon pepper**

■ Stir pumpkin, salt, and pepper into broth mixture. Pour *half* of the soup into 1 or 2 individual freezer containers and freeze as directed. Leave remaining soup in the saucepan and cook immediately. Makes 4 side-dish servings.

TO EAT TWO: Slowly add ½ cup **half-and-half, light cream, *or* milk** to the remaining 2 servings of soup in the saucepan, stirring constantly. Heat through. Ladle soup into individual bowls. If desired, garnish with sliced **green onion *or* chives.**

TO FREEZE TWO: Seal, label, and freeze the freezer containers for up to 3 months. *To serve,* thaw 1 or 2 of the frozen portions in the refrigerator overnight. Place in a saucepan and cook over medium heat till heated through, stirring occasionally. *Or,* place 1 or 2 of the frozen portions in a saucepan. Cover and cook over medium heat about 25 minutes or till heated through, stirring occasionally. For *each* serving, slowly add ¼ cup **half-and-half, light cream, *or* milk** to the soup, stirring constantly. Heat through. Ladle into individual bowls. If desired, garnish with sliced **green onion *or* chives.**

CHILLED SWEET PEPPER SOUP

2 medium carrots, chopped
  (1 cup)
1 large onion, chopped
  (1 cup)
1 tablespoon margarine *or*
  butter

■ In a saucepan cook carrots and onion in hot margarine or butter about 10 minutes or till vegetables are tender, stirring occasionally.

■ **TIME ESTIMATE** ■
Preparation ___ 50 min.
Chilling _____ 4 hrs.

1¼ cups water
1¼ teaspoons instant
    chicken bouillon
    granules
1 sweet yellow pepper,
  chopped

■ Stir in water and bouillon granules. Bring to boiling; stir in sweet yellow pepper. Reduce heat; cover and simmer about 15 minutes or till pepper is tender. Remove from heat and cool slightly.

■ **MENU IDEA** ■
Enjoy this delectable soup with a crisp summer salad.

1 3-ounce package cream
  cheese, cubed and
  softened
½ teaspoon salt
  Dash ground red pepper
  Dash ground nutmeg

■ Stir in cream cheese, salt, ground red pepper, and nutmeg. Pour *half* of the mixture into a blender container or food processor bowl. Cover and blend or process till smooth. Transfer to a mixing bowl. Cover and chill at least 4 hours before serving.

Blend or process the remaining mixture. Pour into 1 or 2 individual freezer containers and freeze as directed. Makes 4 side-dish servings.

■ **PER SERVING** ■
Calories _____ 219
Protein _____ 5 g
Carbohydrate _____ 12 g
Fat (total) _____ 18 g
  Saturated _____ 10 g
Cholesterol _____ 46 mg
Sodium _____ 696 mg
Potassium _____ 290 mg

TO EAT TWO: Stir ¼ cup **half-and-half, light cream,** *or* **milk** into the chilled mixture. Ladle soup into individual bowls. If desired, stir enough additional **half-and-half, light cream,** *or* **milk** into 2 tablespoons dairy **sour cream** to thin slightly; drizzle atop soup.

TO FREEZE TWO: Seal, label, and freeze the freezer containers for up to 6 weeks. *To serve,* let 1 or 2 portions thaw overnight in the refrigerator. For *each* serving, stir 2 tablespoons **half-and-half, light cream,** *or* **milk** into the soup. Ladle soup into a bowl. If desired, for *each* serving, stir enough additional **half-and-half, light cream,** *or* **milk** into 1 tablespoon dairy **sour cream** to thin slightly; drizzle atop soup.

SIDE DISHES

CARROT AND SQUASH STIR-FRY

CARROT AND SQUASH STIR-FRY

To make this quick recipe even faster at mealtime, pre-cut the vegetables and store them in a covered container in the refrigerator. Then at serving time, you'll be ready to stir-fry.

1 tablespoon margarine *or* cooking oil

1 clove garlic, minced

¼ teaspoon dried basil, oregano, *or* Italian seasoning, crushed

1 medium carrot, cut into julienne strips (½ cup)

1 small zucchini *and/or* yellow summer squash, cut into julienne strips (1 cup)

2 medium leeks, thinly sliced (⅔ cup), *or* 2 green onions, thinly sliced (¼ cup)

■ Place margarine or cooking oil in a wok or large skillet. Preheat over medium-high heat. Stir-fry garlic and basil, oregano, or Italian seasoning in hot margarine or cooking oil for 15 seconds. Add carrot. Stir-fry for 1 minute. Add zucchini and/or yellow squash. Stir-fry for 2½ minutes. Add leeks or green onions and stir-fry about 1½ minutes more or till vegetables are crisp-tender.

3 tablespoons grated Parmesan *or* Romano cheese

■ Sprinkle with Parmesan or Romano cheese; toss gently. Serve immediately. Makes 2 servings.

TIME ESTIMATE
Start to finish — 20 min.

MENU IDEA
Serve these crisp garden vegetables alongside pork chops and garnish with some fresh basil.

PER SERVING

Calories	137
Protein	5 g
Carbohydrate	12 g
Fat (total)	8 g
Saturated	3 g
Cholesterol	6 mg
Sodium	231 mg
Potassium	371 mg

GINGER-CREAM ASPARAGUS

8 ounces asparagus spears
¼ cup half-and-half *or* light cream
2 tablespoons water
1 teaspoon cornstarch
¼ teaspoon instant chicken bouillon granules
¼ teaspoon grated gingerroot *or* dash ground ginger
¼ teaspoon finely shredded lemon peel

■ In a medium saucepan cook asparagus spears, covered, in a small amount of boiling water for 4 to 5 minutes or till crisp-tender. Drain.

Meanwhile, for sauce, in a small saucepan combine the half-and-half or light cream, water, cornstarch, chicken bouillon granules, gingerroot or ground ginger, and lemon peel. Cook and stir till thickened and bubbly. Cook and stir for 2 minutes more. Serve sauce over asparagus. Makes 2 servings.

TIME ESTIMATE

Start to finish __ 10 min.

PER SERVING

Calories	73
Protein	4 g
Carbohydrate	7 g
Fat (total)	4 g
Saturated	2 g
Cholesterol	11 mg
Sodium	129 mg
Potassium	396 mg

RECIPE TIME ESTIMATES

The timings listed with each recipe should be used only as general guidelines. Some cooks will work faster and others will work slower than the times given. Here are some other points to remember when referring to these timings:

■ Preparation timings have been rounded to the nearest 5-minute increments.

■ Listings include the time to chop, slice, or otherwise prepare ingredients (such as cooking rice when a recipe calls for cooked rice).

■ When a recipe gives an ingredient substitution (1 cup sliced kiwi fruit or halved strawberries), calculations were made using the first ingredient.

■ When a recipe gives alternate cooking methods (such as broiling or grilling directions), timings refer to the first method.

■ Timings assume some steps can be performed simultaneously. For example, vegetables may be cut up while the water for cooking pasta comes to a boil.

■ The preparation of optional ingredients is not included.

LEMON-ALMOND GREEN BEANS

8 ounces fresh green beans *or* 2 cups loose-pack frozen cut *or* French-style green beans

■ If using fresh green beans, cut crosswise into 1-inch pieces or cut lengthwise into thin strips. Cook, covered, in a small amount of boiling water till beans are crisp-tender. (Allow 20 to 25 minutes for 1-inch pieces or 10 to 12 minutes for lengthwise strips.) If using frozen green beans, cook according to package directions. Drain.

¾ cup sliced fresh mushrooms

1 green onion, thinly sliced (2 tablespoons)

1 tablespoon margarine *or* butter

2 tablespoons slivered almonds *or* chopped pecans, toasted

½ teaspoon finely shredded lemon peel

■ Meanwhile, for sauce, in a small saucepan cook the mushrooms and green onion in hot margarine or butter till tender. Remove from heat. Stir in the almonds or pecans and lemon peel. Toss with hot drained beans. Makes 2 servings.

TIME ESTIMATE

Start to finish — 30 min.

MENU IDEA

Complement fish fillets with these beans, spinach salads, and sourdough rolls.

PER SERVING

Calories	153
Protein	5 g
Carbohydrate	13 g
Fat (total)	11 g
Saturated	2 g
Cholesterol	0 mg
Sodium	74 mg
Potassium	553 mg

LEMON-ALMOND BROCCOLI

8 ounces broccoli, cut into ¾-inch pieces, *or* 2 cups loose-pack frozen broccoli cuts

■ Prepare Lemon-Almond Green Beans as directed above, *except* substitute the broccoli for the green beans. If using fresh broccoli, cook, covered, in a small amount of boiling water for 8 to 12 minutes or till crisp-tender. If using frozen broccoli, cook according to package directions. Drain. Continue as above.

PER SERVING

Calories	133
Protein	5 g
Carbohydrate	8 g
Fat (total)	11 g
Saturated	2 g
Cholesterol	0 mg
Sodium	94 mg
Potassium	466 mg

CREAM-CHEESY CORN

2 slices bacon, cut up

■ In a small saucepan cook bacon till crisp. Remove bacon, reserving 1 tablespoon drippings in saucepan. Drain bacon. Set aside.

3 medium ears of fresh corn
** *or* 1½ cups loose-pack**
** frozen corn**
3 tablespoons water
2 tablespoons finely
** chopped onion**
Dash pepper

■ With a sharp knife cut corn from cobs at two-thirds depth of kernels; do not scrape cob. (You should have about 1½ cups of corn.) Add the fresh or frozen corn, water, onion, and pepper to the saucepan. Bring just to boiling. Reduce heat. Cover and simmer for 5 to 7 minutes or till corn is crisp-tender.

½ of a 3-ounce package
** cream cheese, cubed**
1 tablespoon milk
** (optional)**

■ Add the cream cheese to the *undrained* corn mixture in the saucepan. Stir over low heat till melted. If necessary, stir in the milk to make corn mixture of desired consistency. Stir in reserved bacon. Makes 2 servings.

TIME ESTIMATE

Start to finish — 25 min.

MENU IDEA

Fix Herb-Rubbed Pork Chops (see recipe, page 27) to serve with this creamy corn.

PER SERVING

Calories	276
Protein	7 g
Carbohydrate	23 g
Fat (total)	19 g
Saturated	8 g
Cholesterol	42 mg
Sodium	252 mg
Potassium	385 mg

PASTA AND RICE ON-CALL

To save time later, cook extra pasta or rice and save it. Simply cook the desired amount of pasta or rice according to package directions. (Rinse and drain pasta well.) Place freezer bags in 6-ounce custard cups; place ½ cup of pasta or rice into each freezer bag. Seal, label, and freeze till firm. Remove custard cups. Pasta and rice will keep for up to 6 months in the freezer.

To reheat frozen pasta, remove pasta from freezer bag and use a large spoon to carefully lower pasta into boiling water in a saucepan. Return water to boiling and cook for 1 minute. Drain. *To reheat frozen rice,* remove rice from freezer bag and place in a saucepan. Add 1 tablespoon water for each ½ cup of rice. Cover and heat about 5 minutes or till hot. *To reheat in a microwave oven,* return frozen pasta or rice to custard cups. Micro-cook, covered with waxed paper, on 100% power (high) till hot. Allow 1½ to 2 minutes for one ½-cup portion or 2 to 2½ minutes for 2 portions.

BUTTER BRUSH-ONS

Use flavored butters to give extra zip to vegetables, meats, fish, poultry, or breads. To make any of the following brush-ons, stir the suggested seasonings into softened butter or margarine. These butters will keep for up to 2 weeks in the refrigerator or for 1 month in the freezer, so mix up one or two and keep them on hand. You'll find them delicious and easy to use.

For any of the following recipes, start with ¼ cup softened *butter or margarine.*

TOMATO-PEPPER BUTTER

Stir in 2 tablespoons finely snipped *sun-dried tomatoes* (oil pack) and ¼ teaspoon *cracked black pepper.*

Nutrition information per teaspoon: 24 calories, 0 g protein, 0 g carbohydrate, 3 g total fat (2 g saturated), 7 mg cholesterol, 24 mg sodium, 13 mg potassium

ROASTED RED PEPPER BUTTER

With an electric mixer beat in 2 tablespoons chopped canned *roasted sweet red peppers or pimiento* and 1 clove *garlic,* minced. Stir again before serving.

Nutrition information per teaspoon: 23 calories, 0 g protein, 0 g carbohydrate, 3 g total fat (2 g saturated), 7 mg cholesterol, 22 mg sodium, 3 mg potassium

SESAME BUTTER

Stir in 2 teaspoons *toasted sesame seed.*

Nutrition information per teaspoon: 32 calories, 0 g protein, 0 g carbohydrate, 4 g total fat (2 g saturated), 9 mg cholesterol, 28 mg sodium, 3 mg potassium

LEMON BUTTER

Stir in ¼ teaspoon finely shredded *lemon peel* and 1 teaspoon *lemon juice.*

Nutrition information per teaspoon: 31 calories, 0 g protein, 0 g carbohydrate, 4 g total fat (2 g saturated), 10 mg cholesterol, 30 mg sodium, 2 mg potassium

WINE-TARRAGON BUTTER

With an electric mixer beat in 1 tablespoon snipped *fresh tarragon or dillweed* or ¼ teaspoon *dried tarragon, crushed, or dried dillweed,* and 1 tablespoon *dry white wine or dry sherry.*

Nutrition information per teaspoon: 25 calories, 0 g protein, 0 g carbohydrate, 3 g total fat (2 g saturated), 7 mg cholesterol, 23 mg sodium, 2 mg potassium

MUSTARD-SAGE BUTTER

Stir in 1 tablespoon snipped *fresh sage* or ¼ teaspoon *dried sage,* crushed, and 1 to 2 teaspoons *Dijon-style or prepared mustard.*

Nutrition information per teaspoon: 28 calories, 0 g protein, 0 g carbohydrate, 3 g total fat (2 g saturated), 8 mg cholesterol, 36 mg sodium, 1 mg potassium

CRISPY BAKED POTATOES

2 medium baking potatoes (6 to 8 ounces each)

■ Scrub potatoes thoroughly with a vegetable brush. Cut potatoes in half lengthwise.

2 tablespoons margarine *or* butter, melted
¼ teaspoon seasoned salt *or* garlic salt
⅛ teaspoon pepper
Dairy sour cream, sour cream dip with chives, *or* plain yogurt (optional)

■ In an 11x7x1½- or 9x9x2-inch baking pan, combine melted margarine or butter, seasoned salt or garlic salt, and pepper.

Place potatoes, cut side down, in margarine or butter mixture. Bake in a 450° oven for 25 to 30 minutes or till tender and cut sides of potatoes are browned and crispy. Lift out with a spatula. If desired, serve with sour cream, sour cream dip, or yogurt. Serves 2.

TIME ESTIMATE
Start to finish — 35 min.

MENU IDEA
Barbecued ribs, these potatoes, corn on the cob, and sliced tomatoes make a spectacular summertime meal.

PER SERVING
Calories _____ 288
Protein _____ 4 g
Carbohydrate _____ 43 g
Fat (total) _____ 12 g
  Saturated _____ 2 g
Cholesterol _____ 0 mg
Sodium _____ 301 mg
Potassium _____ 718 mg

CRISPY BAKED POTATO WEDGES

■ Prepare Crispy Baked Potatoes as above, *except* after halving potatoes, cut each half lengthwise into 3 or 4 wedges. Place potatoes, cut side down, in melted margarine mixture in baking pan; turn each wedge over. Continue as above, turning potatoes once during baking.

PER SERVING
Same as *Crispy Baked Potatoes.*

CRISPY BAKED SWEET POTATOES

2 medium sweet potatoes (6 to 8 ounces each)
2 tablespoons brown sugar
⅛ teaspoon ground cinnamon

■ Prepare and bake Crispy Baked Potatoes as above, *except* substitute sweet potatoes for baking potatoes and omit the salt and pepper. When potatoes are tender, turn them cut side up in pan. Sprinkle with brown sugar and cinnamon. Return to oven about 5 minutes more or till brown sugar begins to bubble. Omit sour cream, dip, or yogurt.

PER SERVING
Calories _____ 330
Protein _____ 3 g
Carbohydrate _____ 55 g
Fat (total) _____ 12 g
  Saturated _____ 2 g
Cholesterol _____ 0 mg
Sodium _____ 158 mg
Potassium _____ 646 mg

CREAMY MASHED POTATOES

2½ **cups loose-pack frozen hash brown potatoes *or* 1 *or* 2 potatoes (about 10 ounces total), peeled and coarsely chopped**

- In a medium saucepan cook potatoes, covered, in boiling water for 10 to 15 minutes or till tender. Drain. Mash with a potato masher or beat with an electric mixer on low speed.

⅓ **cup dairy sour cream**
1 **tablespoon margarine *or* butter**
¼ **teaspoon garlic salt**
⅛ **teaspoon pepper**
1 **tablespoon milk (optional)**

- Beat in sour cream, margarine or butter, garlic salt, and pepper. If necessary, gradually beat in enough of the milk to make potatoes smooth and fluffy. If necessary, place potato mixture in saucepan; heat through. Makes 2 servings.

TIME ESTIMATE

Start to finish — 25 min.

MENU IDEA

Buttermilk Fried Chicken (see recipe, page 57), corn on the cob, and these potatoes make a hearty meal.

PER SERVING

Calories _____ 255
Protein _____ 4 g
Carbohydrate ____ 30 g
Fat (total) _____ 14 g
  Saturated _____ 6 g
Cholesterol _____ 17 mg
Sodium_____ 307 mg
Potassium _____ 524 mg

CREAMY MASHED SWEET POTATOES

1 **or 2 sweet potatoes (about 10 ounces total), peeled and coarsely chopped**
2 **tablespoons chopped pecans, almonds, *or* walnuts**
  Brown sugar (optional)

- Prepare Creamy Mashed Potatoes as directed above, *except* substitute sweet potatoes for the potatoes. Omit the garlic salt and pepper. Just before serving, stir in the pecans, almonds, or walnuts. If desired, sprinkle with brown sugar.

PER SERVING

Calories _____ 332
Protein _____ 4 g
Carbohydrate ____ 38 g
Fat (total) _____ 19 g
  Saturated _____ 7 g
Cholesterol _____ 17 mg
Sodium_____ 106 mg
Potassium _____ 348 mg

RATATOUILLE

A touch of lemon adds a different twist to this popular dish from the Provence area of France.

½ **of a small onion, thinly sliced and separated into rings (⅓ cup)**
2 **cloves garlic, minced**
2 **tablespoons olive oil**
1 **cup cubed, peeled eggplant**

■ In a medium skillet cook the onion and garlic in hot olive oil for 5 minutes, stirring occasionally. Add the eggplant. Cook for 10 minutes more, stirring occasionally.

TIME ESTIMATE
Start to finish — 35 min.

MENU IDEA
If you wish, spoon this vegetable relish over veal chops. Then, for accompaniments, serve Buttered Pasta (see recipe, page 184) and crusty Italian bread.

½ **of a medium yellow summer squash, halved lengthwise and cut into ¼-inch-thick slices (⅔ cup)**
½ **of a medium green *or* sweet red pepper, cut into 1-inch squares (½ cup)**
1 **tablespoon snipped fresh basil *or* ½ teaspoon dried basil, crushed**
½ **teaspoon finely shredded lemon peel**
1 **tablespoon lemon juice**
⅛ **teaspoon salt**
Dash pepper

■ Stir the squash, green or sweet red pepper, basil, lemon peel, lemon juice, salt, and pepper into the skillet. Bring to boiling; reduce heat. Cover and simmer for 10 to 12 minutes or till the vegetables are tender.

PER SERVING

Calories	193
Protein	3 g
Carbohydrate	12 g
Fat (total)	17 g
Saturated	2 g
Cholesterol	0 mg
Sodium	140 mg
Potassium	373 mg

½ **cup cherry tomatoes, halved**
1 **tablespoon pine nuts *or* slivered almonds**

■ Add the cherry tomatoes to the vegetable mixture. Toss to combine. Sprinkle with pine nuts or almonds. Makes 2 servings.

GRILLED VEGETABLE TIMINGS

Make supper simple by cooking both your meat and vegetables on the grill. If necessary, before grilling precook vegetables, covered, in a small amount of boiling water for the time specified below. Drain well. Generously brush vegetables with melted margarine or butter (see Butter Brush-Ons, page 177) or olive oil for flavor and to prevent the vegetables from sticking to the grill rack. To grill, place vegetables on grill rack directly over *medium-hot* coals (see tip, page 27). Lay vegetables perpendicular to wires on grill rack so they don't fall into coals. Grill, uncovered, following the timings below and turning occasionally. Grill till vegetables are fork tender and slightly charred.

VEGETABLE	PREPARATION	PRECOOKING TIME	GRILLING TIME
Asparagus	Snap off and discard tough bases of stems. Precook, then tie asparagus in bundles with strips of cooked green onion tops.	3 minutes	3 to 5 minutes
Carrots, tiny whole	Cut off tops. Scrub or peel.	3 minutes	3 to 5 minutes
Eggplant	Cut off stem end and blossom end. Cut eggplant crosswise into 1-inch-thick slices.	Do not precook.	8 minutes
Green, sweet red, or yellow peppers	Halve peppers. Remove stems. Discard seeds and membranes. Cut into 1-inch-wide strips.	Do not precook.	8 to 10 minutes
Leeks	Cut off green tops; trim bulb roots and remove 1 or 2 layers of white skin.	Precook 10 minutes or till tender. Halve lengthwise.	5 minutes
New potatoes	Halve potatoes.	Precook 10 minutes or till almost tender.	10 to 12 minutes
Pattypan squash, small	Trim ends.	3 minutes.	20 minutes
Zucchini	Cut off ends. Quarter lengthwise into wedges.	Do not precook.	5 to 6 minutes

LEMONY FETTUCCINE ALFREDO WITH PEAS

Update this 1920s dish for the '90s by adding lemon peel and peas.

¼ cup light cream,
  half-and-half, *or*
  whipping cream
1 tablespooon margarine
  or butter

■ Let the light cream, half-and-half, or whipping cream and margarine or butter come to room temperature (allow about 30 minutes).

3 ounces packaged
  fettuccine, linguine, *or*
  other pasta
½ cup loose-pack frozen
  peas

■ Meanwhile, cook pasta (see chart, page 185), adding peas the last 5 minutes of cooking. Drain immediately in a colander. Return pasta and peas to the warm saucepan.

¼ cup grated Parmesan
  cheese
½ teaspoon finely shredded
  lemon peel
2 tablespoons broken
  pecans *or* walnuts

■ Add the room-temperature cream and margarine, the Parmesan cheese, and lemon peel to the pasta. Toss gently till pasta and peas are well coated. Transfer to warm individual plates. Sprinkle with pecans or walnuts. Serve immediately. Makes 2 servings.

TIME ESTIMATE
Start to finish — 35 min.

MENU IDEA
Team this side dish with grilled salmon fillets and crisp tossed salads.

PER SERVING
Calories _____ 376
Protein _____ 13 g
Carbohydrate _____ 40 g
Fat (total) _____ 18 g
  Saturated _____ 6 g
Cholesterol _____ 28 mg
Sodium_____ 303 mg
Potassium _____ 225 mg

FETTUCCINE ALFREDO

■ Prepare Lemony Fettuccine Alfredo with Peas as directed above, *except* omit the peas and the lemon peel.

PER SERVING
Same as *Lemony Fettuccine Alfredo with Peas,* except:
Calories _____ 344
Protein _____ 11 g
Carbohydrate _____ 35 g
Sodium_____ 268 mg
Potassium _____ 157 mg

LEMONY FETTUCCINE ALFREDO WITH PEAS

BUTTERED PASTA

3 ounces fresh refrigerated *or* 2 ounces packaged linguine *or* other pasta
1 tablespoon margarine *or* butter

■ Cook linguine or other pasta (see chart, opposite). Drain immediately in a colander. Add margarine or butter and toss lightly. Serve immediately. Makes 2 servings.

TIME ESTIMATE
Start to finish _ 15 min.

PER SERVING

Calories _____ 156
Protein _____ 4 g
Carbohydrate _____ 21 g
Fat (total) _____ 6 g
 Saturated _____ 1 g
Cholesterol _____ 6 mg
Sodium _____ 67 mg
Potassium _____ 53 mg

LEMON-PEPPER PASTA

¼ teaspoon finely shredded lemon peel
⅛ teaspoon pepper

■ Prepare Buttered Pasta as directed above, *except* add lemon peel and pepper with margarine or butter and toss lightly.

PER SERVING

Same as *Buttered Pasta.*

CREAMY PASTA WITH PECANS

2 tablespoons half-and-half *or* soft cream cheese
2 tablespoons grated Parmesan cheese
1 tablespoon chopped pecans, toasted

■ Prepare Buttered Pasta as directed above, *except* omit margarine or butter. Return drained linguine or other pasta to the warm saucepan. Add half-and-half or cream cheese, Parmesan cheese, and toasted pecans. Toss gently till pasta is well coated.

PER SERVING

Same as *Buttered Pasta* except:
Calories _____ 173
Cholesterol _____ 16 mg
Potassium _____ 90 mg

PASTA WITH MUSHROOMS

¼ cup sliced fresh mushrooms
1 tablespoon thinly sliced green onion

■ Prepare Buttered Pasta as above, *except* cook mushrooms and green onion in the margarine till tender. Cook and drain pasta as above. Toss mushroom mixture with pasta.

PER SERVING

Same as *Buttered Pasta* except:
Potassium _____ 94 mg

POPPY SEED AND ORANGE PASTA

¼ teaspoon finely shredded orange peel
2 tablespoons orange juice
1 teaspoon poppy seed

■ Prepare Buttered Pasta as directed above, *except* add orange peel, orange juice, and poppy seed with margarine or butter; toss lightly.

PER SERVING

Same as *Buttered Pasta* except:
Calories _____ 171

COOKING PASTA

In a 3-quart saucepan bring water (about 6 cups of water for 2 to 6 ounces of pasta) to boiling. If desired, add ¼ teaspoon *salt* and 1 teaspoon *olive oil or cooking oil*. Add pasta a little at a time so water does not stop boiling. (Hold long pasta, such as spaghetti, at one end and dip other end into water. As pasta softens, gently curl it around pan and down into the water.) Reduce heat slightly. Boil pasta, uncovered, for time specified or till tender but slightly firm. Stir occasionally. Test often for doneness near end of cooking time. Drain immediately in a colander.

PACKAGED PASTA	COOKING TIME
Acini di pepe	5 to 6 minutes
Angel hair pasta	5 to 6 minutes
Bow ties, large	10 minutes
Bow ties, tiny	5 to 6 minutes
Cavatelli	12 minutes
Corkscrew macaroni	8 to 10 minutes
Fettuccine	8 to 10 minutes
Lasagna noodles	10 to 12 minutes
Linguine	8 to 10 minutes
Mafalda noodles	10 to 12 minutes
Manicotti	18 minutes
Mostaccioli or Penne	14 minutes
Orzo or Rosamarina	5 to 8 minutes
Rigatoni	15 minutes
Ring macaroni	9 to 10 minutes
Rope macaroni	10 minutes
Shell macaroni, jumbo	18 minutes
Shell macaroni, medium	12 to 14 minutes
Shell macaroni, tiny	8 to 9 minutes
Spaghetti	10 to 12 minutes
Spaghetti, thin	8 to 10 minutes
Spaghetti, twisted	15 minutes
Tortellini	15 minutes
Vermicelli	5 to 7 minutes
Wagon wheel macaroni	12 minutes
Ziti	14 to 15 minutes

FRESH REFRIGERATED PASTA	COOKING TIME
Angel hair pasta	1 to 2 minutes
Bow ties	2 to 3 minutes
Fettuccine	1½ to 2 minutes
Linguine	1½ to 2 minutes
Ravioli	6 to 8 minutes
Tortellini	6 to 8 minutes

In recipes that call for packaged pasta, you may substitute 3 ounces fresh refrigerated pasta for 2 ounces of the packaged product.

TOMATO-AND-BASIL-SAUCED PASTA

1 small onion, chopped
   (⅓ cup)
1 clove garlic, minced
1 tablespoon margarine *or*
   butter

■ In a medium saucepan cook the onion and garlic in hot margarine or butter till onion is tender but not brown.

1 14½-ounce can whole
   Italian-style tomatoes,
   cut up, *or* 1 pound ripe
   fresh plum tomatoes,
   peeled and chopped
1 tablespoon snipped fresh
   basil *or* oregano *or* ½
   teaspoon dried basil *or*
   oregano, crushed
¼ to ½ teaspoon sugar
   Dash pepper
2 teaspoons capers,
   drained, *or* 2
   tablespoons sliced
   pitted ripe olives

■ Carefully stir in the *undrained* canned or fresh tomatoes, basil or oregano, sugar, and pepper. Bring to boiling; reduce heat. Simmer, uncovered, about 20 minutes or till of desired consistency. Stir in the capers or ripe olives.

2 ounces packaged
   spaghetti, linguine, *or*
   other pasta

■ Meanwhile, cook the pasta (see chart, page 185). Drain immediately. Serve the sauce over the pasta. Makes 2 servings.

TIME ESTIMATE

Start to finish — 35 min.

MENU IDEA

This side dish, beef steaks, hard rolls, and glasses of Italian red wine is a menu made in heaven.

PER SERVING

Calories	212
Protein	6 g
Carbohydrate	34 g
Fat (total)	7 g
Saturated	1 g
Cholesterol	0 mg
Sodium	451 mg
Potassium	565 mg

CHEESY TOMATO-AND-BASIL-SAUCED PASTA

¼ cup shredded mozzarella
   or provolone cheese
   (1 ounce)

■ Prepare Tomato-and-Basil-Sauced Pasta as directed above, *except* add the drained pasta to the sauce. Toss to coat. Divide pasta mixture between 2 individual au gratin dishes, individual casseroles, or 10-ounce custard cups. Sprinkle with cheese. Place the dishes or custard cups in a baking pan. Bake in a 400° oven for 5 to 8 minutes or till bubbly. Makes 2 servings.

PER SERVING

Calories	248
Protein	10 g
Carbohydrate	34 g
Fat (total)	9 g
Saturated	3 g
Cholesterol	8 mg
Sodium	517 mg
Potassium	577 mg

HOT COOKED RICE

⅔ cup water
⅓ cup long grain *or*
   brown rice
1 teaspoon margarine *or*
   butter
⅛ teaspoon salt *or*
   ½ teaspoon instant
   chicken bouillon
   granules

■ In a small saucepan combine the water, rice, margarine or butter, and salt or chicken bouillon granules. Bring to boiling; reduce heat. Cover and simmer about 15 minutes for long grain rice (about 40 minutes for brown rice) or till rice is tender and liquid is absorbed. Remove from heat. Let stand, covered, for 5 minutes. Makes 2 servings.

TIME ESTIMATE
Start to finish — 25 min.

PER SERVING
Calories ——————— 128
Protein ——————— 2 g
Carbohydrate ——— 24 g
Fat (total) ——————— 2 g
  Saturated ——————— 0 g
Cholesterol ———— 0 mg
Sodium ———— 157 mg
Potassium ———— 36 mg

CONFETTI RICE

2 tablespoons shredded
   carrot
1 green onion, sliced

■ Prepare Hot Cooked Rice as directed above, *except* stir the carrot and green onion into the saucepan along with the rice.

PER SERVING
Same as *Hot Cooked Rice.*

CURRIED RICE

1 stalk celery, thinly sliced
   (½ cup)
2 tablespoons raisins
½ teaspoon curry powder

■ Prepare Hot Cooked Rice as directed above, *except* increase water to ¾ *cup* and stir celery*, raisins, and curry powder into saucepan along with rice. (*For brown rice, stir in celery during the last 15 minutes of cooking.)

PER SERVING
Same as *Hot Cooked Rice*, except:
Calories ——————— 166
Potassium ———— 208 mg

FRUITED RICE

3 tablespoons mixed dried
   fruit bits
⅛ teaspoon ground ginger

■ Prepare Hot Cooked Rice as directed above, *except* increase the water to ¾ *cup* and stir the dried fruit bits and ginger into the saucepan along with the rice.

PER SERVING
Same as *Hot Cooked Rice*, except:
Calories ——————— 166
Potassium ———— 142 mg

PARSLEY-HERB RICE

¼ teaspoon dried basil,
   crushed
2 tablespoons snipped
   parsley

■ Prepare Hot Cooked Rice as directed above, *except* stir the basil into the saucepan along with the rice. Stir the parsley into the cooked rice just before serving.

PER SERVING
Same as *Hot Cooked Rice.*

187

RICE PILAF

With a variety of colors and textures, this rice pilaf dresses up a simple main dish.

⅓ cup long grain *or* basmati rice

2 tablespoons finely chopped prosciutto *or* fully cooked ham

1 clove garlic, minced

1 tablespoon margarine *or* butter

■ In a medium saucepan cook and stir the long grain or basmati rice, prosciutto or ham, and garlic in hot margarine or butter about 5 minutes or till rice is light brown.

TIME ESTIMATE
Start to finish — 30 min.

MENU IDEA
Serve this festive looking rice dish with chicken and sliced zucchini.

¾ cup water

2 tablespoons dried currants *or* raisins

2 tablespoons chopped sweet red *or* green pepper

2 tablespoons dry white wine, apple juice, *or* water

¼ teaspoon instant chicken bouillon granules

⅛ teaspoon dried basil, oregano, *or* Italian seasoning, crushed

2 green onions, sliced (¼ cup)

2 tablespoons pine nuts, slivered almonds, *or* chopped pecans, toasted

■ Carefully stir in the water; currants or raisins; sweet red or green pepper; wine, apple juice, or water; chicken bouillon granules; and basil, oregano, or Italian seasoning. Bring the mixture to boiling; reduce heat. Cover and simmer for 15 to 20 minutes or till the rice is tender and the liquid is absorbed. Stir in the green onions and pine nuts, almonds, or pecans. Serve immediately. Makes 2 servings.

PER SERVING

Calories	266
Protein	7 g
Carbohydrate	35 g
Fat (total)	11 g
Saturated	2 g
Cholesterol	5 mg
Sodium	301 mg
Potassium	263 mg

FRUITY WILD AND BROWN RICE PILAF

Enhance the nutlike flavor of both wild and brown rice by adding almonds to this tasty pilaf.

¼ **cup chopped onion**
¼ **cup chopped celery**
1 **tablespoon margarine *or* butter**

1 **cup water**
2 **tablespoons wild rice, rinsed**
1 **tablespoon dry sherry *or* dry white wine**
½ **teaspoon instant chicken bouillon granules**
¼ **cup regular brown rice**

⅓ **cup chopped nectarines *or* chopped, peeled peaches *or* sliced strawberries**
2 **tablespoons chopped almonds *or* pecans**
¼ **teaspoon finely shredded lemon *or* orange peel**

■ In a medium saucepan cook the onion and celery in hot margarine or butter till the vegetables are tender but not brown.

■ Stir in the water, wild rice, dry sherry or dry white wine, and chicken bouillon granules. Bring to boiling; reduce heat. Cover and simmer for 15 minutes. Stir in the brown rice. Return to boiling; reduce heat. Cover and simmer for 25 to 30 minutes more or till the rice is tender and the liquid is absorbed. Remove from heat.

■ Gently fold in the nectarines, peaches, or strawberries; almonds or pecans; and lemon or orange peel. Makes 2 servings.

TIME ESTIMATE
Start to finish — 55 min.

MENU IDEA
Spoon this two-rice combo alongside grilled turkey tenderloin steaks.

PER SERVING
Calories _____ 248
Protein _____ 5 g
Carbohydrate _____ 32 g
Fat (total) _____ 11 g
 Saturated _____ 2 g
Cholesterol _____ 0 mg
Sodium _____ 310 mg
Potassium _____ 274 mg

BAKED DESSERTS AND BREADS

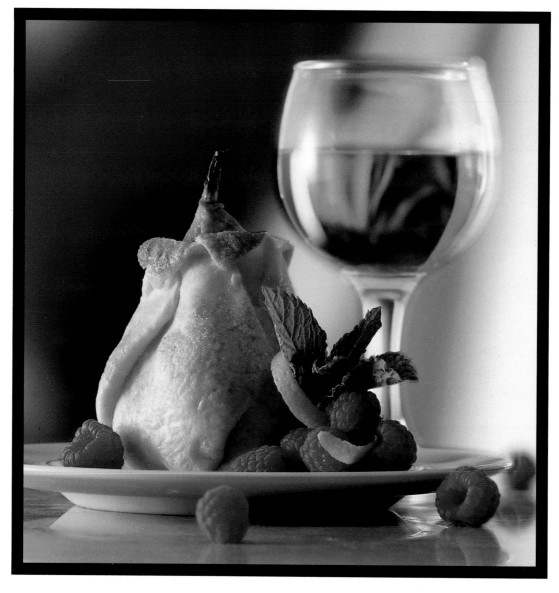

COUNTRY-STYLE PEAR DUMPLINGS

COUNTRY-STYLE PEAR DUMPLINGS

For a presentation with pizzazz, garnish these dumplings with fresh mint leaves, fresh raspberries, and a twist of orange peel.

2 portions Basic Pastry
Dough (see recipe, page
194)
2 tablespoons finely
chopped pecans,
almonds, *or* walnuts
1 tablespoon brown sugar
¼ teaspoon finely shredded
orange *or* lemon peel
Dash ground cinnamon

■ Prepare Basic Pastry Dough as directed. Cover 2 portions and set aside. Lightly grease an 8x8x2-inch baking dish. Set baking dish aside.

In a small bowl stir together the pecans, almonds, or walnuts; brown sugar; orange or lemon peel; and cinnamon. Set aside.

2 small pears

■ Peel pears. Core the pears from the bottom, leaving the stems in place. Press *half* of the nut mixture into the center of *each* pear. Set aside.

On a lightly floured surface, roll each portion of pastry dough into a 7- to 8-inch square. Place a pear in the center of each square. Moisten the edges of the pastry with water. Bring the pastry up around the pear, pleating and pressing to seal around the stem. Roll the pastry back slightly to expose the stem. Place the wrapped pears in the prepared baking dish.

1 slightly beaten egg white
1 tablespoon water
Sugar
Half-and-half *or* light
cream (optional)

■ In a small bowl stir together the egg white and water. Brush egg white mixture over the wrapped pears. Sprinkle with sugar. Bake in a 375° oven about 40 minutes or till the pears are tender and pastry is golden. Cover pears loosely with foil the last 10 to 15 minutes of baking to prevent overbrowning. Serve warm. If desired, serve with half-and-half or light cream. Makes 2 dumplings.

TIME ESTIMATE
Preparation —— 35 min.
Baking ———— 40 min.

MENU IDEA
End an elegant meal with these flaky pastry dumplings and glasses of wine.

PER DUMPLING
Calories	462
Protein	7 g
Carbohydrate	60 g
Fat (total)	23 g
Saturated	5 g
Cholesterol	0 mg
Sodium	165 mg
Potassium	286 mg

BRICKLE-CRUNCH PEACH TARTS

1 tablespoon sugar
1 teaspoon all-purpose
   flour
⅛ teaspoon ground
   cinnamon
1 cup thinly sliced, peeled
   peaches *or* frozen
   unsweetened peach
   slices
1 tablespoon snipped dried
   tart red cherries *or*
   cranberries, *or* raisins
½ teaspoon lemon juice

■ In a medium mixing bowl stir together the sugar, flour, and cinnamon. Add the peaches; cherries, cranberries, or raisins; and the lemon juice. Toss to coat peaches. If using frozen peach slices, let the peach mixture stand for 15 to 30 minutes or till the peaches are *partially* thawed but still icy.

TIME ESTIMATE

Preparation ____ 35 min.
Baking _____ 25 min.

MENU IDEA

Go country-style with Buttermilk Fried Chicken (see recipe, page 57) and a side dish of buttered corn.

PER TART

Calories _____445
Protein _____6 g
Carbohydrate _____56 g
Fat (total) _____23 g
   Saturated _____5 g
Cholesterol _____0 mg
Sodium_____188 mg
Potassium _____243 mg

2 portions Basic Pastry
   Dough (see recipe, page
   194)

■ Prepare Basic Pastry Dough as directed. On a lightly floured surface, roll each portion of dough into a 7½-inch circle. Trim circles to 7 inches. Transfer the circles to an ungreased baking sheet. Stir the peach mixture. Spoon *half* of the peach mixture in the center of each circle, leaving about a 1½-inch border. Fold the border up around peach mixture, crimping pastry to form an edge (see photo, right).

2 tablespoons almond
   brickle pieces
1 tablespoon chopped
   almonds *or* pecans
   Vanilla ice cream
   (optional)

■ Mix brickle pieces and almonds. Sprinkle over peach mixture. Bake in a 375° oven about 25 minutes or till edges are golden and peaches are tender. Cool tarts slightly on baking sheet on a wire rack. Serve warm. If desired, top with ice cream. Makes 2 tarts.

BRICKLE-CRUNCH APPLE TARTS

1 cup thinly sliced, peeled
   apples

■ Prepare Brickle-Crunch Peach Tarts as directed above, *except* substitute the apple slices for the peach slices.

PER TART

Same as *Brickle-Crunch Peach Tarts,* except:
Potassium _____138 mg

INDIVIDUAL CHERRY PIES

No pie plates required! Just take plump and juicy cherries, encase them in flaky pastry, and bake them on a baking sheet.

2 tablespoons sugar
1½ teaspoons cornstarch
¾ cup pitted tart red cherries *or* frozen unsweetened, pitted, tart red cherries

■ In a medium mixing bowl stir together the sugar and cornstarch. Add the fresh or frozen cherries. Toss till cherries are coated.

TIME ESTIMATE

Preparation ____ 25 min.
Baking _____ 18 min.

PER PIE

Calories _____ 409
Protein _____ 6 g
Carbohydrate _____ 52 g
Fat (total) _____ 20 g
  Saturated _____ 5 g
Cholesterol ____ 107 mg
Sodium _____ 138 mg
Potassium _____ 123 mg

2 portions Basic Pastry Dough (see recipe, page 194)
1 slightly beaten egg yolk
1 tablespoon water

■ Prepare Basic Pastry Dough as directed. On a lightly floured surface, roll each portion of dough into a 6-inch square. Place cherry mixture on one-half of each square. Combine the egg yolk and water. Moisten the edges of each square with some of the egg yolk mixture. Fold dough in half over cherry mixture, forming a rectangle. Seal and crimp edges.

Sugar
Vanilla ice cream (optional)

■ Transfer the pies to an ungreased baking sheet. Cut slits in the top crust to allow steam to escape. Brush with egg yolk mixture and sprinkle with sugar. Bake in a 375° oven about 18 minutes or till edges are golden. Remove pies from the baking sheet and cool slightly on a wire rack. Serve warm. If desired, top with ice cream. Makes 2 pies.

INDIVIDUAL CHERRY-BERRY PIES

½ cup fresh *or* frozen blueberries

■ Prepare Individual Cherry Pies as directed above, *except* decrease the amount of cherries to ½ *cup* and add the blueberries.

PER PIE

Same as *Individual Cherry Pies,* except:
Calories _____ 421

BASIC PASTRY DOUGH

Use this pastry when making any of the dessert recipes on pages 237–239. Since this recipe makes four portions, freeze two for another use.

1¼ cups all-purpose flour
¼ teaspoon salt
⅓ cup shortening

■ In a medium mixing bowl stir together the flour and salt. Using a pastry blender, cut in the shortening till pieces are the size of small peas.

TIME ESTIMATE
Start to finish — 15 min.

3 to 4 tablespoons *cold* water

■ Sprinkle *1 tablespoon* of the water over part of the mixture, then gently toss with a fork. Push moistened dough to the side of the bowl. Repeat, using 1 tablespoon of water at a time, till all dough is moistened. Divide into 4 equal portions. Shape each portion into a ball and flatten slightly. Use 2 of the portions immediately as directed in individual recipes.

■ To store the remaining 2 portions, seal portions of dough in moisture- and vapor-proof wrap, label, and freeze for up to 3 months. To use, let dough stand at room temperature about 1 hour or till thawed. Continue as directed in individual recipes. Makes 4 portions total.

OUT OF BUTTERMILK?

If a recipe calls for buttermilk and you don't have any on hand, sour milk is a good substitute. To make ½ cup of sour milk, place 1½ teaspoons lemon juice or vinegar in a glass measuring cup. Add enough milk to make ½ cup total liquid; stir. Let the mixture stand 5 minutes before using.

CORN BREAD CHERRY COBBLER

Cornmeal in the biscuits gives a new twist to an old favorite.

2 cups pitted tart red cherries *or* ½ of a 16-ounce package frozen unsweetened, pitted, tart red cherries

⅓ cup sugar

1 tablespoon cornstarch

1 tablespoon orange juice *or* water

■ For filling, in a medium saucepan combine the cherries, sugar, cornstarch, and orange juice or water. If using fresh cherries, let the mixture stand for 10 minutes. Or, if using frozen cherries, let the mixture stand for 20 minutes.

3 tablespoons cornmeal

2 tablespoons all-purpose flour

2 teaspoons finely chopped pecans *or* walnuts

1½ teaspoons sugar

½ teaspoon baking powder

1 tablespoon margarine *or* butter

1 slightly beaten egg yolk

2 tablespoons milk

■ Meanwhile, for biscuit topping, in a small mixing bowl stir together the cornmeal, flour, pecans or walnuts, sugar, and baking powder. Cut in the margarine or butter till the mixture resembles coarse crumbs. In a small bowl stir together the egg yolk and milk. Add the egg mixture all at once to the cornmeal mixture. Using a fork, stir *just till moistened.*

1 teaspoon sugar

Dash ground cinnamon

Half-and-half, light cream, *or* vanilla ice cream (optional)

■ Cook and stir the cherry mixture over medium heat till thickened and bubbly. Cook and stir for 1 minute more. Reduce heat.

Immediately spoon biscuit topping into 4 mounds on top of hot cherry mixture. Stir together the sugar and cinnamon. Sprinkle sugar mixture over the biscuit topping. Cover saucepan and simmer over low heat about 10 minutes or till a wooden toothpick inserted in the topping comes out clean. Serve warm. If desired, serve with half-and-half, light cream, or ice cream. Makes 2 servings.

TIME ESTIMATE
Start to finish — 35 min.

PER SERVING
Calories ———— 414
Protein ———— 6 g
Carbohydrate ——— 76 g
Fat (total) ———— 11 g
  Saturated ———— 2 g
Cholesterol ——— 108 mg
Sodium ———— 153 mg
Potassium ———— 284 mg

BLUEBERRY AND COCONUT CRISP

Create luscious sundaes by serving the crisp over scoops of vanilla ice cream.

1½ **cups fresh** *or* **frozen blueberries** *or* **unsweetened, pitted, tart red cherries**
2 **tablespoons coconut**

2 **tablespoons rolled oats**
2 **tablespoons sugar** *or* **brown sugar**
1 **tablespoon all-purpose flour**
1 **tablespoon margarine** *or* **butter, softened**
⅛ **teaspoon ground ginger, nutmeg,** *or* **cinnamon**
2 **tablespoons chopped pecans, walnuts,** *or* **almonds (optional)**
Vanilla ice cream, half-and-half, *or* **light cream (optional)**

■ For filling, thaw fruit, if frozen. *Do not drain.* In a medium mixing bowl toss the blueberries or cherries with the coconut. Divide fruit-coconut mixture between two 10-ounce custard cups.

■ For topping, in a small mixing bowl stir together the oats, sugar or brown sugar, flour, margarine or butter, and ginger, nutmeg, or cinnamon. If desired, stir in the chopped pecans, walnuts, or almonds. Sprinkle topping over filling.

   Bake in a 375° oven for 25 to 30 minutes or till fruit is tender and topping is golden. Serve warm. If desired, serve with ice cream, half-and-half, or light cream. Serves 2.

TIME ESTIMATE
Preparation ____ 10 min.
Baking _____ 25 min.

MENU IDEA
Grill Cheesy Sour Cream and Onion Burgers (see recipe, page 148) and serve with a handful of potato chips.

PER SERVING
Calories _____ 216
Protein _____ 2 g
Carbohydrate _____ 36 g
Fat (total) _____ 8 g
   Saturated _____ 3 g
Cholesterol _____ 0 mg
Sodium_____ 75 mg
Potassium _____ 139 mg

CHEESY APPLE CRISP

1½ **cups sliced, peeled apples**
2 **tablespoons finely shredded cheddar** *or* **Swiss cheese**
2 **tablespoons water** *or* **apple juice**

■ Prepare Blueberry and Coconut Crisp as directed above, *except* substitute the apples for the blueberries or cherries and substitute the cheddar or Swiss cheese for the coconut. Add *1 tablespoon* of the water or apple juice to the cheese-fruit mixture in *each* custard cup.

PER SERVING
Same as *Blueberry and Coconut Crisp,* except:
Calories _____ 210
Carbohydrate _____ 31 g
Fat (total) _____ 9 g
Cholesterol _____ 7 mg
Sodium_____ 112 mg
Potassium _____ 127 mg

SIMPLE WHITE CAKE WITH CHOCOLATE GLAZE

⅔ cup all-purpose flour
⅓ cup sugar
1 teaspoon baking powder
⅓ cup milk
1 egg *or* 1 egg white
2 tablespoons margarine *or* butter, softened
½ teaspoon vanilla

■ Grease and lightly flour an 8x4x2- or 7½x3½x2-inch loaf pan. Set pan aside.

In a medium mixing bowl stir together flour, sugar, and baking powder. Add the milk, egg or egg white, margarine or butter, and vanilla. Beat with an electric mixer on low to medium speed about 30 seconds or till combined. Beat on medium to high speed for 1 minute. Pour batter into prepared pan.

■ Bake in a 350° oven 20 to 25 minutes for the 8-inch pan or 25 to 30 minutes for the 7½-inch pan or till a wooden toothpick inserted near the center comes out clean. Cool on a wire rack for 5 minutes. Remove cake from pan. Cool thoroughly on a wire rack.

2 squares (2 ounces) semisweet chocolate, cut up
1 tablespoon margarine or butter
¾ cup sifted powdered sugar
1 tablespoon hot water

■ For chocolate glaze, in a small saucepan melt chocolate and margarine or butter over low heat, stirring frequently. Remove from heat. Stir in the powdered sugar and hot water. Stir in additional hot water, if needed, to make glaze of drizzling consistency.

Spoon glaze over cake, allowing excess to drip down the sides. Makes 4 servings.

TIME ESTIMATE

Preparation ____ 10 min.
Baking _____ 20 min.
Cooling _____ 1 hr.

PER SERVING

Calories _____ 390
Protein _____ 5 g
Carbohydrate _____ 61 g
Fat (total) _____ 16 g
  Saturated _____ 5 g
Cholesterol _____ 55 mg
Sodium _____ 201 mg
Potassium _____ 125 mg

STRAWBERRY-CREAM-CHEESE TORTE

½ cup soft-style cream cheese with strawberry
1 cup sliced strawberries
½ cup whipped cream (optional)

■ Prepare Simple White Cake with Chocolate Glaze as directed above, *except* omit chocolate glaze. Split cake in half horizontally.

Spread the cream cheese over the bottom layer. Add cake top. Serve with strawberries and, if desired, whipped cream. Store leftovers in the refrigerator. Makes 4 servings.

PER SERVING

Calories _____ 243
Carbohydrate _____ 37 g
Fat (total) _____ 9 g
  Saturated _____ 2 g
Sodium _____ 177 mg
Potassium _____ 140 mg

STRAWBERRY SHORTCAKE WITH CREAM CHEESE SAUCE

Strawberries got their name from the way the berries originally were sent to market—strung on straw. Heap some luscious berries atop flaky biscuits for a delightfully all-American dessert.

2 cups sliced strawberries
1 tablespoon sugar (optional)

■ Grease a baking sheet. Set aside. In a medium bowl stir together the strawberries and, if desired, the sugar. Set aside.

½ cup all-purpose flour
¾ teaspoon baking powder
⅛ teaspoon cream of tartar
⅛ teaspoon baking soda
2 tablespoons margarine *or* butter
¼ cup buttermilk *or* sour milk (see tip, page 194)

■ For dough, in a medium mixing bowl stir together the flour, baking powder, cream of tartar, and baking soda. Cut in the margarine or butter till mixture resembles coarse crumbs. Make a well in the center of the dry ingredients, then add the buttermilk or sour milk all at once. Using a fork, stir *just till moistened.*

Sugar (optional)

■ Drop dough into 2 mounds onto the prepared baking sheet. If desired, sprinkle with sugar. Bake in a 450° oven for 10 to 12 minutes or till golden.

Cream Cheese Sauce or ¾ cup whipped cream

■ Split shortcakes into 2 layers. Place bottom layers into 2 individual bowls. Spoon some of the strawberries and Cream Cheese Sauce or whipped cream over the bottom layers. Add top layers. Spoon more strawberries and the remaining Cream Cheese Sauce or whipped cream over tops. Serve immediately. Pass any remaining berries. Makes 2 shortcakes.

TIME ESTIMATE
Start to finish — 40 min.

MENU IDEA
In the spring or early summer, dish up this luscious dessert after a meal of grilled steaks, whole tiny new potatoes, and crisp lettuce salads.

PER SHORTCAKE
Calories _____ 395
Protein _____ 7 g
Carbohydrate _____ 40 g
Fat (total) _____ 23 g
    Saturated _____ 9 g
Cholesterol _____ 29 mg
Sodium_____ 407 mg
Potassium _____ 402 mg

CREAM CHEESE SAUCE

¼ cup dairy sour cream
2 tablespoons soft-style cream cheese
1 teaspoon sugar

■ In a small mixing bowl stir together the sour cream, soft-style cream cheese, and sugar till smooth.

STRAWBERRY SHORTCAKE WITH CREAM CHEESE SAUCE

ALMOND-PRALINE CHOCOLATE UPSIDE-DOWN CAKE

Since this cake is super satisfying served warm, place any leftover cake on a microwave-safe plate and reheat it on 100 percent power (high) about 30 seconds.

2 tablespoons margarine *or* butter
⅓ cup packed brown sugar
2 tablespoons half-and-half *or* light cream
¼ cup coarsely chopped almonds *or* pecans

■ For syrup, in a small saucepan melt the margarine or butter. Stir in the brown sugar and half-and-half or light cream. Cook and stir *just till blended.* Pour syrup into an 8x4x2-inch loaf pan or divide between two 10-ounce custard cups. Sprinkle almonds or pecans evenly over the syrup. Set pan or custard cups aside.

½ cup all-purpose flour
½ cup sugar
2 tablespoons unsweetened cocoa powder
½ teaspoon baking powder
¼ teaspoon baking soda
⅓ cup milk
2 tablespoons margarine or butter, softened
1 egg *or* 1 egg white
¼ teaspoon vanilla

■ For batter, in a medium mixing bowl stir together the flour, sugar, cocoa powder, baking powder, and baking soda. Add milk, margarine or butter, egg or egg white, and vanilla. Beat with an electric mixer on low to medium speed about 30 seconds or till combined. Beat on medium to high speed for 1 minute. Gently pour or spoon the batter over the syrup and nuts in the pan or custard cups. If using custard cups, place on a baking sheet.

Whipped cream *or* vanilla ice cream

■ Bake in a 350° oven for 25 to 30 minutes or till a wooden toothpick inserted near the center comes out clean. Cool on a wire rack for 5 minutes. Loosen sides and invert the cake onto a plate. Serve cake warm with whipped cream or ice cream. Serves 4.

TIME ESTIMATE
Preparation ____ 15 min.
Baking _____ 25 min.

MENU IDEA
Beany Ham Soup (see recipe, page 168) and an assortment of crackers are a good prelude to this delectably delicious cake.

PER SERVING
Calories _____ 468
Protein _____ 7 g
Carbohydrate _____ 59 g
Fat (total) _____ 24 g
   Saturated _____ 8 g
Cholesterol _____ 78 mg
Sodium _____ 266 mg
Potassium _____ 244 mg

FUDGE BROWNIES WITH COCOA GLAZE

½ cup sugar
¼ cup margarine *or* butter
3 tablespoons unsweetened cocoa powder
1 egg
½ teaspoon vanilla

■ Grease a 9x5x3-inch loaf pan; set aside. In a small saucepan stir together sugar, margarine or butter, and cocoa powder. Cook and stir over medium heat till margarine melts. Remove from heat; cool for 5 minutes. Add the egg and vanilla. Beat lightly by hand *just till combined.*

⅓ cup all-purpose flour
¼ teaspoon baking powder
⅛ teaspoon salt
¼ cup chopped walnuts
Cocoa Glaze

■ Stir in flour, baking powder, and salt. Stir in walnuts. Spread batter into the prepared pan. Bake in a 350° oven for 12 to 15 minutes or till a wooden toothpick inserted near the center comes out clean. Cool completely. Frost with Cocoa Glaze. Makes 6 servings.

TIME ESTIMATE

Preparation	15 min.
Baking	12 min.
Cooling	1 hr.
Frosting	5 min.

PER SERVING

Calories	260
Protein	3 g
Carbohydrate	33 g
Fat (total)	14 g
Saturated	3 g
Cholesterol	36 mg
Sodium	180 mg
Potassium	90 mg

COCOA GLAZE

½ cup sifted powdered sugar
1 tablespoon unsweetened cocoa powder
1 tablespoon margarine *or* butter, softened
¼ teaspooon vanilla

■ In a small mixing bowl combine the powdered sugar and cocoa powder. Beat in margarine or butter, vanilla, and enough *hot water* (2 to 4 teaspoons) to make a smooth glaze.

TOASTING NUTS

Toasting nuts brings out their full flavor and aroma. It also helps keep them crisp when they're added to moist mixtures, such as salad dressings, sauces, and fruit salads. To toast less than ¼ cup of nuts, place the nuts in a small skillet. Cook over medium heat for 5 to 7 minutes or till nuts are golden brown, stirring often. To toast more than ¼ cup of nuts, place the nuts in a shallow baking pan. Bake in a 350° oven for 5 to 10 minutes or till nuts are golden brown, stirring once or twice.

CHOCOLATE-CHIP OAT COOKIES

⅔ **cup rolled oats**

■ For oat flour, place the oats in a blender container. Cover and blend till the oats turn into a powder. Set aside.

TIME ESTIMATE
Preparation ____ 15 min.
Baking ____ 8 min.

¼ **cup sugar**
¼ **cup packed brown sugar**
¼ **cup margarine *or* butter, softened**
1 **egg**
½ **teaspoon vanilla**

■ In a large mixing bowl use a wooden spoon to stir together the sugar, brown sugar, and margarine or butter. Mix till smooth. Stir in the egg and vanilla.

PER COOKIE
Calories ____ 139
Protein ____ 2 g
Carbohydrate ____ 18 g
Fat (total) ____ 7 g
 Saturated ____ 2 g
Cholesterol ____ 18 mg
Sodium ____ 70 mg
Potassium ____ 67 mg

⅓ **cup all-purpose flour**
¼ **teaspoon baking soda**
½ **cup semisweet chocolate pieces**
¼ **cup chopped nuts (optional)**

■ Add the oat flour, all-purpose flour, and baking soda. Stir till combined. Stir in the chocolate pieces and, if desired, nuts.

Drop dough from a rounded teaspoon 2 inches apart onto an ungreased cookie sheet. Bake in a 375° oven for 8 to 9 minutes or till edges are lightly browned. Remove from cookie sheet; cool. Makes 12 cookies.

COCONUT-LEMON OAT COOKIES

½ **cup coconut**
½ **teaspoon finely shredded lemon peel**

■ Prepare Chocolate-Chip Oat Cookies as directed above, *except* omit chocolate pieces. In a small bowl toss coconut with lemon peel. After stirring in all the dry ingredients, stir in the coconut mixture and, if desired, nuts.

PER COOKIE
Same as *Chocolate-Chip Oat Cookies,* except:
Calories ____ 118
Potassium ____ 53 mg

ALMOND OAT COOKIES

⅓ **cup toasted chopped almonds**
¼ **cup almond brickle pieces**

■ Prepare Chocolate-Chip Oat Cookies as directed above, *except* omit chocolate pieces and optional nuts. After stirring in all the dry ingredients, stir in the almonds and almond brickle pieces.

PER COOKIE
Same as *Chocolate-Chip Oat Cookies,* except:
Sodium ____ 87 mg
Potassium ____ 69 mg

CINNAMON AND SUGAR SLICES

¼ **cup shortening**
¼ **cup margarine *or* butter**
1½ **cups all-purpose flour**
½ **cup sugar *or* packed brown sugar**
1 **egg *or* 1 large egg white**
1 **tablespoon milk**
½ **teaspoon vanilla**
¼ **teaspoon baking soda**
⅛ **teaspoon salt**

1 **tablespoon sugar**
½ **teaspoon ground cinnamon *or* ¼ teaspoon ground nutmeg**

■ In a large mixing bowl beat shortening and margarine or butter with an electric mixer on medium to high speed about 30 seconds or till softened.

Add about *half* of the flour to the shortening mixture. Then add the sugar or brown sugar, egg or egg white, milk, vanilla, baking soda, and salt. Beat till thoroughly combined, scraping sides of bowl occasionally. Beat or stir in the remaining flour.

■ Shape dough into two 4-inch rolls. Wrap the rolls in waxed paper or plastic wrap. Chill for 4 to 24 hours or till dough is firm enough to slice. *Or,* store in the freezer for up to 3 months.

To bake, cut each roll of dough into 12 to 16 slices. Place slices on an ungreased cookie sheet. Stir together the sugar and cinnamon or nutmeg. Sprinkle over cookies.

Bake in a 375° oven for 8 to 10 minutes or till edges are firm and the bottoms are lightly browned. Remove cookies and cool on a wire rack. Makes 24 to 32 cookies.

TIME ESTIMATE
Preparation ___ 15 min.
Chilling _____ 4 hrs.
Baking_____ 8 min.

MENU IDEA
Pack 'em for a picinic along with Pastrami Kabob Sandwiches (see recipe, page 146), your favorite snack chips, and fresh fruit.

PER COOKIE
Calories _____86
Protein_____1 g
Carbohydrate ____11 g
Fat (total) _____4 g
Saturated _____1 g
Cholesterol _____9 mg
Sodium_____45 mg
Potassium _____13 mg

VANILLA-DIPPED CHOCOLATE SLICES

¼ **cup unsweetened cocoa powder**
1 **cup vanilla-flavored pieces *or* cut-up vanilla-flavored candy coating**

■ Prepare Cinnamon and Sugar Slices as directed above, *except* reduce flour to *1¼ cups* and add cocoa powder with the stirred-in sugar. Omit sprinkling dough with cinnamon-sugar mixture. Continue as directed above.

In a small saucepan melt the vanilla-flavored pieces or candy coating over low heat. Dip *half* of each cooled baked cookie into the melted coating. Place on waxed paper and let stand till coating is set.

PER COOKIE
Calories _____119
Protein_____1 g
Carbohydrate ____15 g
Fat (total) _____6 g
Saturated _____3 g
Cholesterol _____9 mg
Sodium_____45 mg
Potassium _____22 mg

BEVY OF BREADS

Pull piping hot bread from the oven, anytime. It's a cinch when you keep this no-knead bread dough on hand. Mix up the dough (right), then use it in the recipes on pages 254–257. Now, homemade bread is truly one of life's *simple* pleasures.

EASY-MIX YEAST BREAD

3¾ cups all-purpose flour
 1 package active dry yeast
 ½ teaspoon dried dillweed, *or* dried
    sage *or* basil, crushed (optional)
1¼ cups milk
 ¼ cup margarine, butter, *or* shortening
 2 to 4 tablespoons sugar
 ½ teaspoon salt
 1 egg *or* 2 egg whites

■ In a large mixing bowl combine *1½ cups* of the flour, the yeast, and, if desired, herb.

In a medium saucepan heat and stir milk; margarine, butter, or shortening; sugar; and salt *just till warm* (120° to 130°) and margarine almost melts.

Add to flour mixture. Add egg. Beat with an electric mixer on low to medium speed for 30 seconds, scraping bowl. Beat on high speed for 3 minutes. Stir in the remaining flour. Divide dough into halves or quarters.

■ *To chill,* cover portions and refrigerate for at least 2 hours or up to 3 days.

Or, to freeze, wrap the portions in plastic wrap and place in freezer bags. Seal, label, and freeze for up to 3 months. To use, let dough stand at room temperature about 2½ hours or till thawed. (*Or,* thaw overnight in the refrigerator.)

Note: For whole wheat version, substitute 1 cup *whole wheat flour* for 1 cup of the stirred-in all-purpose flour. For cheese version, stir in 1 cup shredded *cheddar or mozzarella cheese* with the stirred-in flour.

205

BEVY OF BREADS

DEEP-DISH PIZZA

Have hot, homemade pizza your way—just pile on your favorite toppings. (Pictured on pages 204–205.)

- ½ of a recipe Easy-Mix Yeast Bread (see recipe, page 205)
- 1 8-ounce can pizza sauce
- 6 ounces bulk pork sausage *or* ground beef, cooked and drained
- ½ cup chopped green pepper *or* sliced fresh mushrooms
- 1 cup shredded mozzarella cheese (4 ounces)

■ With lightly greased fingers, pat dough into the bottom and up the sides of a greased 11x7x1½- or 9x9x2-inch baking pan.

■ Cover and let rise in a warm place till *nearly* double (about 30 minutes). Bake in a 375° oven about 10 minutes or till light brown. (If necessary, lightly press down center of crust.)

■ Spread pizza sauce over hot crust. Sprinkle with meat and green pepper or mushrooms; add cheese. Bake for 15 to 20 minutes more or till crust is golden brown. Serves 2.

Nutrition information per serving: 985 calories, 42 g protein, 111 g carbohydrate, 40 g total fat (14 g saturated), 127 mg cholesterol, 1,746 mg sodium, 545 mg potassium

CHEESY CALZONE

Pizza's close cousin, the calzone, was so named by its Neapolitan inventor because it resembled the style of men's trousers at the time.

- 1 cup shredded mozzarella *or* cheddar cheese (4 ounces)
- ¾ cup ricotta cheese
- ¼ cup sun-dried tomatoes (oil pack), drained and snipped (see tip, page 157) (optional)
- ½ of a recipe Easy-Mix Yeast Bread (see recipe, page 205)
- 1 tablespoon milk
- 1 tablespoon grated Parmesan cheese

■ In a mixing bowl stir together mozzarella or cheddar cheese, ricotta cheese, and, if desired, sun-dried tomatoes. Set aside.
   On a lightly floured surface roll bread dough into a 10-inch circle. Transfer to a large baking sheet.

■ Spread cheese mixture over *half* of the circle to within 1 inch of edge. Moisten edges of dough with water. Fold dough in half over cheese mixture. Seal edges by pressing together with fingers. Cut slits in top. Brush top with milk. Sprinkle with Parmesan cheese.
   Bake in a 375° oven for 25 to 30 minutes or till crust is golden brown. Serves 2.

Nutrition information per serving: 934 calories, 43 g protein, 105 g carbohydrate, 37 g total fat (18 g saturated), 141 mg cholesterol, 849 mg sodium, 459 mg potassium

DINNER ROLLS

They're as simple as a little roll here and a tiny twist there. (Pictured on pages 204–205.)

¼ of a recipe Easy-Mix Yeast Bread (for each shape) (see recipe, page 205)

■ *Butterhorns:* On a floured surface roll dough into an 8-inch circle. If desired, brush with 1 tablespoon melted *margarine or butter.* Cut circle into 6 wedges. Starting at wide end of each wedge, roll toward point. Place, point side down, on a greased baking sheet. Cover; let rise in warm place till *nearly* double (about 30 minutes). Bake in a 375° oven 10 to 12 minutes or till golden brown. Makes 6 rolls.

■ *Cloverleaves:* Divide dough into 18 pieces. Shape each piece into a ball, pulling edges under to make smooth tops. Place *three* balls *each* in six greased muffin cups, smooth side up. Let rise and bake as above. Makes 6 rolls.

■ *Rosettes:* On a floured surface divide dough into 6 pieces. Roll each piece into a 12-inch rope. Tie rope in a loose knot, leaving two long ends. Tuck top end under knot. Bring bottom end up; tuck into center of knot (see photo, page 205). Place on a greased baking sheet. Let rise and bake as above. (If desired, before baking, brush with a mixture of 1 *egg yolk* and 1 tablespoon *water.*) Makes 6 rolls.

Nutrition information per roll: 102 calories, 3 g protein, 17 g carbohydrate, 3 g total fat (1 g saturated), 10 mg cholesterol, 76 mg sodium, 50 mg potassium

BRAIDED BREAD

Blend cheese and herb into the dough for this charming loaf. (Pictured on pages 204–205.)

¼ of a recipe Easy-Mix Yeast Bread (see recipe, page 205)

■ On a lightly floured surface divide bread dough into 3 portions. Roll each portion into a 12-inch rope. Line up the 3 ropes, 1 inch apart, on a greased baking sheet.

■ Starting in the middle, loosely braid the ropes by bringing the left rope *underneath* the center rope; lay it down (see photo, page 204). Bring right rope under new center rope; lay it down. Repeat braiding to end.

■ On the other half, braid by bringing the outside ropes alternately *over* the center rope. Press ends together to seal; tuck under.

■ Cover braid and let rise in a warm place till *nearly* double (about 30 minutes).

■ Bake in a 375° oven for 20 to 25 minutes or till golden brown and bread sounds hollow when tapped. Makes 1 loaf (12 slices).

Nutrition information per slice: 51 calories, 1 g protein, 8 g carbohydrate, 1 g total fat (0 g saturated), 5 mg cholesterol, 38 mg sodium, 25 mg potassium

BEVY OF BREADS

CINNAMON ROLLS

Irresistible! (Pictured on pages 204–205.)

¼ of a recipe Easy-Mix Yeast Bread
  (see recipe, page 205)
1 teaspoon margarine *or* butter
2 tablespoons sugar *or* brown sugar
½ teaspoon ground cinnamon
2 tablespoons chopped nuts *or*
  miniature semisweet chocolate
  pieces (optional)
½ cup sifted powdered sugar
¼ teaspoon vanilla
2 to 3 teaspoons milk

■ On a floured surface roll or pat dough into a 6-inch square. Melt margarine or butter; brush atop dough. In a bowl combine sugar or brown sugar and cinnamon. Sprinkle over dough. If desired, sprinkle dough with nuts or chocolate pieces. Roll up dough jelly-roll style, starting from any side. Pinch seam to seal. Cut roll into 6 slices.

Place slices cut side down in a greased 8x4x2-inch loaf pan. Cover; let rise in a warm place till *nearly* double (about 30 minutes). Bake in a 375° oven about 20 minutes or till golden. Cool slightly; remove from pan.

For icing, in a bowl combine powdered sugar and vanilla. Stir in milk, *1 teaspoon* at a time, till icing is smooth and of drizzling consistency. Drizzle over rolls. Makes 6 rolls.

Nutrition information per roll: 157 calories, 3 g protein, 29 g carbohydrate, 3 g total fat (1 g saturated), 10 mg cholesterol, 85 mg sodium, 54 mg potassium

CARAMEL ROLLS

1 recipe Cinnamon Rolls (at left)
2 tablespoons margarine *or* butter
2 tablespoons brown sugar
2 teaspoons light corn syrup *or* maple-
  flavored syrup
2 tablespoons chopped nuts

■ Prepare Cinnamon Rolls as directed, *except* omit icing. Before adding dough slices to pan, melt the margarine or butter in a small saucepan. Stir in the brown sugar and light corn syrup or maple-flavored syrup. Cook and stir just till blended. Pour into loaf pan. Sprinkle nuts evenly in the bottom of pan. Add dough slices to pan. Let rise and bake, as directed. Invert rolls onto a wire rack or serving plate. Makes 6 rolls.

Nutrition information per roll: 198 calories, 3 g protein, 28 g carbohydrate, 9 g total fat (2 g saturated), 10 mg cholesterol, 132 mg sodium, 82 mg potassium

CINNAMON BREAD

1 recipe Cinnamon Rolls (at left)

■ Prepare Cinnamon Rolls as directed, *except* do not cut roll of dough into slices. Pinch ends of dough closed; tuck under. Place in a greased 7½x3½x2-inch loaf pan. Let rise and bake, as directed. Drizzle with icing. Makes 1 loaf (12 slices).

Nutrition information per slice: 79 calories, 1 g protein, 15 g carbohydrate, 2 g total fat (0 g saturated), 5 mg cholesterol, 42 mg sodium, 27 mg potassium

APPLE-GLAZED ROLLS

A tummy-tempting breakfast treat. (Pictured on pages 204–205.)

    1 tablespoon sugar
    1 teaspoon cornstarch
    ⅛ teaspoon ground cinnamon *or*
         ginger (optional)
    2 tablespoons frozen apple, orange, *or*
         pineapple juice concentrate
    1 tablespoon margarine *or* butter
    ¼ of a recipe Easy-Mix Yeast Bread
         (see recipe, page 205)

■ For glaze, in a small saucepan stir together sugar, cornstarch, and, if desired, spice. Stir in juice concentrate and margarine or butter. Cook and stir till thickened and bubbly. Cook and stir for 1 minute more. Cool.

■ Divide dough into 6 pieces. Shape each piece into a ball, pulling edges under to make smooth tops. Place in a greased 7½x3½x2-inch loaf pan. Cover and let rise in a warm place till *nearly* double (30 to 45 minutes).

Bake rolls in a 375° oven for 20 to 25 minutes or till golden brown. (If necessary, cover with foil the last 5 minutes to prevent overbrowning.) Remove rolls from the pan. Cool 5 minutes on a wire rack; brush rolls with half of the glaze. Cool 5 minutes more; brush with remaining glaze. Makes 6 rolls.

Nutrition information per roll: 138 calories, 3 g protein,
22 g carbohydrate, 4 g total fat (1 g saturated),
10 mg cholesterol, 100 mg sodium, 77 mg potassium

SWEET CHEESE ROLLS

An exquisite combination of sweet sugar and savory cheese. (Pictured on pages 204–205.)

    ¼ of a recipe Easy-Mix Yeast Bread
         (see recipe, page 205)
    3 tablespoons margarine *or* butter,
         melted
    ½ cup finely shredded Edam *or* Gouda
         cheese (2 ounces)
    2 teaspoons sugar

■ On a floured surface roll dough into an 18x10-inch rectangle. Brush with *2 tablespoons* of the margarine. Sprinkle with cheese. With a sharp knife, cut rectangle lengthwise into two 18x5-inch strips. Roll up each strip, jelly-roll style, from a long side. Seal. Cut each rolled strip crosswise into 3 pieces. Roll each piece of dough into a rope 10 inches long.

To shape rolls, make a loop in the center of each rope, leaving about 3 inches free at each end. Bring ends together in front of the loop (see photo, page 204). Pinch the ends together to seal. Lift the loop over the top of sealed ends. Place rolls 3 inches apart on a greased baking sheet. Cover and let rise in a warm place till *nearly* double (40 to 45 minutes).

Bake in a 375° oven for 12 to 15 minutes or till golden brown. Transfer rolls to a wire rack. Brush with remaining margarine. Sprinkle with sugar. Makes 6 rolls.

Nutrition information per roll: 192 calories, 5 g protein,
18 g carbohydrate, 11 g total fat (3 g saturated), 18 mg
cholesterol, 234 mg sodium, 71 mg potassium

BANANA-BRICKLE BREAD

Prevent ledges from forming on the edges of your bread by greasing the pan on the bottom and only ½ inch up the sides. The batter will cling to the pan sides instead of sliding down during baking.

1 cup all-purpose flour
1 teaspoon baking powder
¼ teaspoon baking soda
   Dash salt

■ Grease a 7½x3½x2-inch loaf pan; set aside. In a medium mixing bowl stir together the flour, baking powder, baking soda, and salt. Make a well in the center of the dry ingredients. Set aside.

1½ teaspoons instant coffee crystals
1 tablespoon hot water
1 slightly beaten egg
⅔ cup mashed ripe banana (2 medium)
½ cup sugar
2 tablespoons cooking oil
¼ cup almond brickle pieces

■ In a small mixing bowl dissolve the coffee crystals in the hot water. Add the egg, banana, sugar, and oil. Stir till combined. Then stir the banana mixture into the dry mixture *just till moistened* (batter should be lumpy). Fold in the brickle pieces.

■ Pour batter into the prepared pan. Bake in a 350° oven for 35 to 40 minutes or till a wooden toothpick inserted near the center comes out clean.

Cool the bread in the pan for 10 minutes. Remove from pan and cool slightly on a wire rack. Serve warm or cool. Makes 1 loaf (12 slices).

TIME ESTIMATE

Preparation —— 20 min.
Baking ———— 35 min.

MENU IDEA

For an afternoon snack, spread the bread slices with soft-style cream cheese.

PER SLICE

Calories ————— 125
Protein ——————2 g
Carbohydrate ——21 g
Fat (total) ————4 g
  Saturated ———— 0 g
Cholesterol ——— 18 mg
Sodium————— 75 mg
Potassium ——— 72 mg

CHOCOLATE-CHIP BANANA BREAD

¼ cup miniature semisweet chocolate pieces

■ Prepare Banana-Brickle Bread as directed above, *except* substitute miniature chocolate pieces for the almond brickle pieces.

PER SLICE

Same as *Banana-Brickle Bread,* except:
Saturated Fat———1 g
Sodium————— 58 mg
Potassium ——— 84 mg

PEPPERONI-PARMESAN BREAD

For a crispy, crunchy version, pop slices of this bread into the toaster.

1½ cups all-purpose flour
 ¼ cup grated Parmesan *or* Romano cheese
 2 tablespoons sugar
 1 tablespoon snipped chives
1½ teaspoons baking powder

■ Grease an 8x4x2- or 7½x3½x2-inch loaf pan; set aside. In a medium mixing bowl stir together the flour, Parmesan or Romano cheese, sugar, chives, and baking powder. Make a well in the center of dry ingredients.

 1 beaten egg
 ¾ cup milk
 2 tablespoons cooking oil
 ½ cup chopped pepperoni (2 ounces)

■ In another bowl stir together the egg, milk, and cooking oil. Add the liquid ingredients all at once to the dry ingredients. Stir *just till moistened* (batter should be lumpy). Fold in the pepperoni.

 2 teaspoons grated Parmesan *or* Romano cheese

■ Pour batter into the prepared pan. Sprinkle the Parmesan or Romano cheese over the top. Bake in a 350° oven for 40 to 45 minutes or till a wooden toothpick inserted near the center comes out clean. If necessary, cover with foil the last 10 minutes of baking to prevent overbrowning. Cool in the pan for 5 to 10 minutes. Remove loaf from the pan and cool slightly on a wire rack. Serve warm or cool. Store in refrigerator. Makes 1 loaf (12 slices).

TIME ESTIMATE
Preparation ____ 20 min.
Baking _____ 40 min.

MENU IDEA
Match slices of this savory bread with relishes and hearty bowls of soup.

PER SLICE
Calories _____ 132
Protein _____ 4 g
Carbohydrate _____ 15 g
Fat (total) _____ 6 g
  Saturated _____ 2 g
Cholesterol _____ 22 mg
Sodium _____ 182 mg
Potassium _____ 65 mg

CINNAMON 'N' SPICE OATMEAL MUFFINS

⅔ cup all-purpose flour
⅓ cup rolled oats
¼ cup sugar
1 teaspoon baking powder
½ teaspoon ground
    cinnamon
¼ teaspoon ground nutmeg
⅛ teaspoon salt
    Dash ground cloves

1 beaten egg
⅓ cup milk
2 tablespoons cooking oil
½ teaspoon vanilla
¼ cup chopped walnuts,
    pecans, *or* almonds

■ Grease six 2½-inch muffin cups or line them with paper bake cups. Set muffin cups aside.

In a medium mixing bowl stir together the flour, rolled oats, sugar, baking powder, cinnamon, nutmeg, salt, and cloves. Make a well in the center of the dry ingredients.

■ In another bowl combine the egg, milk, oil, and vanilla. Add the liquid ingredients all at once to the dry ingredients. Stir *just till moistened* (batter should be lumpy). Fold walnuts, pecans, or almonds into the batter.

Spoon batter into prepared muffin cups, filling each ⅔ full. Bake in a 400° oven 17 to 20 minutes or till tops are golden. Remove from muffin cups and cool slightly on a wire rack. Serve warm. Makes 6 muffins.

TIME ESTIMATE

Preparation ____ 20 min.
Baking _____ 17 min.

MENU IDEA

Need breakfast in a hurry? Team these muffins with bowls of sliced peaches and strawberries and cups of coffee.

PER MUFFIN

Calories _____ 193
Protein _____ 4 g
Carbohydrate ____ 24 g
Fat (total) _____ 9 g
  Saturated _____ 1 g
Cholesterol _____ 37 mg
Sodium _____ 111 mg
Potassium _____ 89 mg

BLUEBERRY-OATMEAL MUFFINS

⅓ cup fresh *or* frozen
    blueberries

■ Prepare Cinnamon 'n' Spice Oatmeal Muffins as directed above, *except* substitute the blueberries for the nuts.

PER MUFFIN

Same as *Cinnamon 'n' Spice Oatmeal Muffins,* except:
Calories _____ 166
Fat (total) _____ 6 g

APPLE-OATMEAL MUFFINS

⅓ cup shredded apple

■ Prepare Cinnamon 'n' Spice Oatmeal Muffins as directed above, *except* stir the apple into the egg mixture and omit the nuts.

PER MUFFIN

Same as *Cinnamon 'n' Spice Oatmeal Muffins,* except:
Calories _____ 165
Fat (total) _____ 6 g

(see recipes, pages 214, 217, and 212)

(see recipes, pages 216 and 215)

BIT-OF-CHOCOLATE BANANA MUFFINS, SWEET YOGURT SCONES, CINNAMON 'N' SPICE OATMEAL MUFFINS, BUTTERMILK CORN SCONES, AND JAM-FILLED BISCUITS

BIT-OF-CHOCOLATE BANANA MUFFINS

Pack 'em for a snack. Then, during a work break, sink your teeth into these tender cakelike muffins that are speckled with chocolate. (Pictured on page 213.)

¾ **cup all-purpose flour**
1 **teaspoon baking powder**
¼ **teaspoon salt**

■ Grease six 2½-inch muffin cups. Set muffin cups aside. In a small mixing bowl stir together the flour, baking powder, and salt. Set aside.

¼ **cup packed brown sugar**
3 **tablespoons margarine**
  or **butter**
½ **cup mashed ripe banana**
1 **egg**
2 **tablespoons milk**
¼ **cup miniature semisweet**
  chocolate pieces

■ In a medium mixing bowl beat the brown sugar and margarine or butter with an electric mixer on medium to high speed till light and fluffy. Add the banana, egg, and milk. Beat till combined. Add the flour mixture. Beat on low to medium speed *just till combined.* Fold the chocolate pieces into the batter.

Spoon batter into the prepared muffin cups, filling each cup almost full. Bake in a 400° oven for 15 to 18 minutes or till the muffin tops are golden. Remove muffins from muffin cups and cool slightly on a wire rack. Serve warm. Makes 6 muffins.

TIME ESTIMATE
Preparation ____ 20 min.
Baking _____ 15 min.

PER MUFFIN
Calories _____ 211
Protein _____ 3 g
Carbohydrate ____ 30 g
Fat (total) _____ 9 g
  Saturated _____ 3 g
Cholesterol _____ 36 mg
Sodium_____ 222 mg
Potassium _____ 169 mg

BANANA-NUT MUFFINS

¼ **cup chopped walnuts or**
  pecans

■ Prepare Bit-of-Chocolate Banana Muffins as directed above, *except* substitute the walnuts or pecans for the chocolate pieces.

PER MUFFIN
Same as *Bit-of-Chocolate Banana Muffins.*

BANANA-SPICE MUFFINS

½ **teaspoon ground**
  cinnamon
¼ **teaspoon ground nutmeg**

■ Prepare Bit-of-Chocolate Banana Muffins as directed above, *except* stir the cinnamon and nutmeg into the flour mixture and omit the chocolate pieces.

PER MUFFIN
Same as *Bit-of-Chocolate Banana Muffins,* except:
Calories _____ 176
Fat (total) _____ 7 g
  Saturated _____ 2 g
Potassium _____ 145 mg

BASIC BUTTERY BISCUITS

Biscuits aren't just for breakfast! Serve them along with bowls of soup for lunch or supper. (Jam-Filled Biscuits pictured on page 213.)

  1 **cup all-purpose flour**
1½ **teaspoons baking powder**
1½ **teaspoons sugar**
  ¼ **teaspoon cream of tartar**
  ⅛ **teaspoon salt**
  ¼ **cup butter *or* margarine**
  ⅓ **cup half-and-half, light cream, *or* milk**

■ In a medium mixing bowl stir together the flour, baking powder, sugar, cream of tartar, and salt. Using a pastry blender, cut in the butter or margarine till mixture resembles coarse crumbs. Make a well in the center of the dry ingredients, then add the half-and-half, light cream, or milk all at once. Using a fork, stir *just till moistened.*

■ Turn the dough out onto a lightly floured surface. Quickly knead the dough by gently folding and pressing the dough for 10 to 12 strokes or till the dough is *nearly* smooth. Pat or lightly roll the dough to ½-inch thickness. Cut dough with a floured 2½-inch biscuit cutter, dipping the cutter into flour between cuts.

Place biscuits on an ungreased baking sheet. Bake in a 450° oven for 10 to 12 minutes or till the biscuits are golden brown. Remove the biscuits from the baking sheet and serve hot. Makes 5 or 6 biscuits.

TIME ESTIMATE
Preparation —— 15 min.
Baking ———— 10 min.

MENU IDEA
Serve bowls of Vegetable Beef Soup (see recipe, page 164) and glasses of milk for a tummy-warming meal.

PER BISCUIT
Calories ———— 200
Protein ————— 3 g
Carbohydrate —— 21 g
Fat (total) ——— 11 g
  Saturated ——— 7 g
Cholesterol —— 31 mg
Sodium———— 235 mg
Potassium ——— 57 mg

JAM-FILLED BISCUITS

  2 **tablespoons apricot, strawberry, *or* cherry jam *or* preserves**

■ Prepare Basic Buttery Biscuits as directed above, *except* make an indentation in the center of each biscuit with your thumb. Spoon *1 teaspoon* of jam or preserves into *each* indentation. Bake as directed.

PER BISCUIT
Same as *Basic Buttery Biscuits,* except:
Calories ———— 218
Carbohydrate —— 26 g
Potassium ——— 63 mg

BUTTERMILK CORN SCONES

Extra easy! There's no kneading or rolling—just drop the batter from a spoon. (Pictured on page 213.)

¾ cup all-purpose flour
½ cup yellow cornmeal
1 tablespoon sugar
1½ teaspoons baking powder
¼ teaspoon salt
2 tablespoons margarine, butter, *or* shortening

1 beaten egg
½ of an 8¾-ounce can (½ cup) cream-style corn
⅓ cup buttermilk *or* sour milk (see tip, page 194)

■ Grease a baking sheet; set aside. In a medium mixing bowl stir together the flour, cornmeal, sugar, baking powder, salt, and ⅛ teaspoon *pepper.* Using a pastry blender, cut in the margarine, butter, or shortening till mixture resembles coarse crumbs. Make a well in the center of the dry ingredients.

■ In a small mixing bowl stir together the egg, corn, and buttermilk or sour milk. Add liquid ingredients all at once to the dry ingredients. Using a fork, stir *just till moistened.*

Drop batter from a rounded tablespoon onto prepared baking sheet. Bake in a 400° oven about 15 minutes or till golden. Serve warm. Makes 8 scones.

TIME ESTIMATE	
Preparation	20 min.
Baking	15 min.

PER SCONE	
Calories	132
Protein	3 g
Carbohydrate	21 g
Fat (total)	4 g
Saturated	1 g
Cholesterol	27 mg
Sodium	219 mg
Potassium	74 mg

CHEDDAR-PECAN CORN SCONES

⅓ cup shredded cheddar cheese
¼ cup chopped pecans *or* walnuts

■ Prepare Buttermilk Corn Scones as directed above, *except* fold the cheese and chopped pecans or walnuts into the batter.

PER SCONE	

Same as *Buttermilk Corn Scones,* except:

Calories	175
Fat (total)	8 g
Sodium	248 mg

BUTTERMILK CORN BREAD

■ Prepare Buttermilk Corn Scones as directed above, *except* pour batter into a greased 9x5x3-inch loaf pan. Bake in a 425° oven for 20 to 25 minutes or till a wooden toothpick inserted near the center comes out clean. Cut into squares. Serve warm. Makes 8 servings.

PER SERVING	

Same as *Buttermilk Corn Scones.*

SWEET YOGURT SCONES

For a twist of lemon, stir ½ teaspoon finely shredded lemon peel along with ¼ cup chopped walnuts into the dry mixture. Then, substitute lemon yogurt for the plain yogurt. (Sweet Yogurt Scones pictured on page 213.)

1 cup all-purpose flour
2 tablespoons sugar
1½ teaspoons baking powder
⅛ teaspoon salt
¼ cup margarine *or* butter

■ In a large bowl stir together the flour, sugar, baking powder, and salt. Using a pastry blender, cut in the margarine or butter till mixture resembles coarse crumbs. Make a well in the center of the dry ingredients.

1 beaten egg
⅓ cup plain yogurt *or* dairy
  sour cream

■ In a small mixing bowl stir together the egg and yogurt or sour cream. Add the yogurt mixture all at once to the dry ingredients. Using a fork, stir *just till moistened.*

1 teaspoon sugar
¼ teaspoon ground
  cinnamon

■ Turn dough out onto a lightly floured surface. Quickly knead dough by folding and pressing dough gently for 8 to 10 strokes or till dough begins to hold together. Pat or lightly roll dough into a 6-inch circle. Using a sharp knife, cut into 6 wedges.

In a small bowl stir together the sugar and cinnamon. Sprinkle sugar mixture over the wedges. Place wedges 1 inch apart on an ungreased baking sheet. Bake in a 425° oven for 11 to 13 minutes or till golden. Remove from baking sheet and cool for 5 minutes on a wire rack. Serve warm. Makes 6 scones.

TIME ESTIMATE

Preparation	20 min.
Baking	11 min.

PER SCONE

Calories	184
Protein	4 g
Carbohydrate	22 g
Fat (total)	9 g
Saturated	2 g
Cholesterol	36 mg
Sodium	226 mg
Potassium	67 mg

ORANGE AND RAISIN SCONES

¼ cup raisins
½ teaspoon finely shredded
  orange peel
⅓ cup orange yogurt

■ Prepare Sweet Yogurt Scones as directed above, *except* stir raisins and orange peel into the dry ingredients and substitute orange yogurt for the plain yogurt or sour cream.

PER SCONE

Same as *Sweet Yogurt Scones,* except:

Calories	210
Potassium	114 mg

217

Breakfasts

BACON AND AVOCADO PUFFY OMELET

BACON AND AVOCADO PUFFY OMELET

Treat this omelet like a taco by omitting the bacon and sprouts. Then, sprinkle cheese, avocado, tomato, ½ cup shredded lettuce, and 2 tablespoons sliced pitted ripe olives over the top. Drizzle with ¼ cup taco sauce or salsa.

3 slices bacon
4 eggs
2 tablespoons water

■ In a skillet cook bacon till crisp; drain. Crumble bacon. Preheat the oven to 325°. Meanwhile, separate eggs. In a mixing bowl beat egg yolks with a fork or rotary beater.

In a large clean bowl beat egg whites till frothy. Add water. Continue beating till stiff peaks form (tips stand straight). Gradually pour yolks over beaten egg whites, gently folding to combine.

1 tablespoon margarine *or* butter

■ In a 10-inch ovenproof skillet heat margarine or butter till a drop of water sizzles when dropped into the skillet. Pour in egg mixture, mounding it slightly higher at the sides. Cook, uncovered, over low heat for 8 to 10 minutes or till egg is puffed, set, and golden brown on the bottom.

Immediately place skillet in the 325° oven. Bake for 8 to 10 minutes or till a knife inserted near the center comes out clean. Loosen sides of the omelet with a metal spatula. Invert omelet onto a warm plate.

¾ cup shredded Monterey Jack *or* cheddar cheese (3 ounces)
½ of a small ripe avocado, seeded, peeled, and chopped
1 small tomato, chopped (½ cup)
½ cup alfalfa sprouts (optional)
Dairy sour cream

■ Sprinkle omelet with Monterey Jack or cheddar cheese. Then sprinkle with avocado, tomato, alfalfa sprouts (if desired), and cooked bacon. Cut into wedges. Dollop with sour cream. If desired, garnish with fresh tarragon. Makes 2 servings.

TIME ESTIMATE
Start to finish — 30 min.

MENU IDEA
For an accompaniment, spread your favorite jam or jelly over Sweet Yogurt Scones (see recipe, page 217) or toasted bagels.

PER SERVING
Calories _____ 488
Protein _____ 27 g
Carbohydrate _____ 7 g
Fat (total) _____ 40 g
  Saturated _____ 15 g
Cholesterol _____ 471 mg
Sodium _____ 576 mg
Potassium _____ 544 mg

ITALIAN BREAKFAST FRITTATA

Hold the sauce! This breakfast-style pizza has a tender egg crust topped with onion, salami, and cheese.

4 **eggs**
¼ **teaspoon dried oregano,
   basil, *or* Italian
   seasoning, crushed**
⅛ **teaspoon salt**
⅛ **teapoon pepper**
⅓ **cup cooked orzo, acini di
   pepe, *or* rice**

■ In a medium mixing bowl beat the eggs; oregano, basil, or Italian seasoning; salt; and pepper. Stir in the orzo, acini di pepe, or rice. Set aside.

1 **green onion, thinly sliced
   (2 tablespoons), *or* 1
   tablespoon finely
   chopped onion**
1 **clove garlic, minced**
1 **tablespoon margarine *or*
   butter**
¼ **cup thinly sliced salami,
   Canadian-style bacon,
   or fully cooked ham
   cut into thin strips**

■ In an 8-inch broiler-proof or regular skillet cook the onion and garlic in hot margarine or butter till tender but not brown. Stir in the salami, Canadian-style bacon, or ham. Pour the egg mixture into the skillet over the meat mixture.

½ **cup shredded provolone
   or mozzarella cheese
   (2 ounces)**

■ Cook over medium heat. As mixture sets, run a spatula around edge of skillet, lifting egg mixture to allow uncooked portions to flow underneath. Continue cooking and lifting edges till egg mixture is almost set (surface will be moist). Sprinkle with provolone or mozzarella cheese. If using a broiler-proof skillet, place it under the broiler 4 to 5 inches from the heat. Broil for 1 to 2 minutes or just till top is set and cheese is melted. Or, if using a regular skillet, remove from the heat; cover and let stand for 3 to 4 minutes or till top is set and cheese is melted. Makes 2 servings.

TIME ESTIMATE
Start to finish — 25 min.

MENU IDEA
For a complete breakfast, serve this frittata with wedges of cantaloupe and glasses of your favorite fruit or vegetable juice.

PER SERVING
Calories _____ 420
Protein _____ 25 g
Carbohydrate ____ 18 g
Fat (total) _____ 27 g
   Saturated _____ 11 g
Cholesterol ___ 457 mg
Sodium _____ 761 mg
Potassium _____ 260 mg

CHEESY HAM AND EGG BAKE

Are your mornings hectic? Lighten your load by preparing this dish the day ahead. Assemble it as directed, then cover and chill up to 24 hours. Bake, covered, in a 350° oven for 35 to 40 minutes or till heated through.

2 teaspoons margarine *or* butter
2 teaspoons all-purpose flour
Dash pepper
½ cup milk
¼ cup shredded American cheese (1 ounce)

■ For sauce, in a small saucepan melt the margarine or butter. Stir in the flour and pepper. Add the milk all at once. Cook and stir over medium heat till thickened and bubbly. Cook and stir for 1 minute more. Stir in the cheese till melted. Remove from heat. Set aside.

4 eggs
1 tablespoon grated Parmesan *or* Romano cheese
Dash pepper

■ In a small mixing bowl beat together eggs, Parmesan or Romano cheese, and pepper.

1 tablespoon margarine *or* butter
⅓ cup diced fully cooked ham *or* fully cooked smoked turkey
½ of a 2½-ounce jar (¼ cup) sliced mushrooms, drained

■ In a medium skillet melt the margarine or butter. Pour the egg mixture into the skillet. Cook over medium heat, without stirring, till mixture begins to set on the bottom and around the edge. Using a large spoon or spatula, lift and fold partially cooked egg mixture so uncooked portion flows underneath. Cook over medium heat for 2 to 3 minutes more or till the eggs are cooked throughout but still glossy and moist. Remove from heat.

Spoon the eggs into two individual casseroles. Sprinkle with the ham or turkey and mushrooms. Pour the sauce over the tops.

½ of a small tomato, chopped (⅓ cup)
1 green onion, thinly sliced (2 tablespoons)

■ Cover and bake in a 350° oven for 15 to 20 minutes or till heated through. Sprinkle with tomato and green onion. Makes 2 servings.

TIME ESTIMATE
Preparation ___ 20 min.
Baking_____ 15 min.

MENU IDEA
Spread some jam or jelly on toasted English muffins and serve them alongside this luscious egg dish.

PER SERVING
Calories _____ 388
Protein _____ 26 g
Carbohydrate _____ 9 g
Fat (total) _____ 27 g
  Saturated _____ 9 g
Cholesterol _____ 460 mg
Sodium_____ 907 mg
Potassium _____ 431 mg

TURKEY SCRAMBLE FLORENTINE

In early summer, use whole tiny new potatoes in this hearty dish. Because their skins are so tender and such a pretty pink color, skip peeling the potatoes—just scrub 'em up and they're ready to be chopped.

½ cup peeled and chopped
    potato
2 tablespoons finely
    chopped onion
2 tablespoons margarine
    or butter

■ In a medium nonstick or well-seasoned skillet cook the potato and onion in hot margarine or butter over medium heat for 8 to 10 minutes or till tender, stirring often.

4 eggs
1 tablespoon milk
¼ teaspoon dried tarragon
    or thyme, crushed
⅛ teaspoon pepper
¾ cup shredded fresh
    spinach
⅓ cup diced, fully cooked,
    smoked turkey *or* fully
    cooked ham

■ Meanwhile, in a medium mixing bowl beat together the eggs, milk, tarragon or thyme, and pepper. Stir in the spinach and turkey or ham. Pour the egg mixture over the potato mixture in the skillet.

¼ cup finely shredded Swiss,
    Monterey Jack, *or*
    cheddar cheese (1
    ounce) (optional)

■ Cook, without stirring, till the mixture begins to set on the bottom and around the edge. Using a large spoon or spatula, lift and fold partially cooked egg mixture so the uncooked portion flows underneath. Cook for 3 to 4 minutes more or till the eggs are cooked throughout but still glossy and moist. If desired, sprinkle with cheese. Makes 2 servings.

TIME ESTIMATE
Start to finish _ 25 min.

MENU IDEA
Finish breakfast right with small bowls of sliced fresh strawberries sprinkled with granola.

PER SERVING
Calories _____ 343
Protein _____ 20 g
Carbohydrate _____ 14 g
Fat (total) _____ 23 g
    Saturated _____ 6 g
Cholesterol ___ 440 mg
Sodium_____ 487 mg
Potassium _____ 500 mg

HAM AND ASPARAGUS STRATA

Looking for a brunch menu masterpiece? This cheesy make-ahead strata will be the star of the show.

2 **English muffins, torn or cut into bite-size pieces**
⅓ **cup cubed fully cooked ham**
¾ **cup cooked cut asparagus *or* broccoli flowerets**
2 **1-ounce slices process Swiss cheese, torn**

■ In a greased 1-quart casserole layer *half* of the English muffin pieces. Top with the ham, then add the asparagus or broccoli and the cheese. Top with the remaining English muffin pieces.

1 **slightly beaten egg**
1 **slightly beaten egg white**
¾ **cup milk**
2 **tablespoons dairy sour cream**
1 **tablespoon finely chopped onion**
1 **teaspoon Dijon-style *or* prepared mustard**
⅛ **teaspoon caraway seed**
 Dash pepper

■ In a medium mixing bowl combine the egg, egg white, milk, sour cream, onion, mustard, caraway seed, and pepper. Pour over the layers in the casserole. Cover and chill in the refrigerator for 2 to 24 hours.

■ Bake, uncovered, in a 325° oven for 40 to 50 minutes or till a knife inserted near the center comes out clean. Let stand for 5 to 10 minutes before serving. Makes 2 servings.

TIME ESTIMATE

Preparation ___ 20 min.
Chilling _____ 2 hrs.
Baking_____ 40 min.

MENU IDEA

For a glorious brunch, serve fresh strawberries, Cinnamon 'n' Spice Oatmeal Muffins (see recipe, page 212), and coffee.

PER SERVING

Calories _____419
Protein _____28 g
Carbohydrate _____37 g
Fat (total) _____18 g
 Saturated _____9 g
Cholesterol ___ 158 mg
Sodium_____1,264 mg
Potassium _____ 839 mg

223

PUFFED OVEN PANCAKE WITH SPICED APPLE SAUCE

Every bite is just as fabulous as the first. Spoon the sauce into the center of this hot, popoverlike pancake and eat your way from the edges to the middle.

Nonstick spray coating
2 beaten eggs
⅓ cup all-purpose flour
⅓ cup milk
 Dash salt

■ Spray an 8x1½-inch round baking pan or 8-inch ovenproof skillet with nonstick coating. In a mixing bowl beat together the eggs, flour, milk, and salt with a rotary beater till thoroughly mixed. Pour into the prepared pan or skillet. Bake in a 400° oven for 20 to 25 minutes or till golden and puffed.

1 medium apple, peeled, cored, and thinly sliced
1 tablespoon raisins (optional)
2 tablespoons margarine *or* butter
2 tablespoons brown sugar
2 tablespoons apple juice, apple cider, *or* water
2 tablespoons half-and-half, light cream, *or* whipping cream
1 tablespoon apple brandy (applejack) *or* orange juice
¼ teaspoon ground cinnamon *or* apple pie spice
2 tablespoons coarsely chopped walnuts *or* pecans

■ Meanwhile, for sauce, in a medium saucepan cook the apples and, if desired, raisins, in hot margarine or butter till apples are *almost* tender, stirring frequently. Add the brown sugar; apple juice, apple cider, or water; half-and-half, light cream, or whipping cream; apple brandy or orange juice; and cinnamon or apple pie spice. Bring to boiling. Reduce heat; simmer for 2 minutes, stirring occasionally. Remove from heat. Stir in the walnuts or pecans.

 Remove pancake from pan and transfer to a serving platter. Spoon sauce into the center of the pancake. Serve immediately. Makes 2 servings.

TIME ESTIMATE

Preparation	10 min.
Baking	20 min.

PER SERVING

Calories	460
Protein	12 g
Carbohydrate	49 g
Fat (total)	25 g
Saturated	6 g
Cholesterol	222 mg
Sodium	293 mg
Potassium	354 mg

OATMEAL PANCAKES WITH STRAWBERRY-ORANGE SAUCE

½ cup milk
⅓ cup quick-cooking rolled oats

■ In a small saucepan heat milk till hot; remove from heat. Stir in the oats; cover and let stand for 5 minutes.

⅓ cup all-purpose flour
1 tablespoon brown sugar
1 teaspoon baking powder
⅛ teaspoon baking soda
⅛ teaspoon salt

■ Meanwhile, in a medium mixing bowl stir together the flour, brown sugar, baking powder, baking soda, and salt. Stir in oat mixture.

1 beaten egg
1 teaspoon cooking oil

■ In a small bowl stir together the egg and cooking oil; add all at once to flour-oat mixture. Stir mixture *just till blended* but still slightly lumpy.

■ For each pancake, pour about ¼ *cup* of the batter onto a hot, lightly greased griddle or heavy skillet, and let it spread to about a 4-inch circle. Cook the pancakes till they are golden brown, turning to cook the second sides when the pancakes have bubbly surfaces and the edges are slightly dry.

Strawberry-Orange Sauce *or* maple-flavored syrup

■ Serve the pancakes with warm Strawberry-Orange Sauce or maple-flavored syrup. Makes 2 servings.

TIME ESTIMATE
Preparation — 10 min.
Baking — 20 min.

PER SERVING
Calories — 312
Protein — 10 g
Carbohydrate — 48 g
Fat (total) — 9 g
  Saturated — 2 g
Cholesterol — 112 mg
Sodium — 418 mg
Potassium — 408 mg

STRAWBERRY-ORANGE SAUCE

½ cup orange juice
1 teaspoon cornstarch
½ cup sliced fresh strawberries
1 teaspoon margarine *or* butter
1 teaspoon honey

■ In a small saucepan stir together the orange juice and cornstarch. Cook and stir over medium heat till thickened and bubbly. Cook and stir for 2 minutes more. Add the strawberries, margarine or butter, and honey. Stir till the margarine melts. Makes ¾ cup.

CREAM CHEESE WAFFLES

If you're a syrup lover, opt to omit the fresh fruit and flavored yogurt. Instead, drizzle your favorite syrup over these wonderful waffles.

¾ **cup all-purpose flour**
1 **tablespoon brown sugar**
1½ **teaspoons baking powder**
   Dash salt

■ In a medium mixing bowl stir together the flour, brown sugar, baking powder, and salt. Set aside.

2 **tablespoons soft-style**
   cream cheese
1 **egg yolk**
⅔ **cup milk**
1 **tablespoon cooking oil**

■ In a small mixing bowl stir together the cream cheese and egg yolk till smooth. Stir the milk and oil into egg yolk mixture. Add egg yolk mixture to flour mixture all at once. Stir *just till combined* but still slightly lumpy.

1 **egg white**

■ In a small mixing bowl beat the egg white till stiff peaks form (tips stand straight). Gently fold beaten egg white into flour and egg yolk mixture, leaving a few fluffs of egg white in the batter. *Do not overmix.*

Fresh fruit (optional)
Flavored yogurt
   (optional)

■ Pour *half* of the batter onto grid of a preheated, lightly greased waffle iron. Close lid quickly; *do not open* during baking. Bake according to manufacturer's directions. When done, use a fork to lift waffle off grid.

Repeat with remaining batter. If desired, top with fresh fruit and yogurt. Serves 2.

TIME ESTIMATE
Start to finish _ 20 min.

MENU IDEA
If you wish, serve sausage links or ham slices and glasses of fruit juice with these waffles.

PER SERVING
Calories _____ 388
Protein _____ 12 g
Carbohydrate _____ 48 g
Fat (total) _____ 16 g
   Saturated _____ 6 g
Cholesterol __ 128 mg
Sodium_____ 408 mg
Potassium _____ 256 mg

CREAM CHEESE WAFFLES

BANANA-STUFFED FRENCH TOAST

Absolutely awesome! These colossal slices of French bread are stuffed with a mixture of banana and cream cheese, coated with chopped peanuts, and baked to golden perfection.

4 1-inch-thick slices French bread

■ Grease a baking sheet; set aside. Cut a pocket horizontally in each slice of French bread, cutting from the top crust almost to the bottom crust.

¼ cup mashed ripe banana (1 small banana)
3 tablespoons soft-style cream cheese

■ In a small mixing bowl stir together the banana and cream cheese. Spoon *1 rounded tablespoon* of the banana-cream cheese mixture into *each* pocket.

2 eggs
⅓ cup milk
¼ teaspoon vanilla
½ cup finely chopped peanuts *or* pecans
2 tablespoons sugar
¼ teaspoon ground cinnamon

■ In a shallow bowl beat together the eggs, milk, and vanilla. In a pie plate stir together the peanuts or pecans, sugar, and cinnamon. Dip the stuffed bread slices into the egg mixture, then coat with the nut mixture.

Maple-flavored syrup *or* sifted powdered sugar (optional)

■ Place the stuffed bread slices on the prepared baking sheet. Bake in a 450° oven about 6 minutes or till golden. Turn the slices over and bake about 5 minutes more or till golden. If desired, serve with maple-flavored syrup or sprinkle with powdered sugar. Makes 2 servings.

TIME ESTIMATE

Preparation ____ 15 min.
Baking _____ 11 min.

PER SERVING

Calories _____ 654
Protein _____ 26 g
Carbohydrate ____ 65 g
Fat (total) _____ 34 g
　Saturated _____ 9 g
Cholesterol ____ 239 mg
Sodium _____ 719 mg
Potassium _____ 575 mg

CARAMEL-AND-ORANGE BREAKFAST BUNS

3 tablespoons brown sugar
4 teaspoons margarine *or* butter
1 teaspoon light corn syrup

■ In a small saucepan combine the brown sugar, margarine or butter, and the corn syrup. Heat and stir till combined. Pour into an 8x4x2-inch loaf pan. Set pan aside.

¼ cup powdered sugar
¼ cup ground hazelnuts *or* pecans
2 tablespoons margarine *or* butter, softened
½ teaspoon finely shredded orange peel

■ For filling, in a small mixing bowl stir together the powdered sugar, hazelnuts or pecans, margarine or butter, and orange peel. Set aside.

1 cup all-purpose flour
1½ teaspoons baking powder
1 teaspoon sugar
⅛ teaspoon baking soda
⅛ teaspoon salt
¼ cup margarine *or* butter
⅓ cup buttermilk *or* sour milk (see tip, page 194)

■ For dough, in a medium mixing bowl stir together the flour, baking powder, sugar, baking soda, and salt. Using a pastry blender, cut in the margarine or butter till the mixture resembles coarse crumbs. Make a well in the center of the dry ingredients, then add the buttermilk or sour milk all at once. Using a fork, stir *just till moistened.* •

■ Turn the dough out onto a lightly floured surface. Quickly knead the dough by gently folding and pressing the dough for 10 to 12 strokes or till the dough is *nearly* smooth. Lightly roll dough into a 6x5-inch rectangle.

Spread the filling evenly over the dough. Roll up jelly-roll style, starting from one of the long sides. Pinch seam to seal. Cut into six 1-inch-thick slices. Place slices, cut sides down, in the prepared pan. Bake in a 425° oven about 25 minutes or till golden. Let stand in the pan for 1 minute. Invert onto a serving plate. Serve warm. Makes 6 buns.

TIME ESTIMATE
Preparation ____ 25 min.
Baking _____ 25 min.

MENU IDEA
Team these yummy buns with cold glasses of milk and you've got one scrumptious breakfast!

PER BUN
Calories _____ 285
Protein _____ 3 g
Carbohydrate _____ 30 g
Fat (total) _____ 17 g
  Saturated _____ 3 g
Cholesterol _____ 0 mg
Sodium _____ 316 mg
Potassium _____ 97 mg

BLUEBERRY COFFEE CAKE

When fresh, sweet blueberries are spilling over on your grocer's shelves, buy a box and whip up this simple breakfast cake. If you're lucky enough to have some cake left over, serve it as a snack.

¾ cup all-purpose flour
½ cup sugar
⅛ teaspoon salt
¼ cup margarine *or* butter
2 tablespoons finely chopped pecans *or* walnuts
⅛ teaspoon ground nutmeg, cardamom, *or* cinnamon

■ Lightly grease an 8x4x2-inch loaf pan; set aside. For crumb mixture, in a medium mixing bowl stir together the flour, sugar, and salt. Using a pastry blender, cut in the margarine or butter till mixture resembles fine crumbs.

For topping, remove ¼ *cup* of the crumb mixture. Stir the pecans or walnuts and nutmeg, cardamom, or cinnamon into the ¼ cup crumb mixture. Set aside.

¼ teaspoon baking soda
1 slightly beaten egg white
¼ cup buttermilk *or* sour milk (see tip, page 194)

■ For batter, stir the baking soda into the remaining crumb mixture. Make a well in the center of the crumb mixture.

In a small mixing bowl stir together the egg white and buttermilk or sour milk. Add the egg mixture all at once to the crumb mixture. Stir *just till moistened.*

½ cup fresh *or* frozen blueberries

■ Spread the batter in the prepared pan. Top with blueberries. (Do not thaw frozen blueberries.) Sprinkle the topping over the blueberries.

Bake in a 350° oven about 45 minutes or till a wooden toothpick inserted near the center comes out clean. Serve warm. Makes 4 servings.

TIME ESTIMATE

Preparation ___ 20 min.
Baking ___ 45 min.

PER SERVING

Calories ___ 329
Protein ___ 4 g
Carbohydrate ___ 47 g
Fat (total) ___ 14 g
　Saturated ___ 3 g
Cholesterol ___ 1 mg
Sodium ___ 284 mg
Potassium ___ 98 mg

RASPBERRY-SWIRL BUTTERMILK COFFEE CAKE

For a mid-morning pick-me-up, serve this deliciously sweet treat that's swirled with raspberry jam and iced with chocolate pieces.

3 tablespoons margarine *or* butter
¾ cup all-purpose flour
⅓ cup sugar
⅓ cup buttermilk *or* sour milk (see tip, page 194)
1 egg white
¼ teaspoon baking powder
¼ teaspoon baking soda
¼ teaspoon vanilla

■ Grease a 9x5x3-inch loaf pan or an 8x1½-inch round baking pan. For batter, in a medium mixing bowl beat the margarine or butter with an electric mixer on medium to high speed about 30 seconds or till softened.

Add about *half* of the flour to the margarine or butter. Then add the sugar, buttermilk or sour milk, egg white, baking powder, baking soda, and vanilla. Beat on low speed till thoroughly combined, scraping the sides of the bowl. Beat on medium speed for 2 minutes more. Then beat in the remaining flour on low speed just till combined.

3 tablespoons seedless red raspberry *or* strawberry jam
¼ cup chopped pecans *or* almonds

■ Spread the batter into the prepared pan. Dollop jam in small spoonfuls on top of the batter. Using a small narrow spatula or knife, gently swirl preserves into the batter to create a marbled effect. Sprinkle the pecans or almonds over the top.

2 tablespoons semisweet chocolate *or* vanilla-flavored pieces

■ Bake in a 350° oven for 25 to 30 minutes or till a wooden toothpick inserted near the center comes out clean. Remove from oven. Sprinkle chocolate or vanilla-flavored pieces over warm cake. Let stand 5 minutes. Use the tines of a fork to swirl the pieces. Let cake cool an additional 10 minutes before serving. Serve warm or cool. Makes 4 servings.

TIME ESTIMATE

Preparation	15 min.
Baking	25 min.
Cooling	15 min.

PER SERVING

Calories	355
Protein	5 g
Carbohydrate	50 g
Fat (total)	16 g
Saturated	3 g
Cholesterol	1 mg
Sodium	208 mg
Potassium	134 mg

WHITE GRAPE SPRITZERS

Use the fruited ice cubes to dress up glasses of sparkling water and pitchers of lemonade in addition to the spritzers.

Small strawberries *or* carambola (star fruit) *or* peeled kiwi slices

1 **cup unsweetened white *or* red grape juice, chilled**
1 **cup champagne *or* lemon-lime carbonated beverage, chilled**

■ For fruited ice cubes, place fruit in ice cube trays. Fill trays with water. Freeze till firm. Chill 2 wine glasses.

■ In *each* of the 2 chilled wine glasses, combine *half* of the grape juice and *half* of the champagne or carbonated beverage. Add some of the fruited ice cubes. Makes 2 (8-ounce) servings.

TIME ESTIMATE

Preparation _____ 5 min.
Freezing _____ 4 hrs.
Assembling _____ 5 min.

PER SERVING

Calories _____ 170
Protein _____ 0 g
Carbohydrate _____ 23 g
Fat (total) _____ 0 g
    Saturated _____ 0 g
Cholesterol _____ 0 mg
Sodium_____ 18 mg
Potassium _____ 206 mg

NECTARINE AND BERRY WHIRL

2 **medium nectarines, pitted and sliced, *or* 2 small pears, peeled, cored, and sliced (about 1½ cups)**
½ **cup raspberry-cranberry juice drink *or* cranberry juice cocktail, chilled**
⅓ **cup vanilla yogurt**
4 **ice cubes**
  Nectarine *or* pear slices (optional)

■ In a blender container combine the nectarines or pears, raspberry-cranberry juice drink or cranberry juice cocktail, and vanilla yogurt. Cover and blend mixture till smooth. With the blender running, add the ice cubes, one at a time, through the opening in the lid; blend mixture till slushy. Pour into 2 tall glasses. If desired, garnish with nectarine or pear slices. Serve immediately. Makes 2 (8-ounce) servings.

TIME ESTIMATE

Start to finish _ 10 min.

PER SERVING

Calories _____ 142
Protein _____ 3 g
Carbohydrate _____ 32 g
Fat (total) _____ 1 g
    Saturated _____ 0 g
Cholesterol _____ 2 mg
Sodium_____ 21 mg
Potassium _____ 373 mg

INDEX

Apples
Apple and Spinach
  Slaw, 141
Apple-Glazed
  Rolls, 209
Apple-Oatmeal
  Muffins, 212
Brickle-Crunch Apple
  Tarts, 192
Cheesy Apple
  Crisp, 196
Grilled Apple-
  Cheddarwiches, 152
Mustard-Topped
  Halibut with
  Apples, 97
Puffed Oven Pancake
  with Spiced Apple
  Sauce, 224
Turkey Steaks with
  Apple and Maple
  Sauce, 74
Waldorf Chicken
  Salad, 116
Asparagus
Dilled Beef with New
  Potatoes and
  Asparagus, 16
Ginger-Cream
  Asparagus, 174
Ham and Asparagus
  Strata, 223
Mediterranean-Style
  Fish Rolls, 99
Turkey and Asparagus
  Stir-Fry, 71

Bagel Crisps,
  Dilled, 138
Bananas
Banana-Brickle
  Bread, 210

Bananas (continued)
Banana-Nut
  Muffins, 214
Banana-Spice
  Muffins, 214
Banana-Stuffed French
  Toast, 228
Bit-of-Chocolate
  Banana Muffins, 214
Chocolate-Chip Banana
  Bread, 210
Beans
Beans and Brats with
  Mustard Biscuits, 32
Beany Ham Soup, 168
Beef Steak Chili with
  Beans, 166
Black Bean and
  Sausage Burritos, 47
Lemon-Almond Green
  Beans, 175
Polenta with Tomato-
  Bean Sauce, 107
Tuna and White Bean
  Salad, 134
White-Chili-Style Pasta
  Sauce, 112
Beef
Apricot-and-Almond-
  Stuffed Steak, 7
Beef Roast with
  Tomato-Herb
  Sauce, 17
Beef Salad with Potato
  Crisps, 126
Beef Steak Chili with
  Beans, 166
Beef Steak Fajitas, 13
Beef Stew with
  Lentils, 167
Beef Stroganoff, 12

Beef (continued)
Cheesy Sour Cream
  and Onion
  Burgers, 148
Deep-Dish Pizza, 206
Dilled Beef with New
  Potatoes and
  Asparagus, 16
East-West Barbecued
  Beef Kabobs, 11
Greek-Style Pocket
  Sandwiches, 150
Grilled Bacon-Sauced
  Meat Loaf, 20
Hearty Beef and
  Squash Stew, 158
Indian Beef Patties
  with Cucumber
  Sauce, 19
Italian Pepper Steak
  Stir-Fry, 14
Lemon-Dill Meatballs
  in Creamy Tomato
  Sauce, 43
Marinated Beef and
  Garden Vegetable
  Salad, 124
Marinated Beef with
  Spicy Pecan Sauce, 9
Onion-Stuffed Sirloin
  with Mushroom
  Sauté, 10
Pastrami Kabob
  Sandwiches, 146
Peppered Beef Steak
  with Vinaigrette, 8
Pizza-Style Taco
  Salad, 122
Pork and Pear Spinach
  Salad, 129
Rich Onion and Beef
  Soup, 165

Beef (continued)
Saucy Barbecue
  Sandwiches, 153
Savory Almond
  Meatballs, 18
Spinach and Basil Salad
  with Beef, 125
Springtime Pork Salad
  with Strawberry
  Vinaigrette, 132
Steak Pinwheels Stuffed
  with Spinach, 40
Teriyaki Sesame
  Burgers, 149
Veal Ragout with Peas
  and Pasta, 44
Vegetable Beef
  Soup, 164
Wellington-Style Beef
  Tenderloin, 42
Biscuits
Basic Buttery
  Biscuits, 215
Jam-Filled Biscuits, 215
Mustard Biscuits, 32
Blueberries
Blueberry and Coconut
  Crisp, 196
Blueberry Coffee
  Cake, 230
Blueberry-Oatmeal
  Muffins, 212
Breads (see also Biscuits,
  Muffins, Scones)
Apple-Glazed
  Rolls, 209
Banana-Brickle
  Bread, 210
Banana-Stuffed French
  Toast, 228
Blueberry Coffee
  Cake, 230

Breads *(continued)*
Braided Bread, 207
Buttermilk Corn
Bread, 216
Caramel-and-Orange
Breakfast Buns, 229
Caramel Rolls, 208
Cheesy Calzone, 206
Chocolate-Chip Banana
Bread, 210
Cinnamon Bread, 208
Cinnamon Rolls, 208
Cream Cheese
Waffles, 226
Deep-Dish Pizza, 206
Dinner Rolls, 207
Easy-Mix Yeast
Bread, 205
Oatmeal Pancakes with
Strawberry-Orange
Sauce, 225
Pepperoni-Parmesan
Bread, 211
Puffed Oven Pancake
with Spiced Apple
Sauce, 224
Raspberry-Swirl
Buttermilk Coffee
Cake, 231
Sweet Cheese
Rolls, 209
Brownies with Cocoa
Glaze, Fudge, 201
Burgers, Cheesy Sour
Cream and Onion, 148
Burgers, Teriyaki
Sesame, 149
Burritos, Black Bean
and Sausage, 47

Cakes
Almond-Praline
Chocolate Upside-
Down Cake, 200
Simple White Cake
with Chocolate
Glaze, 197
Strawberry-Cream-
Cheese Torte, 197
Strawberry Shortcake
with Cream Cheese
Sauce, 198
Cheese
Buttermilk and Swiss
Fondue, 101
Caramelized Onion
and Blue Cheese
Pizza, 103
Cheddar-Pecan Corn
Scones, 216
Cheese 'n' Nut
Toasts, 138
Cheese Soup with
Pesto, 156
Cheesy Apple
Crisp, 196
Cheesy Bratwurst and
Cabbage, 33
Cheesy Calzone, 206
Cheesy Ham and Egg
Bake, 221
Cheesy Sour Cream
and Onion
Burgers, 148
Cottage-Cheese-
Dressed Potato
Salad, 140
Cream Cheese
Sauce, 198
Cream Cheese
Waffles, 226

Cheese *(continued)*
Cream-Cheesy
Corn, 176
Easy Cheesy Chicken
Ravioli, 78
Grilled Apple-
Cheddarwiches, 152
Ham and Cheese
Sandwich
Spirals, 144
Lentil and Cheese
Burritos, 102
Lentil and Cheese
Tostadas, 102
Mushroom-and-Blue-
Cheese-Stuffed Pork
Chops, 23
Parmesan-Herb
Croutons, 138
Pepperoni-Parmesan
Bread, 211
Sweet Cheese
Rolls, 209
Chicken *(see* Poultry)
Cookies
Almond-Oat
Cookies, 202
Chocolate-Chip Oat
Cookies, 202
Cinnamon and Sugar
Slices, 203
Coconut-Lemon Oat
Cookies, 202
Vanilla-Dipped
Chocolate Slices, 203
Corn
Buttermilk Corn
Bread, 216
Buttermilk Corn
Scones, 216
Cheddar-Pecan Corn
Scones, 216

Corn *(continued)*
Corn Bread Cherry
Cobbler, 195
Corn Salsa over
Chicken, 49
Cream-Cheesy
Corn, 176
Triple-Corn
Chowder, 162
Cornish Hens, Maple-
Glazed Stuffed, 61
Crabs, Cajun-Coated
Soft-Shell, 86
Croutons, Parmesan-
Herb, 138

Desserts *(see also* Cakes,
Cookies)
Basic Pastry
Dough, 194
Blueberry and Coconut
Crisp, 196
Brickle-Crunch Apple
Tarts, 192
Brickle-Crunch Peach
Tarts, 192
Cheesy Apple
Crisp, 196
Corn Bread Cherry
Cobbler, 195
Country-Style Pear
Dumplings, 191
Cream Cheese
Sauce, 198
Fudge Brownies with
Cocoa Glaze, 201
Individual Cherry-
Berry Pies, 193
Individual Cherry
Pies, 193

Eggs

Bacon and Avocado
Puffy Omelet, 219
Cheesy Ham and Egg
Bake, 221
Ham and Asparagus
Strata, 223
Italian Breakfast
Frittata, 220
Moo Shu Vegetable
and Egg Crepes, 109
Turkey Scramble
Florentine, 222

Fish (see also Shellfish, Shrimp)

Caraway Fish
Chowder, 159
Flounder and
Vegetables en
Papillote, 88
Fresh Salmon Salad
Niçoise, 133
Grilled Tuna Steaks
with Pineapple
Salsa, 95
Mediterranean-Style
Fish Rolls, 99
Mediterranean Tuna
Pockets, 143
Mustard-Topped
Halibut with
Apples, 97
Pasta with Salmon
Cream Sauce, 94
Poached Fillets with
Orange Sauce, 87
Salmon and Green
Peppercorn
Strudel, 92

Fish (continued)
Swordfish and Mixed
Vegetable Stir-
Fry, 91
Swordfish
Margarita, 96
Trout in White Wine
Sauce, 89
Tuna and White Bean
Salad, 134

Fruit (see also Apples, Bananas, Blueberries, Strawberries)

Brickle-Crunch Peach
Tarts, 192
Chicken Quesadillas
with Papaya Salsa, 68
Country-Style Pear
Dumplings, 191
Fresh Fruit and
Chicken Plates, 118
Fruited Rice, 187
Fruited Turkey Salad
with Creamy Orange
Dressing, 120
Fruity Wild and Brown
Rice Pilaf, 189
Glazed Chicken and
Grapes, 54
Melon Salad with
Creamy Apricot
Dressing, 141
Pork and Pear
Spinach Salad, 129
Roast Pork with Warm
Fruit Sauce, 34
Summer Fruit and
Barley Salad, 123

Ham

Beany Ham Soup, 168
Cheesy Ham and Egg
Bake, 221
Ham and Asparagus
Strata, 223
Ham and Cheese
Sandwich
Spirals, 144
Ham with Chunky
Cranberry Sauce, 31
Lemon and Wild Rice
Soup with Ham, 160

Lamb

Greek-Style Pocket
Sandwiches, 150
Lamb Chops
Teriyaki, 37
Lamb Chops with Leek
Sauce, 36
Lentil and Cheese
Burritos, 102
Lentil and Cheese
Tostadas, 102

Muffins

Apple-Oatmeal
Muffins, 212
Banana-Nut
Muffins, 214
Banana-Spice
Muffins, 214
Bit-of-Chocolate
Banana Muffins, 214
Blueberry-Oatmeal
Muffins, 212
Cinnamon 'n' Spice
Oatmeal
Muffins, 212

Nectarine and Berry

Whirl, 232
Nuts, Spiced, 138
Nuts, Sugar-Coated, 138

Pancakes with

Strawberry-Orange
Sauce,
Oatmeal, 225
Pancake with Spiced
Apple Sauce, Puffed
Oven, 224
Pasta
Buttered Pasta, 184
Chicken Spirals with
Basil Alfredo, 59
Creamy Pasta with
Pecans, 184
Garden Vegetable and
Pasta Salad, 139
Greek-Style Pasta and
Shrimp Salad, 135
Lemon-Pepper
Pasta, 184
Lemony Fettuccine
Alfredo with
Peas, 182
Pasta with
Mushrooms, 184
Pasta with Salmon
Cream Sauce, 94
Poppy Seed and
Orange Pasta, 184
Spinach-Stuffed Pasta
Shells, 110
Tomato-and-Basil-
Sauced Pasta, 186
Tortellini and Fresh
Spinach Soup, 161
Turkey Tetrazzini-Style
Casseroles, 81

Pasta *(continued)*
  Veal Ragout with Peas
    and Pasta, 44
  White-Chili-Style Pasta
    Sauce, 112
Peppers Stuffed with
  Cinnamon Bulgur, 106
Pesto, 156
Pizza
  Caramelized Onion and
    Blue Cheese
    Pizza, 103
  Cheesy Calzone, 206
  Deep-Dish Pizza, 206
  Pizza-Style Taco
    Salad, 122
  Spicy Sausage Pizza in
    Potato Crust, 46
Pork *(see also* Ham,
  Sausage)
  Beef Salad with Potato
    Crisps, 126
  Cheesy Sour Cream
    and Onion
    Burgers, 148
  Chinese-Style Pork and
    Vegetables, 29
  Coriander-and-Honey-
    Glazed Pork
    Ribs, 30
  Grilled Bacon-Sauced
    Meat Loaf, 20
  Herb-Rubbed Pork
    Chops, 27
  Indian Beef Patties
    with Cucumber
    Sauce, 19
  Lemon-Dill Meatballs
    in Creamy Tomato
    Sauce, 43

Pork *(continued)*
  Marinated Beef and
    Garden Vegetable
    Salad, 124
  Mushroom-and-Blue-
    Cheese-Stuffed Pork
    Chops, 23
  Picatta-Style Pork, 28
  Pizza-Style Taco
    Salad, 122
  Pork and Cranberry
    Pies, 45
  Pork and Pear Spinach
    Salad, 129
  Pork Chops with
    Currant-Nut
    Stuffing, 24
  Pork Chops with
    Peanut Ginger
    Sauce, 26
  Roast Pork with Warm
    Fruit Sauce, 34
  Saucy Barbecue
    Sandwiches, 153
  Savory Almond
    Meatballs, 18
  Springtime Pork Salad
    with Strawberry
    Vinaigrette, 132
  Teriyaki Sesame
    Burgers, 149
  Veal Chops with
    Vegetable Sauce, 21
  Veal with Artichokes
    and Hollandaise
    Sauce, 22
Potatoes
  Beef Salad with Potato
    Crisps, 126
  Caraway Potato
    Chowder, 159

Potatoes *(continued)*
  Chicken with Sweet
    Potatoes, 52
  Cottage-Cheese-
    Dressed Potato
    Salad, 140
  Creamy Mashed
    Potatoes, 179
  Creamy Mashed Sweet
    Potatoes, 179
  Crispy Baked
    Potatoes, 178
  Crispy Baked Potato
    Wedges, 178
  Crispy Baked Sweet
    Potatoes, 178
  Dilled Beef with New
    Potatoes and
    Asparagus, 16
  Spicy Sausage Pizza in
    Potato Crust, 46
Poultry
  Buttermilk Fried
    Chicken, 57
  Cheesy Sour Cream
    and Onion
    Burgers, 148
  Chicken Ginger, 60
  Chicken Meatball
    Soup, 157
  Chicken Quesadillas
    with Papaya Salsa, 68
  Chicken Spirals with
    Basil Alfredo, 59
  Chicken with Brandied
    Cherry Sauce, 58
  Chicken with Sweet
    Potatoes, 52
  Chutney-Filled Chicken
    and Pastry
    Bundles, 76

Poultry *(continued)*
  Cobb-Style Chicken
    Sandwich, 154
  Corn Salsa over
    Chicken, 49
  Easy Cheesy Chicken
    Ravioli, 78
  Fresh Fruit and
    Chicken Plates, 118
  Fruited Turkey Salad
    with Creamy Orange
    Dressing, 120
  Glazed Chicken and
    Grapes, 54
  Greek-Style Pocket
    Sandwiches, 150
  Ham and Cheese
    Sandwich
    Spirals, 144
  Hearty Turkey Sausage
    and Vegetable
    Skillet, 70
  Hot Curried Chicken
    Salad with Crispy
    Pita Chips, 117
  Indian Beef Patties
    with Cucumber
    Sauce, 19
  Italian-Style Chef Salad
    with Creamy Pesto
    Dressing, 128
  Lemon Chicken
    Salad, 115
  Lemon-Dill Meatballs
    in Creamy Tomato
    Sauce, 43
  Lemon-Herb Chicken
    and Vegetable
    Kabobs, 50
  Maple-Glazed Stuffed
    Cornish Hens, 61

Poultry *(continued)*
Paella-Style Brown
Rice and
Chicken, 53
Pecan-Coated Chicken
Kiev, 66
Picadillo Chicken
Loaves, 77
Pizza-Style Taco
Salad, 122
Pork and Cranberry
Pies, 45
Roast Chicken with
Lemon Stuffing, 63
Saucy Barbecue
Sandwiches, 153
Saucy Italian Chicken
and Artichokes, 56
Spinach-Chicken à la
King, 64
Tangy Barbecued
Chicken Breasts, 62
Teriyaki Sesame
Burgers, 149
Turkey and Asparagus
Stir-Fry, 71
Turkey and Vegetable
Tortilla Roll-Ups, 80
Turkey Scramble
Florentine, 222
Turkey Steaks with
Apple and Maple
Sauce, 74
Turkey Tetrazzini-Style
Casseroles, 81
Turkey with Cranberry
and Fig Chutney, 72
Waldorf Chicken
Salad, 116
Wilted Spinach and
Chicken Salad, 119

*R*ice
Confetti Rice, 187
Curried Rice, 187
Fruited Rice, 187
Fruity Wild and Brown
Rice Pilaf, 189
Hearty Spinach and
Tofu Risotto, 113
Hot Cooked Rice, 187
Lemon and Wild Rice
Soup, 160
Lemon and Wild Rice
Soup with Ham, 160
Paella-Style Brown
Rice and
Chicken, 53
Parsley-Herb Rice, 187
Pilaf Primavera, 104
Rice Patties Florentine
with Yogurt
Sauce, 105
Rice Pilaf, 188

*S*alad Dressings
Creamy Pesto
Dressing, 128
Fruited Turkey Salad
with Creamy Orange
Dressing, 120
Garlic Vinaigrette, 137
Honey-Mustard
Dressing, 137
Lemon-Nut
Vinaigrette, 136
Melon Salad with
Creamy Apricot
Dressing, 141
Oriental
Vinaigrette, 137
Pepper
Vinaigrette, 137

Salad Dressings *(continued)*
Strawberry
Vinaigrette, 132
Tomato-Basil
Vinaigrette, 139
Salads, Main-Dish
Beef Salad with Potato
Crisps, 126
Fresh Fruit and
Chicken Plates, 118
Fresh Salmon Salad
Nicoise, 133
Fruited Turkey Salad
with Creamy Orange
Dressing, 120
Greek-Style Pasta and
Shrimp Salad, 135
Hot Curried Chicken
Salad with Crispy
Pita Chips, 117
Hot Sausage and Lentil
Slaw, 130
Italian-Style Chef Salad
with Creamy Pesto
Dressing, 128
Lemon Chicken
Salad, 115
Marinated Beef and
Garden Vegetable
Salad, 124
Pizza-Style Taco
Salad, 122
Pork and Pear Spinach
Salad, 129
Springtime Pork Salad
with Strawberry
Vinaigrette, 132
Summer Fruit and
Barley Salad, 123
Tuna and White Bean
Salad, 134

Salads, Main-Dish
(continued)
Waldorf Chicken
Salad, 116
Wilted Spinach and
Chicken Salad, 119
Salads, Side-Dish
Apple and Spinach
Slaw, 141
Cottage-Cheese-
Dressed Potato
Salad, 140
Garden Vegetable and
Pasta Salad, 139
Melon Salad with
Creamy Apricot
Dressing, 141
Sandwiches
Cheesy Sour Cream
and Onion
Burgers, 148
Cobb-Style Chicken
Sandwich, 154
Greek-Style Pocket
Sandwiches, 150
Grilled Apple-
Cheddarwiches, 152
Ham and Cheese
Sandwich
Spirals, 144
Mediterranean Tuna
Pockets, 143
Pastrami Kabob
Sandwiches, 146
Red Hot Brats in
Beer, 151
Saucy Barbecue
Sandwiches, 153
Teriyaki Sesame
Burgers, 149
Vegetarian Reuben
Sandwich, 145

Sauces
    Cream Cheese
        Sauce, 198
    Hollandaise Sauce, 22
    Indian Beef Patties
        with Cucumber
        Sauce, 19
    Strawberry-Orange
        Sauce, 225
    Tomatoey Sauce, 110
Sausage
    Beans and Brats with
        Mustard Biscuits, 32
    Black Bean and
        Sausage Burritos, 47
    Cheesy Bratwurst and
        Cabbage, 33
    Deep-Dish Pizza, 206
    Hot Sausage and Lentil
        Slaw, 130
    Red Hot Brats in
        Beer, 151
    Spicy Sausage Pizza in
        Potato Crust, 46
Scones
    Buttermilk Corn
        Scones, 216
    Cheddar-Pecan Corn
        Scones, 216
    Orange and Raisin
        Scones, 217
    Sweet Yogurt
        Scones, 217
Shellfish
    Cajun Coated Soft-Shell
        Crabs, 86
    Rumaki-Style Scallop
        Kabobs, 85
    Seafood Lasagna Roll-
        Ups, 98

Shrimp
    Garlic and Herb
        Shrimp Sauté, 84
    Greek-Style Pasta and
        Shrimp Salad, 135
    Hot-and-Sour
        Shrimp, 83
Soups, Main-Dish
    Beany Ham Soup, 168
    Beef Steak Chili with
        Beans, 166
    Beef Stew with
        Lentils, 167
    Caraway Fish
        Chowder, 159
    Caraway Potato
        Chowder, 159
    Cheese Soup with
        Pesto, 156
    Chicken Meatball
        Soup, 157
    Hearty Beef and
        Squash Stew, 158
    Lemon and Wild Rice
        Soup with Ham, 160
    Rich Onion and Beef
        Soup, 165
    Vegetable Beef
        Soup, 164
Soups, Side-Dish
    Chilled Sweet Pepper
        Soup, 171
    Fresh Tomato
        Soup, 169
    Lemon and Wild Rice
        Soup, 160

Soups, Side-Dish
    (continued)
    Pumpkin and
        Vegetable Soup, 170
    Tortellini and Fresh
        Spinach Soup, 161
    Triple-Corn
        Chowder, 162
Spreads
    Lemon Butter, 177
    Mustard-Sage
        Butter, 177
    Roasted Red Pepper
        Butter, 177
    Sesame Butter, 177
    Tomato-Pepper
        Butter, 177
    Wine-Tarragon
        Butter, 177
Strawberries
    Strawberry-Cream-
        Cheese Torte, 197
    Strawberry-Orange
        Sauce, 225
    Strawberry Shortcake
        with Cream Cheese
        Sauce, 198

Tomatoes
    Beef Roast with
        Tomato-Herb
        Sauce, 17
    Fresh Tomato
        Soup, 169
    Lemon-Dill Meatballs
        in Creamy Tomato
        Sauce, 43

Tomatoes (continued)
    Marinated Beef and
        Garden Vegetable
        Salad, 124
    Polenta with Tomato-
        Bean Sauce, 107
    Tomato-and-Basil-
        Sauced Pasta, 186
    Tomato-Basil
        Vinaigrette, 139
    Tomatoey Sauce, 110
    Tomato-Pepper
        Butter, 177
Turkey (see Poultry)

Veal
    Veal Chops with
        Vegetable Sauce, 21
    Veal Ragout with Peas
        and Pasta, 44
    Veal with Artichokes
        and Hollandaise
        Sauce, 22
Vegetables (see also
        Asparagus, Beans,
        Corn, Potatoes,
        Tomatoes)
    Carrot and Squash Stir-
        Fry, 173
    Chilled Sweet Pepper
        Soup, 171
    Flounder and
        Vegetables en
        Papillote, 88
    Garden Vegetable and
        Pasta Salad, 139
    Hearty Turkey Sausage
        and Vegetable
        Skillet, 70

Vegetables *(continued)*
  Lemon-Herb Chicken
    and Vegetable
    Kabobs, 50
  Lemony Fettuccine
    Alfredo with
    Peas, 182
  Marinated Beef and
    Garden Vegetable
    Salad, 124
  Mixed Vegetable and
    Tofu Chow
    Mein, 108
  Moo Shu Vegetable
    and Egg Crepes, 109
  Peppers Stuffed with
    Cinnamon
    Bulgur, 106
  Pilaf Primavera, 104
  Pumpkin and
    Vegetable Soup, 170
  Ratatouille, 180
  Swordfish and Mixed
    Vegetable Stir-
    Fry, 91
  Turkey and Vegetable
    Tortilla Roll-Ups, 80
  Veal Chops with
    Vegetable Sauce, 21
  Vegetable Beef
    Soup, 164
  Vegetarian Reuben
    Sandwich, 145

*W*affles, Cream
  Cheese, 226
White Grape
  Spritzers, 232

TIPS
  Butter Brush-ons, 177
  Buttermilk,
    Out of, 194
  Dried Tomatoes, 157
  Grilling Basics, 27
  Healthy Choices, 90
  Ingredients to Keep
    on Hand, 51
  Leftovers, Easy
    Ideas for, 152
  Meal Planning, 33
  Microwave Magic, 67
  Pasta and Rice On-
    Call, 176
  Peppers, Handling Hot
    Chili, 12
  Pork Update, 31
  Recipe Time
    Estimates, 174
  Roasting Fresh
    Peppers, 21
  Shopping Strategies,
    Smart, 96
  Special Dinners, 54
  Speedier Cooking,
    Steps to, 103
  Toasting Buns, Rolls,
    and Bread, 150
  Toasting Nuts, 201
  Wrap-It-Up, 161

CHARTS
  Broiling and Grilling
    Fish, 87
  Broiling and Grilling
    Poultry, 73
  Broiling Meat, 38
  Cooking Pasta, 185
  Grilling Meat, 39
  Grilling
    Vegetables, 181

**NUTRITION
CALCULATIONS**
*Keep track of your daily
nutrition needs by using the
information we provide at
the end of each recipe. We've
analyzed the nutritional
content of each recipe serving
for you. When a recipe gives
an ingredient substitution, we
used the first choice in the
analysis. Ingredients listed as
optional weren't included in
the calculations.*

METRIC COOKING HINTS

By making a few conversions, cooks in Australia, Canada, and the United Kingdom can use the recipes in Better Homes and Gardens® *Cooking for Two* with confidence. The charts on this page provide a guide for converting measurements from the U.S. customary system, which is used throughout this book, to the imperial and metric systems. There also is a conversion table for oven temperatures to accommodate the differences in oven calibrations.

Volume and Weight: Americans traditionally use *cup* measures for liquid and solid ingredients. The chart (top right) shows the approximate imperial and metric equivalents.

If you are accustomed to weighing solid ingredients, here are some helpful approximate equivalents:
- 1 cup butter, caster sugar, or rice = 8 ounces = about 250 grams
- 1 cup flour = 4 ounces = about 125 grams
- 1 cup icing sugar = 5 ounces = about 150 grams

Spoon measures are used for smaller amounts of ingredients. Although the size of the teaspoon is the same, the size of the tablespoon varies slightly among countries. However, for practical purposes and for recipes in this book, a straight substitution is all that's necessary.

Measurements made using cups or spoons always should be *level*, unless stated otherwise.

Product Differences: Most of the ingredients called for in the recipes in this book are available in English-speaking countries. However, some are known by different names. Here are some common American ingredients and their possible counterparts:
- Sugar is granulated or caster sugar.
- Powdered sugar is icing sugar.
- All-purpose flour is plain household flour or white flour. When self-rising flour is used in place of all-purpose flour in a recipe that calls for leavening, omit the leavening (baking soda or baking powder) and salt.
- Light corn syrup is golden syrup.
- Cornstarch is cornflour.
- Baking soda is bicarbonate of soda.
- Vanilla is vanilla essence.

USEFUL EQUIVALENTS

⅛ teaspoon = 0.5ml
¼ teaspoon = 1ml
½ teaspoon = 2ml
1 teaspoon = 5ml
¼ cup = 2 fluid ounces = 50ml
⅓ cup = 3 fluid ounces = 75ml
½ cup = 4 fluid ounces = 125ml

⅔ cup = 5 fluid ounces = 150ml
¾ cup = 6 fluid ounces = 175ml
1 cup = 8 fluid ounces = 250ml
2 cups = 1 pint
2 pints = 1 litre
½ inch = 1 centimetre
1 inch = 2 centimetres

BAKING PAN SIZES

American	Metric
8x1½-inch round baking pan	20x4-centimetre sandwich or cake tin
9x1½-inch round baking pan	23x3.5-centimetre sandwich or cake tin
11x7x1½-inch baking pan	28x18x4-centimetre baking pan
13x9x2-inch baking pan	32.5x23x5-centimetre baking pan
12x7½x2-inch baking dish	30x19x5-centimetre baking pan
15x10x2-inch baking pan	38x25.5x2.5-centimetre baking pan (Swiss roll tin)
9-inch pie plate	22x4- or 23x4-centimetre pie plate
7- or 8-inch springform pan	18- or 20-centimetre springform or loose-bottom cake tin
9x5x3-inch loaf pan	23x13x6-centimetre or 2-pound narrow loaf pan or pâté tin
1½-quart casserole	1.5-litre casserole
2-quart casserole	2-litre casserole

OVEN TEMPERATURE EQUIVALENTS

Fahrenheit Setting	Celsius Setting*	Gas Setting
300°F	150°C	Gas Mark 2
325°F	160°C	Gas Mark 3
350°F	180°C	Gas Mark 4
375°F	190°C	Gas Mark 5
400°F	200°C	Gas Mark 6
425°F	220°C	Gas Mark 7
450°F	230°C	Gas Mark 8
Broil		Grill (watch time and heat)

Electric and gas ovens may be calibrated using Celsius. However, increase the Celsius setting 10 to 20 degrees when cooking above 160°C with an electric oven. For convection or forced-air ovens (gas or electric), lower the temperature setting 10°C when cooking at all heat levels.